RURAL DEVELOPMENT ADMINISTRATION

RURAL DEVELOPMENT ADMINISTRATION

By

RAJBIR SINGH

ANMOL PUBLICATIONS PVT. LTD.
NEW DELHI - 110 002 (INDIA)

ANMOL PUBLICATIONS PVT. LTD.
4374/4B, Ansari Road, Daryaganj
New Delhi - 110 002
Ph.: 23261597, 23278000
Visit us at: www.anmolpublications.com

Rural Development Administration

First Published, 2004

ISBN 81-261-1737-0

PRINTED IN INDIA

Published by J.L. Kumar for Anmol Publications Pvt. Ltd., New Delhi - 110 002 and Printed at Mehra Offset Press, Delhi.

Contents

Contents

Preface

Rural development has today become an objective not only of the local and regional concern, but a pragmatic objective fully backed by national government and international organizations. Integrated Rural Development Programme is the most important poverty alleviation programme launched by Government of India after Independence. It was started in 1978-79 in 2300 selected Blocks all over the country and was extended to all the remaining Blocks since October 2, 1980. It is a target group programme in which the persons belonging to BPL families are provided assistance in form of loan and subsidy to purchase potential assets and to generate extra income so that they can cross the poverty line. As the programme got high publicity during the 6th and 7th Plans, researchers could not remain unconcerned to it and various studies were conducted at various levels by the individuals and the institutions. But no comprehensive work has been done so far on this topic in the State of Haryana in general and District Bhiwani in particular. Hence, a modest attempt has been made through the present study to fill up the gap. The present study might provide information about various programmes of rural development undertaken by the Government of India with special emphasis on IRDP, profile of the area of study, administrative structure of IRDP, its process of implementation, performance of IRDP and perception of Officials and Beneficiaries with remarkable findings and suitable suggestions. The basic assumptions of the study are: the success of any development programme like IRDP depends on the administrative structure responsible for its implementation, its process of implementation, Officials-Beneficiaries perception and that of infra-structural support available.

The focus of the present study is on the administration of IRDP in Haryana in general and District Bhiwani in particular. The area of study is District Bhiwani in which nine villages spread over three Blocks-Bhiwani, Badhara and Loharu, have been taken for field survey. The data used in the study are up to 1996. The periods of research is from 1980-1996 whereas for field work Beneficiaries assisted during the period 1990-95 have been taken for interview.

Broadly speaking the study is exploratory and analytic in nature and the conclusion are tentative which are primarily based on empirical evidences collected from respondent Officials and Beneficiaries with the help of specially prepared questionnaires for each group which consisted of both open-ended and close-ended questions. The techniques used in collection of primary data were interview, observation and discussion. For taking sample at each level, the following procedure was adopted. First of all, District Bhiwani was taken purposively for in-depth study. Secondly, three Blocks from the district were selected with the help of simple random sampling on the basis of total number of beneficiaries assisted so far and the same method was applied for selection of villages from each Block. A sample of 240 Beneficiaries was taken from the District with simple random sampling of which 80 Beneficiaries were selected from each Block on the basis of their strength proportionate to sample size in each selected village. The other source of primary data was all the 20 officials of IRDP. The secondary data were collected from various guidelines of Government of India, Reserve Bank of India and NABARD, manuals of poverty alleviation programmes, correspondence between Central and State Governments, and with local Government agencies, books, journals, newspapers etc.

It is my privilege top work under the worthy guidance of Dr. D.S. Chaudhary, Professor, Jawaharlal Nehru Chair, Department of Political Science, Maharshi Dayand University, Rohtak. His provocative comments, critique view and consistent encouragement went to a long way in crystallizing my understanding of the issues involved in the study. My gratitude for him is too deep for words.

I am thankful to Dr. Pratap Singh, Professor and Head, Department of Political Science for his valuable help and guidance.

I am grateful to all the other members of faculty in the Department of Political Science who extended their support to me whenever and wherever desired.

I express my deep sense of gratitude to Sh. S.K. Garg, Lecturer in English, Government National College, Sirsa for his valuable help in the course of study and some other fellows who help me at various intervals during the study.

I am sincerely indebted to my wife Saroj Devi and little sons Hemant and Deepak whose cooperation and sincerity helped me to complete this work. I am highly thankful to my parents for their constant inspiration which kept my morale high.

I feel obliged to all the concerned officials of various departments particularly that of DRDAs, Bhiwani, Hisar and Sirsa, District Statistics Officers, Bhiwani and Sirsa, Directorate of Rural Development, Haryana, Economic and Statistical Organization, Haryana and Ministry of Rural Development, Government of India and that of the various Banks who helped me a lot in collecting the data and for their response about the programme in personal discussion.

The facilities provided by Indian Institute of Public Administration, New Delhi, NIRD, Hyderabad, libraries of CCSHAU, Hisar, MD University, Rohtak, Kurukshetra University Kurukshetra etc. can not be underestimated. I should be failing in my duty if I do not place on record my gratitude to the respondent Beneficiaries and public opinion leaders for their cooperation and help in extracting the primary data.

I am indebted to many scholars and authors whose scholarly writings and view points have been made use of at several stages in this study.

I am also thankful to Mr. Vinod Godara, Mr. Ajay Jain and Mr. Kapil Kumar for their cooperation and sincerity while typing the script.

I would also like to extent my gratitude to Anmol Publication Pvt. Ltd., New Delhi and its Production Manager Sh. K.D. Joshi particularly to be kind enough and to cooperate in publication of the present Book.

Rajbir Singh

Abbreviations

ADC	Additional Deputy Commissioner
AL	Agricultural Labourer
APO	Assistant Project Officer
BC	Backward Classes
BDO	Block Development Officer
BPL	Below Poverty Line
CAD	Command Area Development
CAPART	Council for Advancement of People's Action and Rural Technology
CCI	Cement Corporation of India
CD	Community Development
CDP	Community Development Programme
CEO	Chief Executive Officer
CLCC	Central Level Consultative/Coordination Committee
CS	Chief Secretary
DDP	Desert Development Programme
DK	Do not Know
DLCC	District Level Consultative Committee
DMI	Directorate of Marketing and Inspection
DPAP	Drought Prone Area Programme
DRDA	District Rural Development Agency
DWCRA	Development of Women and Children in Rural Areas
FWP	Food for Work Programme
GIC	General Insurance Corporation

GOI	Government of India
HAD	Hill Area Development
HKGB	Haryana Kshetarya Gramin Bank
HYV	High Yielding Varieties
IAAP	Intensive Agricultural Area Programme
IADP	Intensive Agricultural District Programme
IRDP	Integrated Rural Development Programme
ISB	Industry, Service and Business
ISD	International Subscriber Dialing
JRY	Jawahar Rojgar Yojana
Km.	Kilometer
KVIB	Khadi and Village Industries Board
KVIC	Khadi and Village Industries Commission
KWH	Kilo Watt Hour
LDC	Lower Division Clerk
LIC	Life Insurance Corporation
MD	Managing Director
MF	Marginal Farmer
MFAL	Marginal Farmers and Agricultural Labourers Agency
MLAs	Members of Legislative Assembly
MNP	Minimum Needs Programme
MPs	Members of Parliament
NAL	Non Agricultural Labourer
NABARD	National Bank for Agriculture and Rural Development
NES	National Extension Services
NGOs	Non Governmental Organizations
NIRD	National Institute of Rural Development
NREP	National Rural Employment Programme
NSC	Non Scheduled Castes

NSSO	National Sample Survey Organization
OT	Other
PEO	Planning and Evaluation Organization
PH	Physically Handicapped
PIERP	Pilot Intensive Rural Employment Programme
PNB	Punjab National Bank
PRIs	Panchayati Raj Institutions
RA	Rural Artisan
RBI	Reserve Bank of India
RLEGP	Rural Landless Employment Guarantee Programme
SC	Scheduled Caste
SF	Small Farmer
SFDA	Small Farmers Development Agency
SLCC	State Level Consultative Committee
ST	Scheduled Tribe
STD	Subscriber Trunk Dialing
TADP	Tribal Area Development Programme
TRYSEM	Training of Rural Youths for Self-Employment
U	Uncertain
UNICEF	United Nations Institute for Children Emergency Fund
UTs	Union Territories
VLW	Village Level Worker

1

Introduction

Rural development has today become an objective not only of the local and regional concern, but a pragmatic objective fully backed by national government and international organizations like the United Nations, the International Bank for Reconstruction and Development, World Bank and the International Fund for Agricultural Development. Rural development is advocated today as a basic strategy for economic development all over the world.[1] The sheer largeness for the numbers who continue to live and work in the rural areas in the developing countries attract our attention to this important and neglected sector of economy. No country can achieve the desired goal if a large section of its population is living under unhygienic and destitute conditions. India, being a developing country, whose large population is living in rural areas, has necessity to pay special attention to the improvement of the economic, social and educational conditions of rural masses. Before Independence, the Britishers whose only and exclusive motto was expoitation of the country, did not bother about the improvement of living conditions of rural population. Hence during freedom struggle Mahatma Gandhi, Jawaharlal Nehru and other leaders came in contact with rural masses and knew about the destitute and unhygienic conditions of rural people's living under. Though a few steps were taken before Independence for rural development, these are too few to tackle the problem.

In 1947, when India achieved independence, eighty per cent of her population was dependent on agriculture and until the lot of this vast majority was improved, the picture of India would not look brighter.[2] The per capita yearly income at that time was Rs. 200 and there was great disparity in the income of upper, middle and lower classes.[3] Coupled with the problems of acute food shortage and general poverty of the masses, were the problems of illiteracy and public health. Only 14.4 per cent of people could read and write, 9 per cent of the school going children were in schools and only half of them reached the fourth grade.[4] The average life of an Indian was 29 years. Among the children, the death rate was 146 per 1000. Taking the country's population as a whole, there was one doctor for every 6,300 people but most of them were concentrated in urban areas. In the villages, it was estimated that there was one doctor at every 8,500 population. It was under this condition that independent India launched her career as a welfare state. Most of the people living in rural areas could not satisfy even their basic needs and there was dominance of illiteracy, poverty, unemployment, ignorance, diseases and other scourges of mankind. So it was necessary for the Government to make special provisions for elimination of the above said evils, without which a smooth and spontaneous progress was impossible and it was difficult to create an environment free from deficiency with various kinds of restraints. Hence the Government of India after independence, adopted various programmes for rural development starting from Community Development Progamme in 1952[5]. With the adoption of planning for development the country embarked upon a long, silent, arduous and non-violent socio-economic revolution for ensuring social equality and economic justice for every citizen of the country. The nature of Government tasks in post independence India has thus underwent a sea-change. Its emphasis shifted from maintenance of law and order to social welfare and individual progress. A suitable administrative setup was called for, to plan and implement, the development tasks. Unfortunately, this did not happen and the existing administrative setup designed by her colonial ruler-the Britishers, with minor changes in its traditional characteristics was made responsible for planning, implementation, coordination and vigilance of these new developmental programmes[6]. Development planning was adopted in the hope that the existing administrative machinery would be able to cope successfully with various demands that would be made on it[7]. Efforts were made to make these programmes more and more development oriented and accordingly changes were made in administrative setup to make it more and more development oriented. But these programmes could not achieve the desired goals and the later events clearly demonstrated that the existing administrative machinery was quite inefficient to deliver the goals. It not only impeded development, but also led to a fall in the growth rate.[8] The Government brought new programme to cover the failure of earlier one, but the administrative setup continue to remain almost the same with minor changes. As the success of a scheme is determined by various factor and the machinery responsible for its implementation is the major one. A specific programme requires a specific type of administrative setup for implementing it efficiently so that the attitudes and orientations of people towards the programme as well as the administrative setup should respond effectively. Rigidity, elitist feelings, power lust and overload of work on the required administrative setup were some of the major causes of failure of these schemes. As a result despite four decades of planned economic development, the poor remained poor, living below the minimum standard of consumption of Rs. 20/- (twenty) per capita per month at 1960-62 or Rs. 71/- (seventy-one) at 1971-72 price or Rs. 180/- (one hundred eighty) at 1981-82. They form the bulk of the poorest thirty (30) per cent of the population. For the majority of the people who are poor and belong to the socio-economically weaker sections in society, social and economic justice is still a far cry and an empty slogan.

Thus the problem of rural development has presented numerous problems to planners, administrators and social workers. The first five-year-plan was based on the idea of "all-round development" followed by the "socialistic pattern of society" approach in the second five-year-plan. "Increasing national income and improving conditions of the rural masses" was the goal set before the third five-year-plan. The fourth five-year-plan aimed at "growth with stability" and the emphasis was laid on "removal of poverty" in the fifth five-year-plan. "The alleviation of rural poverty" was the prime objective of sixth five-year-plan. Thus from early fifties, with the launching of first five-year-plan development of rural areas has been one of the abiding concerns of national endeavour. Hence various approaches to rural development were adopted starting from trickle down to specific area approach followed by target group approach. It all started with Community Development Programme (1952) which was instrumental in establishing a network of the basic extension and development service in the village.[9] How far these were helpful in ameliorating the lot of the rural poors is a question which is debatable, but it, undoubtedly, helped in creating awareness in the rural masses about the potential and means of development which made quicker adoption of major technological advances in the field of agriculture, community service and creation of basic infrastructure, were essential for development in latter years.

The awareness acted as a spur for many of reformative measures undertaken by the central and the state governments, like abolition of intermediary landlords, reforms of land tenure system, mechanization of farming and transforming of agriculture operations on scientific lines. Also the total investment made in five year plans on agriculture, irrigation facilities, various inputs like seeds etc., setting up of fertilizer plants, rural electrification and power generation did bring about a qualitative change in the rural scene. It led to the creation of essential physical and institutional infrastructure for socio-economic development in many rural areas. Efforts were also made to evolve schemes and programmes especially designed for the development of small and marginal farmers and the landless and agricultural labourers in particular[10]. With the objective of specific area development the programmes like the development of drought prone areas and desert areas and tribal people were launched in the seventies. Simultaneously various programmes for rural wage and employment for work were introduced to provide opportunities for work for the rural poors during the bleak seasons, when the farmers were not engaged in sowing or harvesting operation. Their aim was to create additional employment in rural areas with the help of available surplus food stock and their wages were partially paid in cash and partially in form of food grains or works of durable utility to the community. A series of these programmes and schemes specially designed for the upliftment of rural areas would reveal that the objective sought to be realized through their implementation have not always materialized. The Small Farmers Development Agency programme aimed at increasing the income level of small and marginal farmers and agricultural labourers has been in operation since 1971. The objective of the programme was to assist specifically identified persons to raise their income level. This was to be achieved by helping them to adopt improved agricultural technology, acquire means of increasing agricultural production like minor irrigation and diversify their farm economy.

The actual impact of the programme on the income of the beneficiary varied a great deal and in many cases has been of doubtful significance. It was found that the small and marginal farmers who constituted over 70 (seventy) per cent of the land holders held barely 24 per cent of the land holdings and that of top 10 per cent held as much as 51 per cent of the assets while the lower 40 per cent held barely 2.1 per cent[11]. Since the rural people derive their livelihood primarily from agriculture, their living conditions depend to a significant extent upon the performance of this sector. The incidence of rural poverty is found to be inversely related to agricultural production per head of rural population. This asserts the existence of trickle down mechanism in India. However, the power of trickle down process has been found to be very limited and at the same time weakening over time. This under-scores the importance of some specific measures in the alleviation of rural poverty by increasing production, employment in rural areas and by maintaining the rural wages rate at a reasonable level.

The agricultural labour households and the primarily cultivator households consisting of marginal and small farmers are identified as the rural poor. The 32nd round (1977-78) of the National Sample Survey Report revealed that about 50 per cent of the agricultural labour households and 31.7 per cent of the household self-employed in agriculture (a large section of whom are marginal and small farmers) were living below poverty line in India. The two groups of households together constituted 79.32 per cent of rural poor. The report also revealed that casual labourers were among the poorest segment of the total work force in agriculture whereas 58.2 per cent of the casual workers and 49.3 per cent of the regular wage workers were living below poverty line. 31.7 per cent of the self employment households in agriculture were found to be living in poverty[12]. The programme of land reforms started in the fifties, had made a little progress. Regional imbalances were glaring and poverty was wide spread and disconcerting. Hence the Integrated Rural Development Programme was introduced in 1978-79 to assist the rural population to derive economic benefits from the developmental assets of each area. The programme consists of small and marginal farmers, agricultural labourers, landless labourers and rural artisans etc. Under the programme, the largest coverage has been under improved agricultural category followed by animal husbandry and fisheries. The programme was comprehensive in scope and sought to secure fuller exploitation of the local potentials[13]. Training of Rural Youths for Self-Employment (TRYSEM), started in 1979 for providing self-employment to rural youths and Agency for Development of Women and Children, could not get satisfactory assistance from other rural development programmes, were associated with IRDP in 1983[14]. According to the official estimates, the pattern of growth, emerging from the development strategy and implementation of special poverty alleviation programmes has brought down the number of rural poor living below poverty line. According to the Planning Commission, the decline has been from 51.2 per cent in 1977-78 to 40.4 per cent in 1983-84, 39.9 per cent in 1985-86 and 28.2 per cent in 1989-90[15]. The Sixth Plan envisaged the reduction of the percentage of people below poverty line to less than 10 per cent by 1994-95[16]. However, the success of the programme like IRDP largely depends upon its effective implementation in the field. At the national level, the experience in implementing this programme in the past has shown that though it did have some measure of success in terms of physical and financial achievements, yet certain shortcomings have been noticed in its implementation. These includes wrong identification of Beneficiaries, leakage, lack of proper infrastructure, low level of investment and low percentage of people crossing poverty line.

Haryana is predominantly a rural state with over 75 per cent population living in rural areas. As to the incidence of poverty among the rural population, the 1990-91 household survey had brought out 37 per cent of the total families living below the poverty line. In Haryana too, like other states, the major poverty alleviation programme of IRDP has been implemented since its very inception in 1978-79 with the twin objective of removal of poverty and unemployment among the rural masses. In view of the exceedingly increased importance attached to this programme in the state, it is considered appropriate to study the implementation of this programme in order to ascertain the extent to which it has met the desired objectives in the past and what are its weaknesses. So for no comprehensive study has been undertaken in this regard in the state in general and Bhiwani District in particular on the problem of Administration of Integrated Rural Development Programme in Haryana. It is fruitful and essential to conduct a study to fill up the gap on this subject. The study might provide information about various development programmes with special emphasis on Integrated Rural Development Programme, its performance, administrative setup, process of implementation, perception of officials associated with the scheme and that of the Beneficiaries and to highlight the loop-holes in the implementation of programme with suitable suggestions. Moreover, the study might open new vistas for further research on the problem.

Basic Assumptions

The basic asusmptions of the present study include: 1. The success of any scheme for development is determined to a large extent by the administrative setup responsible for its implementation and its method and procedure of working. 2. The administrative structure for development programmes should be flexible, goal-oriented and development-oriented in nature. 3. The performance of the administrators depends on their mental make up and a developmentalist is needed to implement development policies. 4. The success of a development scheme is determined by the perception of both the officials concerned and that of the people for whom it is going to be implemented. 5. Training of personnel in management technology specially in areas of project planning and sharpening of professional skills determined the success of a scheme. 6. The approach of officials towards people should be that of persuasion, cooperation and mutual understanding. 7. A programme of integrated nature like the IRDP cannot get the expected results without proper coordination and communication among various agencies. 8. The Beneficiaries' positive attitudes towards the development schemes will be essential for maximizing their output. 9. Operational deficiency in proper monitoring hampers the desired success of the development programmes. 10. The success of IRDP depends on infrastructural support available.

With these assumptions in brief our aim was to analyse:

- The various programmes of rural development undertaken by the Government of India so far with special reference to Integrated Rural Development Programme in the State of Haryana in general and District Bhiwani in particular.
- To study the profile of the area of study.
- To examine the administrative structure of IRDP at various levels.

- To study the process of implementation of IRDP.
- To study the performance of IRDP.
- To study the perception of Officials concerned and that of the Beneficiaries.
- To review the progress and actual implementation of IRDP and its utility in present context.
- To suggest suitable measures for effective implementation of the programme.

Focus of the Study

The focus of the present study is on the Administration of Integrated Rural Development Programme in Haryana with special focus on District Bhiwani which is situated on the South-Western parts of the State, though forms the part of Indo-Gangetic Alluvial Plain, yet largely it is dry and sandy. In spite of the fact that the climatic conditions of the district are not favourable, it has an edge over the other districts so far as the development activities are concerned. It is the second largest district in the State constituting 11.6 per cent of the total area and 7 per cent of the total population. More than four-fifths of the districts population is inhabiting in rural areas and most of them are engaged in agriculture and other allied activities for their livings. The district is sparsely populated and majority of the population is Hindus. The Scheduled Castes constitutes about one-fifth of its population. The district is not evenly populated and the density in the South-Western parts is less than half to the North-Eastern parts. About one-fourth of district population forms the main work force of which more than two-thirds are engaged in primary sector. Agriculture is the backbone of the rural economy of the district. In spite of all the oddities the district has presented an eventful growth in all fronts of development. All the villages are enjoying the facilities of electricity, safe drinking water and metalled roads in addition to the satisfactory network of health, transport and communication services. The execution of various irrigation projects has transformed the rural scenario in the district and it has brought a prominent change in its economy. The district has not only a fragile network of industry, but also is centralized in some parts. The area of the study was chosen Bhiwani District in which nine Gram Panchayats, spread over three Blocks-Bhiwani, Badhara and Loharu, have been taken up for identification of sample

Beneficiaries for collecting primary data. The other source of primary data is IRDP officials of DRDA, Bhiwani. Various programmes of rural development undertaken by the Government of India have been discussed with special emphasis on Integrated Rural Development Programme. Besides, review of IRDP at various levels, its administrative structure and process of implementation have been critically examined. The main focus of study is on the perception of Beneficiaries and that of Officials with a view to assessing the impact of this programmes. The data given in the study are up to 1995-96. The period of study has been 1980-96. However, for field work Beneficiaries assisted during the period from 1990-95 have been interviewed.

Methodology

Broadly speaking the study is exploratory in nature and the conclusions are tentative. In term of scope, the study seeks to provide an initial step towards understanding the various programmes of rural development with special emphasis on Administration of Integrated Rural Development Programme in Haryana. The study is primarily based on empirical evidences collected by conducting interviews with selected respondent Beneficiaries and that of the IRDP Officials. Simple random sampling technique has been adopted for the selection of Beneficiary respondents. For the selection of the sample at each level, the following procedure was adopted. First, Bhiwani district was taken for the purpose of in-depth study, of course the following factors have been taken into account while selecting the District Bhiwani for in-depth study of the problem:

- Not much work has been done in Haryana so far. However, not even a single study is available on the present problem of District Bhiwani.
- The proximity and acquaintance of the area and the people was also one of the considerations for choosing the Bhiwani District.
- The district is average in its demographic features as well as from the point of families assisted under IRDP in the state.
- The district is both agriculturally as well as industrially among the most backward districts in the state.

Second, the selection of Blocks in the District has been done by applying simple random sampling technique on the basis of families assisted under IRDP since 1980-1995. Out of the total eight Blocks in the district: Tosham (6381), Badhra (5589), Bawani Khera (5505), Bhiwani (5003), Dadri-I (4621), Loharu (4544), Dadri-II (4236) and Siwani (3445), three have been taken for sampling. Thus, the selected Blocks are Bhiwani, Badhara and Loharu. Third, for choosing the Gram Panchayats from each Block, the lists of Gram Panchayats covered under IRDP during the above mentioned period were taken from the DRDA's Office. The number of Gram Panchayats assisted under IRDP in each selected Block was Bhiwani (61), Badhara (78) and Loharu (79). From each of the selected Blocks, three Gram Panchayats were chosen on the basis of number of Beneficiaries assisted during 1980-95 with simple random sampling. Thus the selected Gram Panchayats are: Mitathal, Devsar and Tigrana in Bhiwani Block, Allauddinpur, Gagarwas and Jhumpa Kalan in Loharu Block and Gopi, Bandhwa and Pichopa Kalan in Badhara Block. The number of Beneficiaries in the selected Gram Panchayats during the above mentioned period was Devsar (172), Tigrana (133), Mitathal (94), Gopi (116), Bhandwa (84), Pichopa Kalan (69), Jhumpa Kalan (131), Allauddinpur (98) and Gagarwas (39). Fourth, the respondents were of two types i.e. the Beneficiaries of IRDP and the Officials of DRDA, Bhiwani. For interview, a sample of 240 respondent Beneficiaries was taken form the District Bhiwani, taking 80 Beneficiaries from each selected Block. The number of respondent Beneficiaries taken from each selected Gram Panchayat was proportionate to the size sample. These respondent Beneficiaries have been spread over the nine selected Gram Panchayats. To identify the Beneficiaries simple random sampling technique has been applied. For this the lists of IRDP Beneficiaries during 1990-95 was taken from DRDA, Bhiwani. As the number of IRDP officials in the district was 20. Hence all of them have been chosen for interview. There was no need of sampling in this case. Besides, all the nine Branch Managers of concerned Rural Development Banks and nine public opinion leaders/Sarpanchas of the selected Gram Panchayats have been interviewed to evaluate their perceptions and participation in the programme to make the study more comprehensive and indepth. The primary data for the study were collected from the sample Beneficiaries and Officials concerned with the help of carefully prepared questionnaires consisting of both structured and unstructured questions. The questionnaires were designed to elicit responses relating to the respondents background information, administrative structure of IRDP, its process of implementation and Officials-Beneficiaries perceptions about each other as well as about the programme on the whole. Data were also collected through the techniques of observation and discussions. The personal knowledge gained through stay in villages and informal discussions with officials have provided a lot of useful information for the study. For collection of primary data, separate sets of questionnaires have been used - one each for IRDP Beneficiaries, IRDP Staff, Bank Officials and Sarpanch/public opinion leaders. These schedules/questionnaires were administered personally with the respondents. The responses were collected from the respondents individually, though group discussions were also utilized in the study. Bank Branches were also visited to verify the facts relating to financial aspects.

In addition to the information collected from the respondents, the secondary data were collected from the relevant official records including various guidelines of the programmes and schemes, the manuals, correspondence between Government of India, State Government and between State Government and lower level agencies, the progress reports, agenda notes and the proceedings of various meetings conducted at Central and State levels. The data were collected from the office records of the DRDAs, Branches of concerned Banks in the District, District Statistics Office, District Development and Panchayat Office, Country and Town Planning Office, the Directorates of Economics and Statistics, and Rural Development. Moreover, a number of publications and evaluation reports of Ministry of Rural Development, Planning Commission, National Institute of Rural Development (NIRD), Government of India, Rural Development and Panchayati Raj, and Economics and Statistics Departments of the Government of Haryana were extensively used in the course of the present study. The information from books, journals, research articles and news papers were also used in the study. However, a question often asked in empirical studies is about the general conclusions of the study because there is always a problem of generality. The reasons might be the limitations of time, the universe of study, place and size of sample etc. Some times, the tools of analysis also pose a problem in making generalization. But this does not mean that there can not be any specific conclusion.

Plan of Chapterization

The data and information collected through various sources for the study have been classified in seven chapters including the concluding chapter.

Chapter 1 touches upon the problem of administration of Integrated Rural Development Programme, importance of study, review of literature, conceptual frame, basic assumptions, the universe of study and the methodology.

Chapter 2 is concerned with the historical perspective of Rural Development Programmes, review of literature and conceptual frame of IRDP.

Chapter 3 deals with the profile of the State of Haryana, District Bhiwani and that of the selected Blocks in the District of Bhiwani. It gives information about the administrative history, demographic, geographical and economic aspects about each of the above mentioned levels.

Chapter 4 examines the administrative structure of Integrated Rural Development Programme at Central, State, District and Block levels. It provides knowledge about the organizational setup of IRDP, composition of consultative committee and other subsidiary organizations at various levels with a critical view.

Chapter 5 describes the process of implementation of IRDP. In this chapter, the various step taken in the implementation of IRDP particularly at Block and District levels have been discussed. It consists of information about identification of BPL families, formulation and approval of annual action plans, organization of credit camps, processing of loan applications, disbursement of loan, purchasing of assets, monitoring and recovery of loans.

Chapter 6 deals with the actual implementation of IRDP. In this chapter, the performance of IRDP at State and District levels has been presented. It provides information about the BPL families-caste and category wise, number of families assisted, their caste and category wise composition, financial allocation, sector wise coverage of Beneficiaries and per capita investment at District and State levels.

Chapter 7 highlights the perception of IRDP Officials and that of Beneficiaries towards each other and the programme as a whole. It consists of information about the background of Beneficiaries, process of implementation of the programme and Officials-Beneficiaries perception about administrative structure of IRDP, its process of implementation, its performance, the evaluation as a whole and their views about each other.

Chapter 8 deals with the thread of the preceding chapters in the form of conclusions. Along with the findings of the study, some suggestions have also been offered in this chapter.

In the next chapter we have attempted to describe in brief the historical perspective of various Rural Development Programmes including origin of IRDP review of literature and conceptual frame of IRDP with its salient features.

REFERENCES

1. Srivastava, A.K., *Integrated Rural Development Programme in India: Policy and Administration* (New Delhi: Deep and Deep Publications, 1988), p. 17.
2. Bala Krishna, S., "Some Demographic Features of Rural India", (ed.) *Rural Development in India.* (Hyderabad: National Institute of Rural Development, 1979), p. 51.
3. *Ibid.,* p. 68.
4. *Ibid.,* p. 54
5. Rao, B.G., "Community Development in Maharashtra", Panandikar, V.A. Pai, (ed.), *Decade of Planning in India,* (Bombay: Popular Prakashan, 1969), pp. 131-147.
6. Mathur, Kuldeep, *Administrative Institutions, Political Capacity and India's Strategy for Rural Development* (Asian Center for Development Administration, 1975).
7. Datta, B.C., "Planning for Rural Areas', *Khadi Gramdyog,* Vol. 21, No. 3, December, 1974, pp. 179-182.
8. Mathur, Kuldeep, *Bureaucratic Response to Development,* (Delhi: National, 1972), p. 121.
9. Singh, Hoshiar, (ed.), *Rural Development in India: Evaluative Study in Politics and Programme,* (Jaipur: Printwell Publication, 1985), p. 1.

10. Chambers, Robert, *Rural Development: Putting the Last First,* (London: Longman, 1983), p. 147.

11. Tinaikar, S.S., "Anti-poverty Programme — A Critique", *The Public Administrator* (IIPA, Maharashtra Regional Branch, 1984-85), p. 6.

12. Ghosh, Madhusudan, "Agricultural Development and Rural Poverty in India", *Indian Journal of Agricultural Economics,* Vol. 51, No. 3, July-September, 1996, pp. 375-378.

13. Government of India, Department of Rural Development, *Manual for IRDP and Allied Programmes,* Ministry of Agriculture, New Delhi, April, 1991, p. 7.

14. *Ibid,* p. 9.

15. Government of India, Department of Rural Development, *Conference of Ministers of Rural Development and Water Supply - 29th and 30th October, 1990: Agenda,* New Delhi, 1990, p. 7.

16. Government of India, Planning Commission, *Sixth Five Year Plan 1980-85,* New Delhi, pp. 51-52.

2

Historical Perspective and Conceptual Frame of IRDP

This chapter provides information about the historical perspective of rural development programmes including IRDP, review of literature and conceptual frame of IRDP with its salient features.

The concept of Integrated Rural Development Programme (IRDP) is the outcome of a long series of various rural development programmes extended up to Independence or beyond it. Before considering the various aspects of Integrated Rural Development Programme (IRDP), its performance, process of implementation, administrative structure, Beneficiaries officials perception, it is worthwhile to highlight the various schemes or programmes initiated by the Government of India for rural development in brief.

During British Raj rural development, was started as a humanitarian act and the practice was not backed by any executive or legal sanction in the beginning. Legality and legitimacy was provided later. Rural development as a function of government initially began 'as a search for an alternative to laissez-faire', as B.B. Mishra observed.[1] The Famine Commission (1880) observed, 'Agricultural prosperity in ordinary time was the best shield against the difficulties and trails of a season of drought.[2] There were various sporadic attempts at agricultural development but no real beginning was made until technical agricultural personnels were appointed. Mahatma Gandhi gave a big boost to rural development through his 'back to the village' movement and his comprehensive programme which included use of Khadi, promotion of cottage and village industries, and women's upliftment.[3] R.N. Tagore set up his Sriniketan Institute of Rural Reconstruction in 1921 to make the rural folk 'self-reliant and self-respectful'. Mr. F.L. Brayne, the District Collector of Gurgaon started in 1927, a programme of rural reconstruction based on self-help and hard work.[4] In the same year, the Martandam experiment was started in Madras under the leadership of the Youngman' Christian Association 'to bring about a complete upward development towards a more abundant life for rural people, spiritually, mentally, physically, socially and economically'.[5] Similarly in 1932, the princely state of Baroda launched a programme for amelioration of rural ills. Thus, the rural development programmes in India started by R.N. Tagore and Mahatma Gandhi during pre-independence period, which emphasised on self and mutual help, for a change in outlook of villagers as a precondition for development. Material advancement of village was considered less important and the contribution of Britishers and princely states toward rural development was microscopic. Hence large scale rural development programmes of various types were initiated after independence by the Government of India. Some of these were meant for general development of rural areas, others for development of specific area or target groups and still others for rural wage and employment generation. To have a better picture of rural development programmes, it is worthwhile here to mention a brief review of these programmes. The emphasis of general rural development programmes was on agriculture. The general programmes include Community Development Programme, National Extension Scheme, Panchayati Raj Institutions, Co-operative Movement, Intensive Agricultural District Programme (IADP), Intensive Agricultural Area Programme (IAAP), High Yielding Varieties (HYV) etc.

Under the first-five-year plan (1951-56), the strategy of socio-economic transformation was to establish National Extension Service (NES) as a permanent agency and Community Development as a method to unite government services with people's effort to solve commonly felt problems. The role of National Extension Service (NES) was to bring improved knowledge of agriculture and certain basic services to the very doors of the people, while Community Development Programme (CDP) created the climate and the ground through social education, motivation, group formation, aided-self projects etc. The process of people's participation was the very basis of this approach. In fact, the rationale of combining Community Development with National

Extension Service was to create a social climate of acceptability and group infrastructure so that extension service could reach and serve more people.[6] Thus Community Development Programme was the first in this direction with a view of systematic integrated rural development by making one multi-purpose functionary responsible at the grass-root level for all rural development activities particularly in the field of agricultural development. As a result of this programme, a number of rural facilities were provided and certain degree of development conscience was also created among the rural folk.[7] It was the Community Development Organization through which the government reached down to the villages as an agent for the improvement of agriculture and the transformation of rural society. There was a major change in the functioning of the administrative set up after owning the responsibilities of development and social change by the Government. The administration was given the responsibilities of leadership role in influencing, guiding and managing development process.[8] Though systematic training was imparted but without any training policy[9] and this leads to people's alienation from the development programmes.

By late fifties, it was realized that something was seriously wrong with CDP. It was no more a people's programme but bureaucratic mobilization to fulfil targets set by the centralized planing process. Hence, periodical evaluation of progress of rural development on the basis of CDP led to change in two directions. First, there was the shift in emphasis to economic development, especially agricultural production. Secondly, there was the broadening of popular participation through democratic decentralization as recommended by the Balwant Rai Mehta Committee (1958)[10]. For making CDP more successful, Panchayati Raj Institutions (PRIs) were introduced in 1959 with a three tier structural organization with delegation of authority for decision making and policy implementation. Thus Panchayati Raj was heralded as political revolution that brought democracy to the door steps of the people and ensured their participation in development activities. While every Indian State had adopted the Panchayati Raj system in one form or the other, it has not proved effective in promoting either economic development or political participation at the village level.[11] As Ashok Mehta Committee put it, "some would treat it just as an administrative agency"; and still others as "an extension of democracy at the grass root level"; and still others as a "character of rural local government"[12]. Apart from this, these institutions are bound to be judged by the operational efficiency of their administrative machinery. Within five years, these institutions began to stagnate and score to decline. The trend continued in the eighties and an attempt is being made to restructure and galvanise them into purposive action. Panchayati Raj was considered as an institutional mechanism for rural development. Its twin objectives were development and democracy[13]. Though it has contributed to rural development, the scheme could not become successful in most of the stages due to odd reasons since long. A basic defect of the community development approach was that it thought of the community as a whole without realizing that this was broken up into various social and economic stratifications. It was alleged that both CDP and PRIs catered to the demands of the dominant class and caste groups[14]. Another important instrument of rural development has been the co-operative movement. The blue print of the co-operative development programme as an integral part of rural development was provided by the well known Rural Credit Survey Committee Report. It looked upon co-operation as an alliance of the weak against the dominance of the strong element that is the landlords-trader-moneylender group supported by the banking and trading institutions in the city and metropolitan centers. The blue print of the constructive programme of rural development recommended by the Committee was known as "The Scheme for Integrated Rural Credit". The scheme was for integrated rural credit in this sense that agricultural production was to be linked to agricultural finance and recovery of agricultural loans was to be linked to co-operative marketing and processing. These were essential elements of the crop loans scheme which was also a scheme for supervising credit. The credit was to be linked with standing crop rather than with land security[15]. On the recommendation of the committee, National Co-operative Development Corporation was established to encourage co-operative marketing and processing. As the institution was designed to provide short term and medium term credit, for long term credit there was a system of land mortgage banks now known as Land Development Banks. In the past, provided finance only for redemption of credit with the establishment of the Agricultural Refinance Corporation in 1963.

They were geared more and more to provide long term finance for purpose like digging tube wells, land reclamation, horticulture, mechanization etc. As in the case of CDP, the benefit of co-operative development have also gone largely to the richer and middle peasants rather than to small farmers and tenants. Some programmes of agricultural development existed outside the pale of CDP and Co-operative movement. They were essentially the programmes of a technical nature, like supply of improved seeds, improvement of agronomical practices, development of green manure and compost, popularization of chemical fertilizer etc. They were all of a general nature and not particularly developed for the small farmers or weaker sections. It is not as if community development had not emphasised on agriculture. However, the efforts for food production were not the monogamous.

Lack of technology was an inherent weakness for accelerating agricultural production, in spite of sincere endeavours of the CD staff. The need for greater concentration on food production itself, almost in preference to the concept alround development prevalent then, was reflected in the 'Report on India's Food Crisis and Steps to Meet It (1959) by a team led by Dr. Sherman E. Johnson under the auspices of Ford Foundation. It observed that "The rate of increase must be tripled to meet the third plan target. If India's food production increases no faster than the present rates, the gap between supplies and targets will be 28 million by 1965-66. This will be about 25 per cent short fall in term of need. No conceivable programme of imports or rationing can meet a crisis of this magnitude." Food production must be given the highest priority and selected crops and selected areas in each state should be chosen which have the greatest increased potentialities".[16] These recommendations led to the strategy for locating well endowed districts and farms therein capable of yielding high agricultural production and marketable surplus. Consequently, more concentration was put on improving productivity per acre than on extending the acreage. A package programme was launched as the Intensive Agricultural District Programme (IADP) in the last year of the Second Plan (1960-61) and 37 districts in 14 states were covered by 1970[17]. This was followed by the Intensive Agricultural Area Programme (IAAP) in 1964-65 which also adopted the strategy of IADP, but less intensively. By 1966, 117 Districts covering 1,596 blocks and by 1970, 150 Districts were brought under this programme. IADP advocated a selective area approach to agricultural development and the achievement of intensity of cropping. Towards this, packages for extension services and for improved production practices were designed. Both knowledge and inputs were made available. Preparation of farm plan was stressed incorporating the 'package' needed for output increase. The programme was quite successful. The drought years of 1964-66 were really a harrowing experience but out of this crucible emerged the focus on the utilization of the High Yielding Varieties (HYV) representing the needed mix of research results and farm application. The infrastructure and the experience in IADP to some extent and the technology of the new varieties largely contributed the optimism on the food production front. The HYV which was originally launched in 1963-64, expanded sufficiently to cover 37 million hectares by 1977-78.[18] Though these programmes (IAAP and HYV) contributed to the 'Green Revolution' and increased in agricultural production, these remained largely confined to regions with better natural advantages. At the same time, they greatly increased economic polarization in rural areas and also contributed to increasing social antagonisms between landlords and tenants and land owners and labourers.[19]

Associated with poverty in the rural areas are the problems of unemployment and under-employment. These are the two basic factors which effects the poorest segment of the rural population and are the major contributory factors of the high incidence of poverty in the rural areas. A substantial reduction in poverty can be achieved only if there are determined efforts at the distribution of income and consumption in favour of the poorer section of the population, hence a number of rural wage and employment generation programmes were launched simultaneously. These includes Rural Manpower Programme (RMP), Crash Scheme for Rural Employment (CSRE), Pilot Intensive Rural Employment Programme (PIREP), Food for Work Programme (FPW), National Rural Employment Programme (NREP). Rural Landless Employment Guarantee Programme (RLEGP) and Jawahar Rojgar Yojana (JRY). The later programme i.e. JRY is presently under implementation in the country and is a culmination of previous efforts in implementing wage employment programmes for the removal of poverty and under employment.

Rural Manpower Programme (RMP) was the first major programme started in 1960-61 to provide employment on the mass scale in the rural areas. The aim was to provide employment for 100 days at least to 2.5 million persons in the country by the end of the third five-year-plan. However, the programme did not gain much grounds due to the availability of limited funds. Therefore, this programme came to an end in 1968-69[20]. In the early Seventies, when the planning strategy emphasised a direct attack on poverty, the Crash Scheme for Rural Employment was introduced in April, 1971. The purpose of Crash Scheme was to alleviate the prevailing conditions of unemployment and under-employment in rural areas by generating additional employment through rural works. This programme aimed to generate employment opportunities for 1000 persons in each district for 250 days per year during the three years from 1971-74. Apart from employment generation, the other objective of this programme was to generate assets of a durable nature in the areas of minor irrigation, land development, afforestation and school buildings etc[21]. However, the programme failed to generate substantial employment due to poor planning and weak administrative machinery. The Community Development Programme and 'Green Revolution' could not do much for rural poor. Hence special programmes were needed either on target basis or areas basis. The All India Credit Review Committee (1969) pointed out "If the fruits of development continued to be denied to large section of the rural community, while prosperity accrues to some, the resulting tensions, social and economic, may not only upset the process of orderly and peaceful change in the rural economy but even frustrate the national efforts to keep up agricultural productions.[22] The broad objectives of planning in India has been 'growth with social justice' and it has remained the major concern and focus of the government. In order to achieve the goals of development with social justice, it was necessary to ensure that all patterns of overall economic growth itself is such as to generate adequate income for the weaker sections through its impact on employment generation and on the development of the backward regions.[23] It was considered that growth in economy and agricultural production will automatically 'Trickle down' to the masses and alleviate their poverty. The first setback to this contention came with disillusionment, which was equally quick, with the emerging pattern of growth which 'bypassed a large section of rural population particularly the small farmers, tenants, share croppers and agriculture labourers'.[24]

In the fourth plan, the attention shifted to the weaker sections. It was realized that the gains of development did not percolate to the poor. The basic problem was now to achieve rapid growth with distributive justice. The 'area based' and 'target based' approach was adopted and a number of programmes devised.[25] Special programmes were introduced for the benefit of the poor, relatively less privileged classes and backward areas. The objectives of these programmes were creation of assets, skill development and creation of infrastructure as well as to take up development works in the backward areas. Beneficiary oriented programmes like Small Farmers Development Agency (SFDA), and Marginal Farmers and Agricultural Labourers Agency (MFAL) aimed at helping the specific target groups of Beneficiaries were started in 1971-72.[26] The main objective of the SFDA was to assist the small farmers, with land holdings between 2.5 to 5.0 acres, who had not benefited from the gains of the green revolution. This was to be achieved by helping them to adopt to irrigation and other production increasing measures and diversify their farm economy through subsidiary activities like animal husbandry, dairying, horticulture etc. Subsidy to the extent of 25 per cent was provided to the identified small farmers on capital investments and inputs besides the facility of loans to them from the cooperative and commercial banks. SFDA remained a cent per centrally funded scheme up to 1978 and therefore it came to be funded on 50: 50 sharing basis by centre and state governments. During the fourth five-year-plan, 46 Pilot projects were launched. Each project was expected to cover, during the five year period, approximately 50,000 families of identified small farmers. Similarly the objectives of Marginal Farmers and Agricultural Labourers (MFAL) scheme was to assist the marginal farmers, with land holdings below 2.5 acres and agricultural labourers to improve their productivity and income through a varieties of activities like crop husbandry, increased use of inputs, minor irrigation, animal husbandry etc. The admissible subsidy to the scheme was kept at 33 1/3 per cent, besides the loans on SFDA pattern continued to be floated to them. During the Fourth Five Year Plan, 41 MFAL projects were started. Each project aimed at covering over the five years period, 15,000 marginal farmers and 5000 agricultural labourers out of the identified lists. The two agencies were brought together in 1974 under a combined agency came to be known as SFDA. The basic objective of this agency was to enable selected target groups of marginal and small farmers and agricultural labourers to improve their incomes through undertaking productive activities or improving their existing ones. It consisted of a governing body with a small executive staff, with the collector as the head. Its members were district officers of agriculture, animal husbandry and other departments closely concerned with its programmes. Financial institutions and Zila-Parishads were represented along with some non-officials.[27] It had no staff of its own except few officials at the District level. It depended upon the existing block officials to identify target persons and implementation of the schemes for their benefit. By 1980, the number of SFDAs rose to 168 from 87 in 1972-73, covering 1818 Blocks in 200 District of the country.[28] During the 9 years of the operation of SFDA-MFAL agencies a total of 16.7 million persons from the target groups were identified for assistance in all project Blocks. The assistance was made available to 8 million Beneficiaries of whom 1.3 million belonged to SCs and STs. About 75 per cent (6.1 million) of the Beneficiaries were helped through subsidised supply of inputs, improved implementation etc. The cumulative medium and long term credit advanced to the Beneficiaries till August, 1980 stood at Rs. 382.4 crores and the total money spent up to this period was Rs. 239.7 crore which included subsidy and administrative expenses.[29] SFDA programme which could deliver some benefits to only about Eight million persons, suffered from several limitations. First, the total members identified for assistance did not cover all the target group household which were estimated in 1971 to be 51 million. Secondly, even among the identified beneficiary households only half of these were given some assistance. Thirdly, the assistance in the form of subsidy and loan was too small in many cases to enable the very poor households, which were mostly of marginal farmers and agricultural labourers, to improve their dismal economic lot substantially.

To cover the regional imbalances certain other special programmes like Development of Drought Prone Area (DPAP), Hill Area Development (HAD), Whole Village Development Programme, Command Area Development (CAD), Tribal Area Development (TADP) and Desert Development Programme (DDP) were started in the seventies. These are essentially area-based programme. These programmes, in general aimed at the overall development of the area where they operated. Moreover, these programmes focused on the development of weaker sections of the society.

Drought Prone Area Programme (DPAP) is an area development programme with a thrust on development of irrigation sources, soil and moisture conservation, forestation, livestock development and development of sound dry land farming practices and their adoption. It has occupied special importance as it relates to vast areas which are subject to the hazardous consequences of drought. This programme has been extended to 947 Blocks in 155 District in 13 States, including total area of 746 lakh hectares up to 1994-95. The total expenditure on this programme since its inception in 1973-74 to 1994-95 has been Rs. 1742 crore and has improved the position of an area of 57.29 lakh hectares. Though it is essentially an area development programme, the individual beneficiary approach, similar to that of SFDA has also been adopted in DPAP[30]. Hill Area Development Programme has been in operation in hilly areas with the objective of raising the living standard of the local population. The programme is oriented to the local conditions so as to benefit directly the local population. Area development plans are prepared for the integrated development of hill areas.[31] Tribal Area Development Programme is concerned with the development of triabal areas and to bring a qualitative change in the socio-economic structure of the tribal community. The Integrated Area Plans prepared under this programme focus on the development of tribal communities in general and the weakest sections among the tribals, in particular. The main approach to development has been to cover 50,000 to 70,000 tribal beneficiaries by different agencies under various economic development programmes.[32] In Command Area Development Programme the emphasis is to ensure alround development of the command area with a view to achieve efficient and optimum utilization of the irrigation potential. Though the programme is area-based, special emphasis on weaker sections has also been laid side by side, in order to enable hem to take full advantage of the benefits available to small and marginal farmers under the SFDA programme are also available under this programme with the difference that the target number or Beneficiaries to be covered is not fixed[33]. Desert Development Programme (DDP) was started in the states of

Haryana, Rajasthan, Gujarat, Himachal Pradesh, and Jammu and Kashmir in 1977-78 with the objectives of controlling desertification and promotion of opportunities to raise the level of production, income and employment in areas covered under the programme. The objectives are sought to be achieved by taking up activities like irrigation, afforestation, soil and water conservation, dryland agriculture, ground water development, livestock development etc. The programme covers both hot and cold arid areas and has been extended to 7 States covering 36 Districts and 277 Blocks by 1994-95. From the very beginning of the programme up to 1994-95, a sum of Rs. 597.51 crore has been spend and the position of 5.52 lakh hectares area has been improved. The pattern of funding and allocation for the programme varies according to the extent and severity of aridity. Up to 1978-79, the entire expenditure on the programme was born by the central government. From 1979-80 onwards, the cost is shared equally between the central government and the state government concerned.[34]

Based on the equitable distribution of the benefits of development, a Whole Village Development Scheme was conceived. It was based on the recommendations of the National Commission on Agriculture. The main theme of this scheme was the concentration on multifaceted development endeavour around the village community as a whole and to entrust the programme to suitable voluntary agency if there was one in the area. The programme includes land reforms and consolidation of holdings, land development including soil and water management, maximizing irrigation support and cropping programme for the village as a whole, aiming at maximized use of resources. To start with, it was proposed to take up five pilot projects in four states. Pilot Intensive Rural Employment Project (PIREP) was planned as an action-cum study project to provide employment to the needy rural people in selected areas along with Crash Scheme for Rural Employment. It was introduced in 15 selected Blocks in October, 1972 for a period of three years. Besides employment generation, it was also aimed at studying the nature and dimensions of the problem of unemployment among wage seeking rural workers. It also tried to find out the potential for employment in the secondary and tertiary sectors and the skill training need for such employment.[35] Though PIREP proved to be slightly better programme because of the fact that it threw light on certain characteristics of rural unemployment but it was not rated as successful by the Review Committee on PIREP which pointed out that due to certain organizational deficiencies, this programme could not prove to be of much use in evolving a comprehensive programme for the whole country.[36] Food for Work Programme (FWP) was introduced as a nation wide programme in April, 1977 in view of the abundant availability of food stocks. The basic objectives of the programme were to generate additional gainful employment to a large number of unemployed and under employed persons in the rural areas for raising their income and consequently their nutritional levels; to create durable community assets; and to utilize the surplus food grains for the development of human resources.[37] The distinctive aspect of this programme was to pay a part of the wage in the form of food grains at subsidised prices, which assured minimum food consumption and therefore, minimum nutrition to the Beneficiaries. The work under this programme was on the whole planned and implemented by taking into account the lessons derived from the working of the rural works and crash employment programmes launched earlier. It was evaluated by the PEO of the Planning Commission which pointed out that the major hindrance in the implementation of the programme was its administrative slackness. It continued up to October, 1980 when it was replaced by a more comprehensive programme named National Rural Employment Programme (NREP).

In view of the emphasis laid down in the Sixth Plan on the alleviation of rural poverty and redistribution of income and consumption in favour of the poorer sections of the population by significantly increasing employment opportunities in the rural areas, the Food for Work Programme was redefined and restructured in the form of National Rural Employment Programme (NREP). This programme was started in October, 1980 as a centrally sponsored scheme on 50: 50 sharing basis between the Centre and States.[38] The basic objectives of the programme were generation of additional gainful employment for unemployed and underemployed men and women in the rural areas, creation of durable community assets to strength the rural infrastructure which will lead to a rapid growth of the rural economy and improvement in the overall quality of life in the rural areas.[39] Under NREP, preference was to be given to landless labours, scheduled castes and scheduled tribes for employment and the works which had the potential to provide direct benefits to the poor were preferred. Wages were to be paid partly in cash and partly in food grains. Since its inception up to 1988-89 under NREP, funds to the tune of Rs. 4774.13 crore were utilized against the allocation of Rs. 4986.25 crore. In addition 5.58 million tones of food grains were also utilized. The total mandays generated under NREP were 3252.44 million during this period.[40] NREP has however, had a significant impact in terms of stabilization of wages in the rural areas, containing prices of food grains and the creation of wide variety of community assets which could be expected to raise the levels of living of the rural population.[41] It apparently looked a direct focus on the target group population for whom it was meant.

Rural Landless Employment Guarantee Programme (RLEGP) was launched in August, 1983 to deal with the problem of wide spread poverty among the economically depressed classes of rural people, the landless workers. The objectives of this programme were similar to those of the NREP with the addition that at least one member of every rural landless household would get a guaranteed employment up to 100 days in a year. The programme was entirely funded by the Central Government. The criteria for financial allocation and conditions stipulated for use of funds were similar to those for NREP. Under this programme, since its inception, up to 1988-89, a sum of Rs. 3035.07 crore was utilized against the allocation of Rs. 2674.7 crore. The total mandays generated were 1395.25 millions and the food grains utilized in the above time period was 25.19 lakh tonnes.[42] The report of the Mid Term Appraisal of Seventh Plan and Annual Report of the Department of Rural Development[43] have noted that the programme has been able to create community assets and generate additional employment, in addition to stabilizing the wage rates in the country side. Certain weaknesses have also been observed in its implementation by the studies conducted by the Planning Commission. Jawahar Rojgar Yojana (JRY) came into existence by merging the erstwhile employment programme of NREP and RLEGP. This programme was launched in April, 1989 all over the country with the objectives[44]: generation of additional gainful employment for the unemployed and under-employed persons both men and women in rural areas; creation of sustained employment by strengthening rural economic infrastructure and also assets in favour of rural poor for their direct and continuing benefits and improvement in the overall quality of life in the rural areas. Jawahar Rojgar Yojana is a centrally sponsored scheme on the cost sharing basis between the centre and states in ratio of 80: 20. The target group and administrative setup of the programme are similar to that of IRDP. At the District level, the entire work relating to coordination, review, supervision and monitoring of the programme has been entrusted to DRDA/Zila Parishad. At the village level, the Panchayati Raj Institution (PRIs) are directly sought to be involved in the implementation of the programme. The state level committee for the rural development programmes is responsible for monitoring and review of the programme at state level. Since its inception in 1989-90 up to 1995-96, a sum of Rs. 21335.58 crore has been utilized by the states, constituting 98.18 per cent of the total allocation and has created 5823.54 million mandays against the target of 5936.40 million.[45]

The Fifth Plan (1974-79) recognized that rural development should include agricultural development in its widest sense, so as to embrace, apart from crop production, all allied activities. This integrated development should encompass both spatial and functional integration of all relevant programmes bearing increased agricultural production and reduction of unemployment.[46] It is true that the economic betterment of these weaker sections cannot be achieved without social transformation involving structural changes, educational development, growth in awareness and change in outlook, motivation and attitudes. The policy framework based on these factors should be such as to provide opportunities for the weaker sections to display initiative to stand on their feet. To identify the people living in poverty, a poverty line was drawn, based on the minimum level of the caloric consumption of 2400 calories for rural areas and 2100 calories for urban areas per head per day in India. For the first time the number of persons who could be regarded as poor was estimated on the basis of consumption index i.e. Rs. 240/- at (1960-61 price level) per capita per year by the study group of Planning Commission, the abject poverty line was defined as the level corresponding to Rs.200/-. It was estimated that 164 million people were below the poverty line in 1960-61. In deciding this procedure more widely accepted is to find the lowest equal consumer expenditure level in the observed National Sample Survey data at which the quantum of food intake meets the nutritional requirement and adopt that as the minimum consumption norm[47]. Their composition had a national preponderance among the small landholders but had about 60 million who were landless agricultural labourers or artisans. The percentage of population below poverty line in 1977-78 may be projected at 48 per cent in rural areas and 41 per cent in urban areas. The total number would be 290 million. Hence task to attack this poverty line both by public investment and by activating self-employment was set and Minimum Needs Programme and Adult Education Programme were initiated[48]. Many programmes for target group and area development are under active implementation. It was felt that they did not form part of a unified effort to tackle the different resources endowment in any given area. The inadequacy of the full exploitation of the potentialities in the area and the entire technological build up behind the green and white revolutions had to have much wider impact on the rural areas, became the cause of concern.

The analysis of experience of the target group strategy as well as area development approaches in the late seventies has led to the design of a new programme called Integrated Rural Development Programme (IRDP).[49] Thus the concept of Intergrated Programme for Rural Development which is based on the knowledge of local needs, resource endowment and potentialities was introduced in 1976. The programme was initially started in 20 selected Districts of the country and it was revied in 1978-79 to integrate the methodology and approach of the three major on-going special programmes of Small Farmers Development Agency (SFDA), Command Areas Development (CADP) and Drought Prone Area Programme (DPAP). All the principal contents of these three programmes were integrated into a new programme called Integrated Rural Development Programme and taken up in 2300 Blocks of the country in 1978-79.[50] Up to 1978-79, IRDP was a central sector scheme and 100 per cent funds were provided by the central government. During the 1979-80 the programme was made a centrally sponsored scheme in which funding was shared on 50: 50 basis between the center and the states. In case of Union Territories, however, 100 per cent funds were provided by the Central Government. IRDP was extended to all the Blocks in the country w.e.f. 2nd October, 1980. Since then IRDP continues to be a major instrument of poverty alleviation in rural areas. Over the last fifteen years, since 1980, during which IRDP has been under implementation, a total of 469.96 lakh families have been assisted with total investment of Rs. 22600.80 crore consisting of Rs. 7936.92 crore of subsidy and Rs. 15260.88 crore credit from institutional financing agencies. The per capita investment has been increased from Rs. 2876 in the sixth plan to about Rs. 10200 during the year 1994-95.[51] At the national level, the targets have been achieved in respect of all the qualitative parameters set out in the programme guidelines. However, the programme performance has been uneven between the states.

The emphasis in the IRD and in other special programmes was on developing human resources in the targeted group of small farmers, marginal farmers, landless labourers, rural artisans and other rural poor and equip them to find self-employment in agriculture and allied activities. This necessarily involves concerted efforts by way of training programmes and equipping the 'targeted group' with the necessary knowledge, skills and technology. There are several on going training programmes designed for achieving specific purposes but the problem has not been tackled in its totality. Hence the need for a comprehensive training programme for the rural youth embracing the various facts of economic activity in the rural areas, particularly in agricultural and allied sector was felt.[52] With this end in view, the Government of India approved a comprehensive training programme known as the "National Scheme of Training of Rural Youths for Self-employment" (TRYSEM) on 15th August, 1979 to cover both IRD and non-IRD areas. Its main objective is to train at least two lakh rural youths every year in agricultural and allied activities for self-employment. The main thrust of the scheme is to equip rural youths with necessary skills and technology to enable them to seek self-employment for which the trainee will be given appropriate support from government for setting up their own enterprise.[53] In August, 1993, the scope of the programme was enlarged by including wage employment. On completion of training, the TRYSEM Beneficiaries are assisted under the main programme of IRDP. The Beneficiaries of TRYSEM comprises of youths of the age group of 18-35 from families living below the poverty line. About 50 per cent trained youths should belong to the Scheduled Castes and Scheduled Tribes and a minimum of 40 per cent of youths trained should be women. At least 3 per cent of the benefits should be earmarked for physically handicapped persons. The identified youths are put through a period of training either with a training institution or under a master craftsman. The duration of the training is flexible depending upon types of courses and in normal case it should not exceed six months. TRYSEM trainees are given a stipend and a tool-kit on successful completion of training and they become eligible to get a culmination of subsidy and institutional credit under IRDP for acquisition of income generating assets. The Block Development Officer selects the eligible youths belonging to the families living below the poverty line with the help of the Gram Sachiv or village level workers (VLWs). The administrative structure of this programme at various level is the same as that of IRDP. Under the programme 37.09 lakh youths were given training since 1980-81 to March, 1996. The percentage of trained youths undertaking self-employment and wage employment was 56 per cent. The coverage of Scheduled Castes and Scheduled Tribes was 41 per cent and that of the women was 44 per cent during the above mentioned period. The total expenditure incurred during this period was Rs. 497.96 crore and Rs. 127.22 crore respectively on recurring and non-recurring heads.[54]

Realizing the need for development of rural women and to ensure their better participation in the development activities, a new scheme entitled "Development of Women and Children in Rural Area" (DWCRA) was started in 1982.[55] It was extended to all the Districts up to 1995-96 with UNICEF assistance as a pilot project in 50 selected Districts. The primary objective of the scheme is to focus attention on the women members of rural families below poverty line with a view to provide them opportunities of self-employment on a sustained basis. The need for a special programme designed exclusively for women was felt as it was noticed that women members of IRDP families were not availing the benefits of that programme in adequate measure.[56] The beneficiary group of DWCRA is the same as that of under IRDP i.e. families living below the poverty line. However, the basic difference with IRDP lies in the fact that under DWCRA, it is not individual family who receive the benefits but the group as a whole. The DWCRA scheme envisages the information of group each consisting of 10-15 women for taking up economic activities suited to their skill, aptitude and the local conditions. The group strategy has been adopted under the programme to motivate the rural women to come together who were not hitherto coming forward to take the benefits. DWCRA scheme operates in conjunction with IRDP and TRYSEM. The group members are given training usually under TRYSEM. Each group of women under DWCRA is given a lump-sum grant of Rs. 15,000 as a revolving fund for purchase of the raw materials, marketing and child care etc. This amount is contributed in equal share by the Government of India, State Government and UNICEF. DWCRA like IRDP is also being implemented through the DRDA at the district level. There exists a separate staff on the strength of the DRDAs to supervise and monitor the operation of the programme in the concerned development Blocks in the District. Under DWCRA, 146562 women groups have been organized against the target of 117935 groups formation up to 1995-96 which is 124 per cent of the target. The total membership of the formed groups is about 24.59 lakh members, which comes to an average of 17 members per group and the same is in accordance with the prescribed target of 10-15 members per group. The total funds utilized during this period is Rs. 191.36 crore.[57]

Review of Literature

The vastness of the Rural Development Programme and the attention of the government towards rural development has attracted the attention of the scholars of varied interest to study the impact of the programme. The researchers and scholars could not remain unconcerned with this area and as a result a number of studies have been conducted both by the individuals and institutions. Some studies have emphasised the role of bureaucrats in rural development, others on the necessity of people's participation in rural development programmes and still others have advocated structural and behavioural changes in administrative machinery responsible for its implementation. Some have proposed to integrate under a single agency, some others are of the view to integrate all the service sectors. It seems appropriate here to have a glimpse of the studies in this field in order to have a historical and theoretical perspective of the problem under investigation. These studies can be divided into two parts-General studies regarding rural development and Studies on IRDP conducted at various levels. Some of the important studies relating Rural Development and Administration can be cited here: La

Palombora[58] (ed.) "Bureaucracy and Political Development" (1963) concluded that the upper reaches of a public administrative hierarchy may constitute a paragon of skill, rationality and humanness but all this goes relatively unnoticed if those who deal directly with the public are arrogant, aloof, arbitrary and corrupt in behaviour. A.P. Barnabas[59] "Citizens' Grievances and Administration" (1969) found that the public did not have confidence in administration and the officials themselves were not fully satisfied with what the administration can do for the villagers. More than that, they indicated a lack of confidence among each other and consequently, their alienation from administration. Kuldeep Mathur.[60] "Bureaucratic Response to Development" (1972) has pointed out that the performance of the administrators was dependent on their mental make up and a 'developmentalist' was needed to implement development policies. J.N. Khosla[61] in the article "Research in Development Administration" (1974) pointed out that the key factor in development administration is its capability to enlist mass participation in development schemes. Sharma and Malhotra's[62] "Integrated Rural Development" (1977) concluded that integrated rural development is a liberating force, a dynamic awakening by restructuring and modernization of the traditional society and the rural setting with proper mobilization of local resources in man and material to ensure comprehensive development specially of those segments which could not keep pace with more aggregative developmental processes. J.S. Mathur[63] (ed.) "Rural Development in India" (1979) inferred that various programmes of employment generation in rural areas have made some impact on the vast problems of unemployment and under employment but the new approach of Integrated Rural Development Programme can be expected to provide a working base for tackling this problem. Jai Kant Tiwari[64] "Rural Development Administration: Perspectives and Prospects" (1984) a research on relations between client-bureaucrats for development activities infers that the clients are highly alienated in a bureaucratic structure, more apathetic towards participation in development activities and less universalistic in orientation than bureaucrats. Ramashray Roy[65], et al. in the book "Problems in Rural Development" (1985) has pointed out that Block Level Planning is essential for rural development which can provide people's active participation in shaping their own lives by improving economy and removing poverty and inequality. Bal Ram Jakhar[66] on "Plan Policies for Rural Development in India" (ed.) (1985) briefed out that the success of any programme depends on the synchronization of power, administrative structure and strategies for delivery of local services. Hargain Singh[67] "Panchyati Raj Administration in Haryana" (1985) found that Panchyati Raj Administration in Haryana needs complete overhauling and a modern, cooperative, involvement oriented attitude both of the government as well as of the citizens. The system requires not only structural changes but its backbone also needs to be strengthened by providing adequate funds, suitable guidance and proper supervision and control to bear the bestowed responsibilities. S.R. Maheshwari[68] "Rural Development in India" (1985) pointed out that Rural Development Programmes in India suffer from a high degree of centralization as illustrated by the IRDP. S.R. Singh[69] "Bureaucracy and rural Development" (1988) noted that the rural development programme is the single most important vehicle of government initiated for purposes of socio-economic change. Anil Chaturvedi[70] "District Administration: The Dynamics of Discord" (1988) concluded that most of the interactions that took place between various departments at District level were routine, with emphasis focused on an exchange of information pertaining to current demands, stating of complaints and conferring of decisions already taken unilaterally and there was little interaction between the actors for a purposive review of the past or planning for the future. Mohinder Singh[71] "Rural Development Administration and Anti-Poverty Programmes" (1988) pointed out that small farmers development agency (SFDA) could not attain the desired goal due to lack of proper utilization of physical and human resources. S.K. Jha[72] "Rural Development Administration in India" (1988) has remarked that though the number of employees has been increasing, the efficiency of the bureaucratic machinery and its out put has remained at a low level. L.N. Dahiya[73] "Dynamics of Economic Life in Rural India" (1991) found that the villages are in the process of modernization though the change is not as rapid as it should have been. C.R. Kothari[74] (ed.) "Rural Development: Strategy for Rural Development" (1991) has noted that Rural Development is a part of the same process of socio-economic change and depends upon the will of the people and any scheme of rural development would not make significant impact on the rural scene till it is based on local resources, needs and skills. Kumar B. Das[75] "Rural Development Through Decentralization" (1991) pointed out that the transplantation of growth models without paying proper attention to resource base, imperative of socio-economic setting, institutional and structural characteristics can neither be expected to reduce poverty and inequality nor can ensure a self-propelling development process. O.C. Sud[76] "Administrative Problems of Rural Development in India" (1992) found that the grass rot institutions, which were expected to play a crucial root in bringing about socio-economic change in rural scenario, have been far from satisfactory.

After review of various studies on rural development and administration, now we will review in brief the studies on Integrated Rural Development Programme. T.N. Chathurvedi[77] in the article "Rural Development: The Elusive Horizons" concludes that in order to give a purposive direction to the Integrated Rural Development, effort is called to work out the integration of field programmes in the primary, secondary and tertiary sectors with forward and backward linkages. Amitabh Joshi[78] in the article "Poverty Alleviation Programmes - Target Setting and Removal of Poverty" infers that the term "Integrated Rural Development Programme" is a misnomer. At no stage does the programme seek to provide for an integrated development of the rural society. It is essentially a poverty alleviation programme functioning in isolation of the socio-economic and political realities of rural society. Madhab Prasad Pondyal[79] in the article "Administrative Hurdles to Poverty Eradication: Nepal's Experience with Integrated Rural Development Projects" (1984) asserts that though the 6th five-year-plan of Nepal aimed at eradication of poverty through an integrated approach to rural development, no specific programme addressing the poor people of the project areas has been implemented till now Sudhakar B. Rao[80] in the article "TRYSEM and ISB Component of IRDP" (1986) suggests that sufficient stress needs to be given to increase the non-farm sectors under IRDP. Sanjay Sinha[81] "Poverty Alleviation: Anything Goes" (1986) opines that things have gone wrong at a multitude of levels. First, the DRDA officials, charged with plan formulation, have neither the necessary skill nor the planning experience. Secondly, the pressure for achieving quantitative targets, the related malpractices and the consequent policing role thrust upon the DRDA leave little time for such theoretical exercises as planning.

Thirdly, detailed directive issued by the centre and by the state governments have, in practice, left little room for maneuver on the basis of local conditions. Singh and Lal[82] in the article "Poverty Analysis - Where Does it Lead" (1987) concluded that about 48 per cent of the beneficiary households had erased the poverty line. P.W. Sharma[83] in the article "IRDP and Poverty Alleviation Strategies: An Appraisal" (1988) observed that the experience gained so far has shown that IRDP could not be organically inter-linked with other on-going programmes. Jasbir K. Singh[84] in the article "Socio-Economic Impact of IRDP on Weaker Sections in Punjab" (1988) has remarked that the Integrated Rural Developments Programme is showing its impact on the weaker section served. V.S. Singh[85] in the article "An Insight into Poverty Alleviation Programmes" (1988) concluded that lack of infrastructural facilities, poor technical guidance to the Beneficiaries, lack of coordination among the bank and block officials, delay in setting of insurance claims and under-financing of the project give rise to poor return and renders the scheme unviable. Rao et al.[86] in the study conducted in Warangal District "IRDP Assistance in Andhra Pradesh: An Evaluation" (1988) pointed out various deficiencies prevailing in the whole chain of IRDP in the district which are under-financing, providing cash credits by violating the norms, lack of supervision, lack of knowledge on the part of the Beneficiaries to utilize the assets, lack of adequate training to the schemants, the IRDP loans not being utilized to the extent of their real objectives. Suresh Taneja[87] in the article "Long Search For Savers" (1989) stated that despite tall claims about the success of various anti-poverty measures such as IRDP, NREP, RLEGP and TRYSEM, most of the households are still not able to meet their minimum consumption requirements. Calling it the world most ambitious credit-based poverty alleviation effort, the World Bank[88] in article "Flaws in IRDP" (1989) found the failure of India's IRDP to its inability to ensure continued access to institutional credit for disadvantaged rural households. Kulkarni, et al. in[89] in article "IRDP in Bijapur: An Evaluation of Dairy Scheme" (1989) found out that different socio-economic factors affected the success or failure of different IRDP schemes. L.C. Jain,[90] et al. "Grass Without Roots: Rural Development under Government Auspices" in their fields study of seven blocks spread over five states have observed that even the specifically designed poverty alleviation programmes are not reaching the poor. Nor do they have sufficient depth to make an impression on poverty. Lakshman and Narayan[91] "Rural Development in India" felt that the main inherent flaw in antipoverty programmes was the lack of local participation and more reliance on bureaucracy. Neela Mukherjee[92] in the article "Lessons of Poverty Alleviation Programmes" has contended that in spite of best of intentions and a number of anti-poverty programmes, not much dent could be made into the problem of rural poverty. The specific shortcomings of the poverty alleviation programmes, in Sandeep Bagchee's[93] "Poverty Alleviation Programmes in 7th Plan-An Appraisal" opinion are basically the result of not taking into account the complexities of the environment, of having multiple and conflicting objectives instead of simplifying them by focusing on a single operational goal and designing a suitable and viable strategy on this basis. Bandopadhaya[94] in the article "Direct Intervention Programmes for Poverty Alleviation" recommends linking of these programmes with the programmes of land reforms, better planning and implementation at grass root level. N.J. Kurian[95] in the article "Anti-Poverty Programme: A Reappraisal" has brought out that the IRDP is too much centralized and bureaucratized in its planning and implementation. The benefits under the programme designed for the poor are not reaching them but are largely being taken away by the social process dominated by the rich. Kamta Prasad[96] in the article "Rural Development in the Eighth Plan' deduced the quantum of investment available for per beneficiary under both IRDP and JRY has been very meagre. Sharat Prasher[97] "Rural Development Administration" has pointed out that the present poverty alleviation schemes and programmes though primarily meant for the desperately poor, find it difficult to reach and help them. Sundaram[98] in the study "Anti -Poverty Rural Development in India" has observed that the main reasons for the failure of various rural development programmes are lack of financial resources, proper identification, lack of co-ordination among various programmes and activities of various departments. Upadhyaya[99] "IRD-Basic Approach and Policy" concludes that undoubtedly IRDP did help in enabling Beneficiaries to cross the poverty line but its role, taking into consideration the totality of the problem, has been insignificant.

The implementation of the this programme has been evaluated by a number of individuals and organizations since its inception. Major evaluative studies were carried out by Reserve Bank of India (RBI), National Bank for Agriculture and Rural Development (NABARD), Programme Evaluation Organization (PEO) of Planning Commission. Almost all the studies have pointed out shortcomings in the selection of Beneficiaries, low level of investment, lack of infrastructure, linkages etc.[100] The misidentification of Beneficiaries at the implementation level as assessed by the various evaluative studied are surprisingly high and vary from 15 to 47 per cent.[101] It is the result of a wider socio-economic malady of the country arising on account of the collusion of the politicians and bureaucrats at the grass root level. Thus according to the Kottayan study, income of some 55 per cent of the Beneficiaries increased due to IRDP, 63 per cent of the unemployed Beneficiaries got themselves fully employed after taking assistance under the programme, 17 per cent completed repayment and 72 per cent have been repaying loan.[102] Other case studies of the programme confirm the fact that there have been considerable gains in income and employment to the Beneficiaries. Some studies attribute the low performance of IRDP to the personal characteristics of the Beneficiaries.[103] Studies exclusively devoted to the performance of IRDP in respect of SC and ST Beneficiaries found out that they have not done well in the matter of generating income and employment when compared with the Non-SC Beneficiaries.[104] A study carried out by the NABARD indicated that the programme had helped 57 per cent of the Beneficiaries to cross the poverty line and increased the average income of Beneficiaries by 82 per cent.[105] Similarly, a study of the RBI, indicated that the assistance provided under IRDP had lead to a progressive shift in rural income in respect of 51 per cent of Beneficiaries and 17 per cent have been to cross the poverty line.[106] The Programme Evaluation Organization of the Planning Commission pointed out that 37 per cent households reported some increase in their family assets, 77 per cent households reported improvement in consumption level and 64 per cent felt that their overall status in the village society had been elevated as a consequence of their coverage under IRDP.[107] Nilkant Rath in the article "Garibi Hatao: Can IRDP do It" has pointed out that IRDP has not come any where near its objective of raising at least a third of the rural (population) poor above poverty line. Indira Hirway[108] "Critique of Target group Approach: A Study in Gujarat" has observed that about 55 per cent to 75 per cent of the participants are non-poor and at the same time the non-participants belong to the lowest three declines of consumption level. Kartar Singh[109] has criticized the implementation part of IRDP and suggested the need for rationalization of the promotional system for VLWs, raising of limit of subsidy and strengthening the market facilities. Misra[110] has pointed out the problem of identification of the Beneficiaries, remote control due to centralized planning and implementation, target-oriented approach, and lack of effective coordination between IRDP agencies and other institutions, cumbersome procedure and inadequate supervision mechanism. Sarita Sharda[111] "Administrative Structure and Functioning of IRDP" observed the weak administrative structure as an important factor at various levels for inadequacy of implementation of IRDP. Mukul Sanwal[112] gives certain suggestions for the improvement of the implementation process of the IRDP such as selection of the Beneficiaries in open Gram Sabha, issues of passbooks, effective monitoring and evaluation system, better cooperation between Beneficiaries and implementors and simplifying the loan procedure. Yadav et al.[113], conclude that the personnel of various departments involved in the implementation of different programmes have no clear understanding of the concept of integrated rural development. They work in isolation, without linkages with other agencies, creating serious obstacles to the programme. The scheme undertaken under IRDP are often uneconomic, unsuitable to the area and Beneficiaries. The Concurrent Evaluation of IRDP (GOI, 1988)[114] and (GOI, 1990)[115] revealed that the coverage of the destitute and the very-very poor group had been 71 per cent, 81 per cent Beneficiaries had found the assistance adequate and in 72 per cent cases the assets were found intact and in about 70 per cent cases the assets had generated additional income. An Evaluation study of IRDP conducted by R.N. Tripathi[116] et al. found the shortcoming in staffing pattern, lack of effective supervision and co-ordination as the significant drawbacks of IRDP. In a similar study conducted in Gorakhpur District of Uttar Pardesh[117], the authors found that the staff at block level considers IRDP work as an additionality and an unnecessary imposition on them. Similarly Rohini Nayyar[118] pointed out that there was lack of coordination between the departments, absence of proper planning, lack of infrastructural facilities and absence of appropriate linkages all of which have led to structural and administrative weaknesses in the execution of IRDP at the ground level. Patil and Singh[119] pointed out that the IRDP has failed to a great extent in eliminating rural poverty and unemployment due to lack of technical expertise in respective fields and lack of awareness amongst the poor households about the anti-poverty programmes. The Report on Concurrent Evaluation[120] (GOI, 1996) of IRDP revealed that in 72 per cent of the villages, the BPL survey was conducted and among the Beneficiaries 47 per cent were SC and ST, 1.3 per cent Physically Handicapped and 27 per cent women. Among the families assisted 50 per cent were from primary sector followed by 40 per cent in tertiary sector and 10 per cent in secondary sector. The percentage of families above poverty assisted under the programme was negligible. The selection of Beneficiary families was 52.6 per cent by Gram Sabha, 95 per cent Beneficiaries have purchased the assets of their choice, 85 per cent of the Beneficiaries found the assistance adequate and the quality of assets was good in 70 per cent cases. In 79 per cent the assets were found intact and 55 per cent of the Beneficiaries have crossed the poverty line.

Thus the review of these studies would help to have a clear and indepth understanding about the present problem besides to help in formulation of theoretical framework. The definition of Rural Development and Integrated Rural Development Programme observed by various individuals and institutions are given in the following pages of this chapter with basic assumptions and objectives of the study.

Conceptual Frame

The Rural Development and Integrated Rural Development Programme have been defined in various ways. The concept of rural development was born in the context of agriculture and continued for a long time in coterminous with agricultural development in India.[121] No other person has a better understanding of rural development than Mahatma Gandhi, the father of nation, back in 1936, he wrote in *Harijan*, "I have believed and repeated times without number that India is to be found not in a few cities, but in its 7 lakh villages. Further more, I would say that, if the village perishes, India will perish too".[122] To Gandhi Ji, every village must be self-sufficient. Self-sufficiency and basic needs are two important goals of rural development. The World Bank defines rural development as a strategy designed to improve the economic and social life of a specific group of people, the rural poor. It involves extending the benefits of development to the poorest among those who seek a livelihood in the rural areas. The group includes small scale farmers, tenants and the landless.[123] Bajpai writes that the main aim of rural development is to break the vicious circle of poverty through better and higher production, reasonable distribution, better living standard and balanced development among the regions as well as among the various sections of rural population.[124] Rural development, since the seventies, reflects the reduction of poverty, inequality and exploitation, and is manifested in special programmes for the weaker sections of the rural community and for fighting backwardness.[125] Rural Development means development of villages which constitute the bulk of the population of India. Traditionally, rural development was considered the development of agriculture but now in modern times this concept has changed considerably, now it includes agriculture, small scale industries including social aspects. Reddy defines Rural Development as the process of improving living conditions, providing minimum needs, increasing productivity and employment opportunities and developing potentials of rural resources through integration of spatial, functional and temporal aspects.[126] Haldipur views the rural development as a process of social change which is bound to evoke conflict and resistance from the existing power structure.[127] To Kothari rural development means increasing employment opportunities, production, productivity and similar other measures to bring about economic and social change in the rural areas, especially for the benefits of poorer sections.[128] Desai believed that critical element in the rural development is the improvement of living standard of the poor through opportunities for better utilization of their physical and human resources.[129] Raju contends that rural development is an indigenous process involving a multi-dimensional effort by a variety of institutions. The Beneficiaries of the development process have a distinct role to play.[130] Today, rural development is seen as a process aimed at improving the well-being of people living outside the urbanized areas.[131] Mishra et al. enumerate the rural development as a process of increasing in agricultural productivity; improving the use of scarce land and water resources; supply of capital resources; maximization and creation of employment opportunities and raising the standard of living of rural population.[132] Rutten views the rural development as institutionalization of a revolutionary solidarity movement through the methodology of the mass movement.[133] The ideas of various scholars regarding the concept of rural development is aimed at improvement in the various fields of life of ruralites viz. economic, social and cultural. In other words, rural development means conscious effort made to raise the standard of living of the rural poor by providing them employment opportunities of various types.

After mentioning of various definitions of rural development, it would be pertinent to present here a picture of the concept of Integrated Rural Development Programme (IRDP) which is the central theme of this study. C. Subramanyam defined the Integrated Rural Development Programme as systematic, scientific and integrated use of all our natural resources and as part of this process enabling every person to engage himself in a productive and socially useful occupation and earn an income that would meet at least the basic needs.[134] Lele sees IRDP as scientific management of resources and providing adequate work to the mass of workers in the region and in the process, increasing the internal potentials of growth.[135] Sharma, et al. view the integrated rural development as a strategy to improve the economic and social life of the rural poor and the rural weak in the overall spectrum of development.[136]

Sen defines IRDP as functional and spatial integration mean appropriate location of social and economic activities over a physical space for the balanced development of a region.[137] Sharma and Mishra consider IRDP as a wide and broad concept which includes not only increased productivity, particularly agricultural but also increased and more diversified rural employment to generate higher incomes for the rural poor.[138] Desai and Chaudhary see the IRDP as an approach for tackling the problem of rural poverty.[139] The Integrated Rural Development has been defined as development which can help to increase the purchasing power of the rural poor through the generation of greater opportunities for gainful employment.[140] Mahajan perceives IRDP as an integrated development of agriculture, industry and related activities.[141] In other words the process of integrated rural development under IRDP aims at quick development of small scale rural consumer and agrobased industries and thus reduce the monopoly hold of big manufacturers.[142]

Himachalam views the IRDP as an organized and systematic effort to alleviate mass poverty in rural India and as an area specific and beneficiary oriented programme.[143] Sharma, et al. consider it as an integration of methodology and approach of both Beneficiaries-oriented programmes and development programmes.[144] Shah observed that the term 'integrated development' refers to integration of sectoral with spatial. Rural development aims at the development of all the sectors-agriculture, industry, transport, communication, housing, environment etc.[145] Frankel viewed the IRDP as a programme for direct attack on poverty and attempts toward elimination of poverty among the target groups of small and marginal farmers, agricultural labourers, rural artisans etc. By creating new avenues under secondary and tertiary sectors in the rural areas.[146] In view of Sharma and Malhotra IRDP is a broad concept covering practically all aspects of rural life, agriculture and allied sectors, small cottage industries, social services like health, education, sanitation, recreation, production, employment, transport, commerce, power supply, water, political and social tensions and more than these instituting a programme for institutional changes to ensure mass participation in the massive development efforts.[147] Roy viewed the concept of Integrated Rural Development a multi-level, multi-sector and multi-section concept.[148] Hence IRDP is an organized and systematic efforts to alleviate mass poverty in rural areas with the help of assets purchased through loan. It is an area specific and Beneficiaries oriented programme which aims at eliminating destitution through formulation of projects based on local resources on sound scientific lines.

Main Features of IRDP

The main features of IRDP may be highlighted here. These include:

(i) The Integrated Rural development Programme is basically an anti-poverty programme in which people living below poverty line are identified and provided loans and assistance, in a bid to bring them above the poverty-line, by raising production and productivity in agriculture and allied sectors and by imparting assets and skills to increase the earnings of such vulnerable groups (target groups) in the rural sector.

(ii) Its strategy is to put to optimum use of the local resources-human, biological and natural through available technology to create assets and employment, increase income, remove poverty and minimise inequality.

(iii) It is a target group programme consisting the weaker sections of the rural population, which includes scheduled castes/scheduled tribes, agricultural and non-agricultural labourers, rural artisans, marginal and small farmers and those whose annual income from all sources is below Rs. 6400/- (a figure which determines the poverty line), for the seventh five- year-plan. The cut off line for assistance, however, fixed at Rs. 4800/- so that the poorest can have the benefit of this scheme. For the eighth plan (1992-97), the poverty was redefined and kept at an annual income of Rs. 11,000/- for a family with cut off point of Rs. 8500/- per annum for assistance under the programme. This has been done by taking into account the price rise up to the year 1991-92.

(v) The poorest of the poor is given priority under this programme.

(vi) The assistance from IRDP is given in such a way that at least 50 per cent of the assisted families should be SC and ST and at least 40 per cent of the total Beneficiaries should be women Women-headed households must be given priority and at least 3 per cent of the Beneficiaries should be from the category of physically handicapped. The investments made in IRDP are governed by two principal factors: interest shown by the beneficiary and its acceptability to the Banking Institutions.

(vii) Family is considered to be the unit for purpose of the IRDP and the identified families are to be given assistance in the form of subsidies and loans to enable them to take up economic activities which would raise their income. The pattern of subsidy varies from 25 per cent for small farmers, 33.3 per cent for marginal farmers, agricultural labourers and rural artisans to 50 per cent for SC/ST and physically handicapped. The ceiling on subsidy is Rs. 3000/- per family in normal areas, Rs. 4000/- in DPAP/DDP areas and Rs. 5000/- for SC and ST and physically handicapped. Recently the subsidy limits of IRDP have been enhanced by Rs. 1000/- for each category.

(viii) The linchpin of the IRDP is the DRDA which is responsible for its implementation at the District level.

In the following Chapter an attempt has been made to describe in brief the profile of the state of Haryana and that of District Bhiwani which is the universe of this study.

REFERENCES

1. Mishra, B.B., *District Administration and Rural Development* (Delhi: Oxford University Press, 1983), p. 387.
2. *Ibid,* p. 85.
3. Pinto, Marina R., "Rural Development and Bureaucracy in India", *The Indian Journal of Political Science,* Vol. 53, No. 3, July-September 1992, p. 281.
4. Brayane, F.L., *Better Villages* (Bombay: Oxford University Press, 1946), p. 268.
5. Randhawa, M.S., *Developing Village in India* (Bombay: Orient Longman, 1951), pp. 39-42.
6. Jain, S.C., *Rural Development: Institutions and Strategies* (Jaipur: Rawat Publications, 1985), p. 14.
7. Dubhashi, P.R., "Approaches to Integrated Rural Development in India: Administrative and Organizational Issues", *The Administrative Change,* Vol. 6, No. 1-2, July 1978-June 1979, p. 112.
8. Ahmad, R. Furqun, Development Administration: Need For a New Training Pattern", *Indian Journal of Politics,* Vol. 29, No. 1-2, 1995, p. 152.
9. Gorwala, A.D., *The Role of Administrator: Past, Present and Future* (Pune: Gokhale Institute of Politics and Economics, 1957) p. 8.
10. Pinto, Marino R., "Rural Development and Bureaucracy in India" *op. cit.,* p. 283.

11. Ray, Ramashray, et al., *Problems in Rural Development* (Delhi: Discovery, 1985), p. vi.

12. Government of India, *Report of Ashok Mehta Committee on Panchayati Raj Institution* (New Delhi: Ministry of Agriculture and Irrigation, 1978), p. 6.

13. *Ibid.*, p. 10.

14. Dubhashi, P.R., "Approaches to Integrated Rural Development in India: Administrative and Organizational Issues", *op. cit.*, p. 113.

15. Dubhashi, P.R., "Approaches to Integrated Rural Development in India: Administrative and Organizational Issues", *op. cit.*, p. 113.

16. Government of India, Directorate of Economics and statistic, *Bulletin on Food Statistic 1972,* New Delhi, p. 97: Also see Rau, S.K., "Strategies of Rural Development", in Rau, S.K. (ed.), *Rural Development in India: Some Facets* (Hyderabad: NIRD, 1979), p. 2

17. Rau, S.K., "Strategies of Rural Development" (ed.), in Rau, S.K., *Rural Development in India: Some Facets, op. cit,*. p. 3.

18. Chaturvedi, T.N., "Rural Development: The Elusive Horizon", *The Administrative Change,* Vol. 6, No. 12, July, 1978-June, 1979, p. 215.

19. Reserve Bank of India, *Report of All India Rural Credit Review Committee,* Bombay, 1969, p. 134.

20. Agro-Economics Research Centre, Himachal Pradesh University, *national Rural Employment Programme* (New Delhi: Mittal Publications, 1988), p. 33.

21. Singh, Kartar, *Rural Development: Principles, Policies and Management* (New Delhi: Sage Publications, 1986), p. 206.

22. Reserve Bank of India, *Report of All India Rural Review Committee, op. cit.*, p. 579.

23. Meeta, Krishna, "Poverty Alleviation Programmes", *The Third Concept,* Vol. 10, No. 114, August, 1996, p. 43.

24. Government of India, *Report of the National Commission on Agriculture,* Part-II, Chapter-6, 1976, p. 41.

25. Misra, S.N., *Rural Development and Panchayati Raj* (Delhi: Concept Publishing Company, 1980), p. 36.

26. Government of India, Department of Rural Development, *Manual of IRDP and Allied Programmes, 1991, op. cit.,* p. 1.
27. Marino, R. Pinto, "Rural Development and Bureaucracy", *op. cit.,* p. 287.
28. Khanna, B.S., *Rural Development* in South Asia-I: India (New Delhi: Deep and Deep Publications, 1991), p. 138.
29. Government of India, Ministry of Rural Reconstruction, *Annual Report 1980-81,* pp. 76-77; Jain, S.C., *Rural Development: Institutions and Strategies* (Jaipur: Rawat Publication, 1985), pp. 40-41.
30. Thaha, Mumtaz, "Next Step in Rural Development: Action for Eighties" in (ed.), Lakhsaman and Narayana, *Rural Development in India: A Multi-Dimensional Analysis* (Bombay: Himalaya Publication, 1984), p. 264.
31. Thaha, Mumtaz, "Next Step in Rural Development: Action for Eighties" *op. cit.,* p. 266.
32. *Ibid.,* p. 266.
33. *Ibid.,* p. 267.
34. NIRD, *Administrative Arrangements for Rural Development - A Perspective,* Proceedings of the National Workshop held at NIRD, *op. cit.,* pp. 92-93.
35. Khanna, B.S., *Rural Development in South Asia-I: India, op. cit.,* p. 156.
36. Government of India, Ministry of Irrigation and Agriculture, *Report of the Review Committee on Pilot Intensive Employment Project* (PIREP), New Delhi, 1977, pp. 11-19.
37. Prashad, Kamta, *Planning for Poverty Alleviation* (New Delhi: Agricole Publishing Academy, 1985), p. 37.
38. Government of India, Department of Agriculture, *NREP: Guidelines,* New Delhi, 1985, p. 5.
39. Government of India, Department of Rural Development, *Manual on NREP and RLEGP,* New Delhi, 1986, p. 4.
40. Government of India, Department of Rural Development, *Annual Report 1988-89,* New Delhi, p. 77.
41. Government of India, Department of Rural Development, *Gramin Vikas Newsletter: Rural Development Programme at a Glance,* New Delhi, January, 1989, p. 12.

42. Government of India, Department of Rural Development, *Basic Rural Statistics - 1990,* New Delhi, pp. 68-70.

43. Government of India, Planning Commission, *Mid term Appraisal of the Seventh Plan,* pp. 40-42.

44. Government of India, Department of Rural Development, *Agenda for the Meeting of States Secretaries of Rural Development on JRY: 21st and 22nd September, 1992,* New Delhi, p. 9 and Also see Government of India, Department of Rural Development, *Manual on JRY,* New Delhi, 1991, p. 1.

45. Government of India, Ministry of Rural Areas and Employment, *Annual Report 1996-97,* New Delhi, p. 5.

46. Minhas, B.S., "Rural Poverty, Land Redistribution and Development Strategy: Facts", *Sankhyan* (Indian Journal of Statistics), Series C, Vol. 36, No. 2-4, June-December, 1974, p. 252.

47. Reddy, G.N., *The Rural Poor* (Allahabad: Chugh Publication, 1991), p. 1.

48. Rau, S.K., 'Strategies of Rural Development", *op. cit.,* pp. 7-8.

49. Jain, S.C., *Rural Development: Institutions and Strategies, op. cit.,* p. 5.

50. Government of India, Department of Rural Development, *Manual of IRDP and Allied Programme, 1991, op. cit.,* p. 1.

51. *Ibid.,* p. 1.

52. Government of India, Ministry of Agriculture, *Circular on TRYSEM,* Department of Rural Development, New Delhi, 20-7-79: *Important Circular on IRDP,* Vol. II, April, 1983, p. 587.

53. *Ibid.,* p. 588.

54. Government of India, Ministry of Rural Areas and Employment, *Annual Report,* 1996-97, p. 157.

55. Government of India, Ministry of Rural Development, Circular No., *M. 12012/23/82-IRD III,* New Delhi, 13-7-1982.

56. Government of India, Department of Rural Development, *Manual for IRDP and Allied Programmes 1991, op. cit.,* p. 77.

57. Government of India, Ministry of Rural Areas and Employment, *Annual Report 1996-97,* p. 28.

58. Palombora, Joseph la (ed.), *Bureaucracy and Political Development* (Princeton, N.J.: Princeton University Press, 1963).

59. Barnbas, A.P., *Citizens' Grievances and Administration* (New Delhi: Indian Institute of Pubic Administration, 1969).
60. Mathur, Kuldeep, *Bureaucratic Response to Development* (Delhi: National, 1972).
61. Khosla, J.N., "Research in Development Administration", in Panandikar, Pai (ed.), *Development Administration in India* (Madras: Macmillan ISSD press, 1974), p. 230.
62. Sharma, S.K. and Malhotra, S.L., *Integrated Rural Development: Approach, Strategy and Perspectives* (New Delhi: Abhinav Publication, 1977).
63. Mathur, J.S., "Employment Generation in Rural India" (ed.), *Rural Development in India: Some Facets* (Hyderabad: National Institute of Rural Development, 1979), pp. 442-443.
64. Tiwari, Jaikant, *Rural Development Administration: Perspectives and Prospects* (Allahabad: Chugh Publishers, 1984), p. 196.
65. Ray, Ramashray, *et al., Problems in Rural Development* (Delhi: Discovery, 1985), pp. 176-177.
66. Jakhar, Balram, "Plan Policies for Rural Development in India', in *Rural Development in India* (ed.), Hoshiar Singh (Jaipur: Printwell, 1985), p. 9.
67. Singh, Hargian, *Panchayti Raj Administration in Haryana* (Delhi: India Publisher, 1985), p. 127.
68. Maheshwari, S.R., *Rural Development in India* (New Delhi: Sage Publication, 1985), pp. 225-226.
69. Singh, S.R., *Bureaucracy and Rural Development* (New Delhi: Mittal Publications, 1988), p. 6.
70. Chaturvedi, Anil, *District Administration: The Dynamics of Discord* (New Delhi: Sage Publication, 1988), p. 149.
71. Singh, Mohinder, *Rural Development Administration and Anti-Poverty Programmes* (New Delhi: Deep and Deep Publication, 1988).
72. Jha, S.K., *Rural Development Administration in India* (New Delhi: Commonwealth Publishers, 1988), pp. 345-346.
73. Dahiya, L.N., *Dynamics of Economic Life in Rural India: A Case Study* (New Delhi: Gian Publication House, 1991), p. 161.
74. Kothari, C.R. (ed.), *Rural Development, Vol. 1, Strategy for Rural Development* (Jaipur: Manak Publication (P) Ltd., 1991), p. 42.

75. Das, Kumar B., *Rural Development through Decentralization* (New Delhi: Discovery Publication House, 1991), p. 33.

76. Sud, O.C., *Administrative Problems of Rural Development in India* (Delhi: Kanishaka Publishing House, 1992), p. 246.

77. Chatuvedi, T.N., "Rural development: The Elusive Horizons" *The Administrative Change,* Vol. 6, No. 1-2, July, 1978-June, 1979, pp. 221-223.

78. Joshi, Amitabh, "Poverty Alleviation Programme — Target Setting and Removal of Poverty", *Ibid., pp.* 237-39.

79. Pondyal, M.P., "Administrative Hurdles to Poverty Eradication: Nepal's Experience with Integrated Rural Development Projects", in T.N. Chaturvedi (ed.), *Rural Development: Some Themes and Dimensions* (New Delhi: IIPA, 1986), pp. 143-44.

80. Rao, Sudhakar B., "TRYSEM and ISB component of IRDP", *Kurukshetra,* Vol. 4, No. 8, 1986, p. 19.

81. Sinha, Sanjay, 'Poverty Alleviation: Anything Goes', *Economics and Political Weekly,* Vol. 21, No. 19, May 10, 1986, p. 823.

82. Singh. V.S. and Lal, Banwari, "Poverty Analysis - Where does it lead", *Man and Development,* Vol. 9, No. 3, September, 1987, p. 25.

83. Sharma, P.W., "IRDP and Poverty Alleviation Strategies: An Appraisal", *Kurukshetra,* Vol. 36, No. 6, March, 1988, p. 18.

84. Singh, Jasbir K., "Socio-Economic Impact of IRDP on Weaker Sections in Punjab", *Guru Nanak Journal of Sociology,* Vol. 9, No. 1. April, 1988, p. 80.

85. Singh, V.S., "An insight into Poverty Alleviation Programmes", *Yojana, Vol. 32, No. 6, April 1-15, 1988, p. 25.*

86. Rao, Perumalla D. and Natrajan, R., 'IRDP Assistance in Andhra Pradesh: An Evaluation", *Kurukshetra,* Vol. 36, No. 6, March, 1988.

87. Taneja, Suresh, "Long Search for Savers", *The Tribune,* February 9, 1989, p. 6.

88. World Bank, "Flaws in IRDP", *The Tribune,* September 3, 1989, p. 5.

89. Kulkarni, *et al.,* "IRDP in Bijapur: An Evaluation of Dairy Scheme", *Social Change,* Vol. 19, No. 89, 1989, p. 78.

90. Jain, L.C., Krishanmurthy, B.V., and Tripathi, P.M., *Grass Without Roots: Rural Development Under Government Auspices* (New Delhi: Sage Publications, 1985), pp. 193-95.

91. Lakshman, T.K. and Narayana, B.K. (ed.), *Rural Development in India* (Bombay: Himalaya Publishing House, 1984), p. 41.

92. Mukherjee, Neela, "Lessons of Poverty Alleviation Programmes", *Yojana,* New Delhi, August 15, 1990, pp. 37-40.

93. Bagchee, Sandeep, "Poverty Alleviation Programmes in 7th Plan—An Appraisal", *Economic and Political Weekly,* Vol. 22, No. 4, January 24, 1987, p. 140.

94. Bandopadhaya, D., "Direct Intervention Programmes for Poverty Alleviation", *Economic and Political Weekly,* Vol. 23, No. 24, June 25, 1988, pp. 89-96.

95. Kurian, N.J., "Anti-Poverty Programmes: A Reappraisal", *Economic and Political Weekly,* Vol. 24, No. 12, March 25, 1989, pp. 13-17.

96. Prashad, Kamta, "Rural Development in the Eighth Plan', *Yojana,* Vol. 36, No. 14-15, August 15, 1992, pp. 72-75.

97. Prasher, Sharat, *Rural Development Administration* (Jaipur: Arihant Publishing House, 1994), p. 209.

98. Sundaram, I.S., *Anti-Poverty Rural Development in India* (New Delhi: D.K. Publications, 1984).

99. Upadhaya, Rakesh, *IRD Basic Approach and Policy* (Bombay: Himalaya Publication House, 1989).

100. Government of India, Department of Rural Development, *Gramin Vikas Newsletter: Rural Development Programmes at a Glance,* New Delhi, January, 1989, p. 6.

101. Rath, N., "Garibi Hatao: Can IRD Do it?" *Economic and Political Weekly,* Vol, 20, No. 6, February 9, 1985, p. 241.

102. Department of Applied Economics, *IRDP: Evaluation and Impact Study: Kottayam District* (Cochin University, Cochin, 1984).

103. Kutty Krishana, A.C., "A Case Study of Integrated Rural Development Programme in a Kerala Village"; Gupta, Malay,– "Planning of Rural Development Programme and its Strategies" (Both in) *Indian Journal of Agricultural Economics,* Vol, 39, No, July-September, 1984.

104. Jose, AM and Aziz, Abdul, "IRDP and SC-ST Beneficiaries: A Study of two Blocks in Kerala", paper presented at an *All-India*

Seminar on Development Programmes for SCs and STs, organized by the Department of Applied Economics, Andhra University, Walter, 27-29 March, 1985.

105. Alexander, K.C., "Rural Set up and Problems of Planned Change", in *Rural Transformation,* NIRD, Hyderabad, 1984, pp. 10-30.

106. Government of India, Department of Rural Development, *Annual Report 1984-85,* New Delhi.

107. Rath, Nilkanth "Garibi Hatao: Can IRDP do it" *Economic and Political Weekly,* February 9, 1985, p. 245.

108. Hirway, Indira, "Critique of Target group Approach: A Study in Gujarat", in I*ndian Journal of Agricultural Economics,* Vol. 39, No. 3, July-September, 1984, p. 460.

109. Singh, Kartar, "IRDP: Some Polices and Management Issues", *Kurukshetra,* Vol. 33, No.11, August, 1985, pp. 9-12.

110. Misra, I.S., "Rural development Change before IRDP: A Fresh Look", *Indian Journal of Agricultural Economics,* Vol. 41, No. 4, Oct-Dec., 1986, p. 656.

111. Sharda, Sarita, "Administrative Structure and Functioning of IRDP-A Case Study", *Administrative Change,* Vol. 17, No. 2, July-December, 1989, pp. 73-80.

112. Sanwal, Mukul, "Garibi Hato: Improving Implementation", *Economic and Political Weekly,* Vol. 20, No. 49, December 7, 1985, pp. 2176-78.

113. Yadav, *et al.,* "IRDP-Constraints and Remedies", *Indian Journal of Agricultural Economics,* Vol. 41, No. 4, Oct-Dec 1986, p. 663.

114. Government of India, *Concurrent Evaluation of IRDP-The Main Findings of the Survey for Jan-Dec. 1987,* Department of Rural Development, Ministry of Agriculture, New Delhi, August, 1988.

115. Government of India, *Concurrent Evaluation of IRDP — The Main Findings of the Survey for Jan, 1989 - Sept. 1989,* New Delhi, Department of Rural Development, Ministry of Agriculture, June, 1990.

116. Tripathi, R.N., *et al,* "Evaluation of IRDP in Udhampur and Anantnag Districts of J & K, quoted in NIRD *Research High Lights: Summaries of Studies Conducted in 1987-88,* Hyderabad, pp. 3-9.

117. Tripathi, *et al.*, "Evaluation of IRDP in Gorakhpur District in U.P.", *ibid,* pp. 11-17.
118. Nâyyar, Rohini, "Does Garibi Hatao Work", *Economic and Political Weekly,* Vol. 24, No. 18, April 29, 1989, p. 919.
119. Patil, B.V., and Singh, Gurchran, "Effective Implementation of IRDP: Some Suggestions", *Yojana,* Vol. 35, No. 8, May 15, 1991, pp. 14-16.
120. Government of India, Ministry of Rural Area and Employment, *Report on Concurrent Evaluation of IRDP (September, 1992 to August, 1993),* New Delhi, 1996.
121. *Reports of Royal Commission on Agriculture in India* (Bombay: Government Central Press, 1928), p. 631.
122. Gandhi, M.K., *Harijan,* 16th November, 1934.
123. World Bank, *Rural Development-Sector Policy Paper* (Washington, D.C.: IBRD, 1975), p. 3.
124. Bajpai, S.K., "Rural Development: Some Constraints", *Kurukshetra,* Vol. 30, No. 23, 1982, p. 26.
125. Shah, S.M., *Rural Development: Planning and Reforms* (New Delhi: Abhinav Publication, 1977), p. 40.
126. Reddy, Uday Bhaskar, "The Role of Voluntary Agencies in Rural Development", *The Indian Journal of Public Administration,* Vol. 33, No. 3, July-September, 1987, p. 547.
127. Haldipur, R.N., "Bureaucracy's Response to New Challenge', *Indian Journal of Public Administration,* Vol. 12, No. 1, January-March, 1966, p. 8.
128. Kothari, C.R. (ed.), *Rural Development, Vol. 1, Strategy for Rural Development, op. cit.,* p. 38.
129. Desai, Vasant, *Rural Development, Vol 1 to 6* (New Delhi: Himalaya Publishing House, 1988), p. 144.
130. Raju, Yerram B., "And Plan Rural Credit Better Way", *Yojana,* Vol. 29, No. 24, January 1-15, 1988, p. 16.
131. Shah, S.M., *Rural Development: Planning and Reforms, op. cit.,* p. 40.
132. Mishra, S.N., et al., *Participation and Development* (New Delhi: National Book Organization, 1984), p. 147.
133. Verson, W. Rutten, "Integrated Rural Development Programme - A Skeptical Perspective", *Agricultural Development Council Review,* Singapore, No. 4, 1975.

134. Subramanyam, C., "Strategy of Integrated Rural Development", *Community Development and Panchayati Raj Digest,* Vol. 8, April, 1977; Reddy, Venkta, *Rural Development in India: Poverty and Development* (Delhi: Himalaya Publication House, 1988), p. 127.

135. Lele, Uma, *The Design of Rural Development: Lessons from Africa* (London: The John Hopkins University Press, 1975), p. 26.

136. Sharma, S.K. and Malhotra, S.L., *Integrated Rural Development Programmes: Approach, Strategy and Perspectives, op. cit.,* p. 17.

137. Sen, Lalit K., "Role of Area Development in Multi-Level Planning", *Indian Journal of Public Administration,* Vol. 31, No. 3, 1986, p. 176.

138. Mishra, S.N. and Sharma, Kaushal, *Problems and Prospects of Rural Development in India, op. cit.,* p. 22.

139. Desai, I.P. and Chaudhary, B., *History of Rural Development in India, op. cit.,* p. 211.

140. *Chandrapur District Inventory,* Indian Council of Agricultural Research, Delhi, 1976, p. 1.

141. Mahajan, V.S., *Indian Economy and Regional Development* (New Delhi: Deep and Deep Publications, 1982), p. 108.

142. *Ibid,* p. 109.

143. Himachalam, P., "How for has IRDP Alleviated Poverty?", *Kurukshetra,* Vol. 38, No. 2, 1989, p. 10.

144. Sharma, M.L., *et al.,* "IRDP: Retrospect and Prospect", *Kurukshetra,* Vol. 38, No. 2, p. 118.

145. Shah, S.M., "IRDP-Success or Failure", *Kurukshetra,* Vol. 38, No. 2, 1989, p. 22.

146. Frankel, R. Franeine, "India's New Strategy of Agricultural Development, Political Costs of Agrarian Modernization", *Journal of Asian Studies,* Vol. 28(4), pp. 69-71.

147. Sharma, S.K., Malhotra, S.L., *Integrated Rural Development: Approach Strategy and Perspectives, op. cit.,* pp. 16-17.

148. Roy, Predipto, "Integrated Rural Development: Experiments and Experiences', *Agricultural Development in India-Policy and Problems* (ed.), Shaw, C.H. (Bombay: Orient Longman, 1979), pp. 519-20.

3

Haryana: A Profile

The perception of the people very much depend upon and are influenced by the geographical, economic, social and political background of the area in which they happen to be. As these factors play an important part in shaping a particular political culture and moulding the behaviour of a person residing in that particular environment, the study of these factors becomes of great significance. In this chapter an attempt has been made to describe in brief the profile of the State of Haryana, District Bhiwani and that of the selected Blocks so that one could have an overall picture of the State in general and District Bhiwani in particular. When Punjab was partitioned in 1947 the entire Hindi speaking region of Punjab governed by British remained an integral part of Eastern Punjab. Later in 1948, native states of the region were included in newly formed state Patiala and Eastern Punjab States Union (PEPSU). After some time PEPSU was merged in Punjab in 1956, which later on paved the way for the creation of Haryana. In spite of this political, geographical and administrative unity, the people of Haryana region did not merge their identity with the people of Punjab. In sociocultural and linguistic aspects, they always maintained their own separate identity. The Akalis under the leadership of Saint Fateh Singh demanded for a separate Punjabi State on linguistic basis. The government has to bow before their pressure. Ultimately Central Government agreed to examine the demand on September 23,1965 and appointed a committee under Sardar Hukam Singh, the then Speaker of Lok Sabha and the committee submitted its report to Lok Sabha on March 18,1966. On March 21, 1966, Government of India accepted the recommendations of the Committee in principle for the reorganization of the State. On April 18, 1966, three members Boundary Commission under Justice Shah was appointed. Government accepted the recommendations of the committee. As a result Haryana, the then 17th state in Indian Union came into existence on November 1,1966[1], as a result of bifurcation of the bilingual State of Punjab under 'The Punjab State Reorganization Act, 1966' passed by the Indian Parliament on September 10,1966. This new state of Haryana comprised of the Districts of Gurgaon, Mahendergarh, Rohtak, Hisar, Karnal, some parts of Sangrur (Jind) and Ambala Districts, having an area of 43,188 sq. km. and a population of 75,99,759 at that time.[2]

Haryana is located on the North-Western side of the Indian Union adjoining Delhi. It extends from 27 3 to 31 9, North latitude and 74 5' to 77 6' East longitude, to the East of the State are Uttar Pradesh and Delhi. The State has Rajasthan in the South and West Punjab and Himachal Pradesh in the North.[3] Physically, Haryana falls into the broad natural divisions namely the sub-Himalayan and the Indo-Gangetic Plain which runs in South-Eastern direction almost parallel to each-other. In the North-East, however, a narrow track of Ambala District lies within the outer ranges of Shivalik hills, and in the South-East the District Mahendergarh and Gurgaon form the Northern boundary of Arravali mountain.[4] The Western plain which approximately covers Hisar, Bhiwani, Sirsa, and Mahendergarh Districts, has a higher degree of aridity.

It is a thirsty land clothed by steppe vegetations and with sand dunes of various shapes and sizes. The Eastern-Plain extends from the west of Yamuna up to isohyet line. The plain is flat and its general elevation varies only between 200 to 230 meters above the sea level. No important river passes through the state. Ghaggar, a non-perennial river, flows in the Northern extreme part, while Yamuna, which is fairly a good source of irrigation, flows along the Eastern boundary of the State. Haryana has a semi-arid climate in the South West and Gangetic type in the rest of State. Most of year, the climate of Haryana is of pronounced character. It is very hot in summer and markedly cold in winter. There are two well marked sessions of rainfall in the state–the monsoon period lasting from the middle of June till September and the winter which occurs from December to February.[5] Haryana is a small state with an area of 44.212 sq. km. i.e. 1.35 per cent of the area of India and a population of 1,64,63,648 which is 1.5 per cent of India's total population, out of which 88,27,474 are males and 76,36,174 are females. In Haryana density of population per sq. km was 372 and sex ratio per 1000 males was 865 females in 1991 as compared to 257 and 927 of national level respectively. Out of the total population 1,24,08,904 people (75 per cent) are living in rural areas in 6,998 villages and 40,54,744 people (25 per cent) are living in urban areas in 94 towns.[6] The literacy rate after 6 years onward is 55.33 per cent to the total population in Haryana as compared to 52.21 per cent of India. The population in Haryana has increased 27.41 per cent in last decade as compared to 23.9 per cent at national level.

Table 3.1 reveals that Hisar is the biggest District having an area of 6279 sq. km followed by Bhiwani with an area of 5140 sq. km whereas Panchakula is at the bottom with an area of 816.15 sq. km followed by Sonipat and Rewari. As far as the population is concerned Hisar District is at the top with a population of 18,44,634 followed by Rohtak with 18,08,606 and Faridabad with 14,77,240 where as Panchkula District has the lowest population i.e. 3,19,398 followed by Rewari 6,23,301 and Kurukshetra 6,41,943. Faridabad District has the highest population per sq. km. i.e. 702 followed by Kurukshetra with 527 whereas Sirsa is at the bottom with 211 followed by Bhiwani with 222. The sex ratio is highest in Rewari District i.e. 927 females per 1000 males followed by Mahendergarh with 910 whereas it is lowest in Sonipat District with 841 females per 1000 males followed by Rohtak with 851 females. The total population of Scheduled Castes in Haryana is 32,50,933 out of which 26,75,277 are rurals and 5,77,656 are urbans constituting 82 per cent and 18 per cent of their population respectively. There are 17,47,821 males and 15,03,112 females. Out of the total literate population of Scheduled Castes 7,17,538 are males (72 per cent) and 2,83,940 are females (28 per cent).[7] The religion-wise composition of population in Haryana is Hindu 1,46,86,512, Sikhs 9,56,836, Muslims 7,63,375, Jains 35,296 and followers of other religion 3472.

In Haryana there are 4 Universities, 181 Colleges, 2998 High/ Senior Secondary Schools, 1,499 Middle Schools and 5,501 Primary Schools which provide a very good infrastructure to the people for eduction purposes. The total literate people in the state are 74,49,926 residing in rural areas and 24,74,086 in urban areas.[8] There are 3,071 hospitals, dispensaries and health centres, 447 Ayurvedic, Unani and Homeopathic institutions and 149 family welfare

Table 3.1
Demographic features of Haryana

District	*Area in Sq. Km*	*Males*	*Females*	*Total*	*Persons per Sq. Km.*	*Females 1000 Males*
Ambala	1568.85	418981	378499	797980	508	903
Panchkula	816.15	173557	145841	319398	391	840
Yamuna/N	1756.00	436415	385465	821880	468	883
Kurukshetra	1217.00	341612	300331	641943	527	879
Kaithal	2799.00	443019	377666	820685	293	852
Karnal	1967.00	475056	410741	885797	450	865
Panipat	1754.00	449504	383997	833501	475	854
Sonipat	1385.00	410133	344733	754866	545	841
Rohtak	4411.00	977075	831531	1808606	410	851
Faridabad	2105.00	808223	669017	1477240	702	828
Gurgoan	2760.00	612620	533470	1146090	415	871
Rewari	1559.00	323460	299841	623301	400	927
M/Garh	1683.00	357004	324865	681869	405	910
Bhiwani	5140.00	606378	533340	1139718	222	880
Jind	2736.00	524014	439090	963104	352	838
Hisar	6279.00	991016	853618	1844634	294	861
Sirsa	4276.00	479407	424129	903536	211	885
Total						
1991	44212.00	8827474	7636174	16463648	372	865
1981	44212.00	6909938	6012680	12922618	292	870

Source: Statistical Abstracts of Haryana 1995-96.

centres to provide health care to people whereas 546 Veterinary hospitals and 859 veterinary dispensaries to fulfil the requirement of animals health in the state.[9] The occupational structure of the population in Haryana reveals that there are 47,18,726 main workers 3,84,744 marginal workers and 1,13,60,180 non-workers constituting 28.6 per cent, 2.4 per cent and 69 per cent respectively. Among the main workers one-fourth are residing in urban areas and three-fourths in rural areas. The sector-wise distribution of main workers in Haryana shows that 27,71,028 people are engaged in primary sector, 6,27,654 in secondary sector and 13,20,044 in tertiary sector constituting about 59 per cent, 13 per cent and 28 per cent respectively.[10] The primary sector consists of agriculture and allied activities like livestock, forestry, fishing, plantation etc. whereas the secondary sector includes of mining, household industries and construction and the tertiary sector consists of trade and commerce, transport and communication, and service sector. Among the main workers in the state 18,29,530 are cultivators, 8.96,782 agricultural labourers, 50,561 engaged in mining, livestock, forestry, fishing plantation etc., 72,195 in household industry and 4,26,138 in other than household industry, 1,23,476 in construction, 4,07,010 in trade and commerce, 1,53,459 in transport, storage an communication and 7,59,575 in other services. In the pre-1966 Punjab which was one of the two most prosperous states in the country, the present Haryana region was quite behind to Punjab in economic development though much better developed than other states. The per capita income of Haryana region in 1966-67 was Rs. 343 which rise up to Rs. 2370 in the year 1980-81. During 1994-95 it was Rs. 12,242 at current prices and Rs. 7508 at the prices of 1990-91.[11] The similar figures of India for the said time period were Rs. 8,282 and Rs. 4,983 respectively. Today, Haryana is one of the go-ahead states in the country with an excellent infrastructure. It is very close to Delhi, the National Capital which has a big market for raw materials, finished good and trading etc. The transport and communication network is in a satisfactory condition in the state. It is the first state which linked all its villages and towns by metalled roads up to 1981. The total length of these in state in 22,452 km up to 1994-95. Besides, many state Highways, three National Highways including Grant Trunk Road pass through the state, having total length of 656 km The main railway routes which pass from the state are Delhi to Agra, Ajmer, Ferozpur and Chandigarh. Some parts are under Ambala Division and some others are under Bikaner and Firozpur divisions.[12] The postal and telecommunication network is very-well established and every village is connected with it and almost all the towns and cities are provided with STD/ISD facilities. There was 2588 Post Offices, 394 Telegraph Offices and 750 Telephone Exchange in the state up to 1995-96. Haryana is the first state of Indian Union which has provided electricity, metalled roads and safe drinking water facilities to all its village (6,745) and towns (81) according to 1981 Census. Power generation and distribution system has been augmented many folds in Haryana. The total consumption of power has increased to 78,243 lakh kWh in 1994-95 from 4343 lakh kWh in 1966-67 and the per capita consumption has increased to 446 kWh from 58 kWh in the respective periods.[13] The Power projection is very good and the future is bright in view of a number of Projects that the state has undertaken.

Haryana is basically a rural dominant state and agriculture is the backbone of state's economy though considerable network of industry has been established. Out of total population, 124.09 lakh people (75.37 per cent) are residing in rural areas[14] and the agricultural and allied sectors pay about 40 per cent of the state's gross domestic production (GDP) and 59 per cent of total main workers force is engaged in primary sector. In the state more than 85 per cent of the population has land holdings up to 5 hectares and 60 per cent up to 2 hectares whereas the average size of land holding in the state is 2.43 hectares. The total cultivable area in the state is 37.6 lakh hectares out of which 35.6 lakh is net area sown which is 81.5 per cent of the total land. Almost 3 per cent area is under forest which is thinly populated and 11 per cent is not available for cultivation and 4 per cent is fallow land. Today, Haryana is not only self-sufficient in foodgrains production but also among the top contributors of foodgrains to central pool which stand at 30-35 lakh tonnes.[15] Like agriculture, the associated activity of Animal Husbandry is also well developed in Haryana. Because of the suitable agro-climatic conditions some of the best breed of the country, both milk and draught variety, are found here.

Haryana is beneficiary of the multi-purpose project on Satluj and Beas where it shares benefits with Punjab and Rajasthan. Major irrigation projects are Western Yamuna Canal, Bhakra Canal and Gurgaon Canal. The state has completed Jui and Siwani Lift Irrigation Schemes and Jawaharlal Nehru Irrigation Scheme the biggest of its kind and Loharu Lift Irrigation Scheme. This system has changed the scenario of Southern Haryana particularly that of Bhiwani District. Besides canal irrigation, tube wells are the major sources of irrigation all over the State. The net area irrigated in the state is 27.19 lakh hectares which is 76 per cent of the net area sown. Out of the net area irrigated in the state 13.82 lakh hectares is covered under canal irrigation and 13.04 lakh hectares under tube wells.[16] Various steps have been taken to raise the standard of living of the farmers of Haryana which is the first state to write off their co-operative loans. It has raised the price of sugarcane from Rs. 24 to 35 per genital in 1988-89 and Rs. 90 in 1996-97. The major crops in the state are rice, wheat, bajra, pulses, oil seeds, cotton and sugarcane. The area under various crops is 19.85 lakh hectares wheat, 9.76 lakh hectares rice, 5.69 lakh hectares bajra, 4.74 lakh hectares pulses, 6.18 lakh hectares oil seeds and 5.5 lakh hectares cotton and the production of various crops is 72.97 lakh tones wheat, 22.3 lakh tones rice, 7.2 lakh tones bajra, 8.6 tones oil seeds, 5.2 lakh tones pulses and 2.3 lakh tones cotton. The results of Green Revolution have clearly reflected in the state which has witnessed a phenomenal increase in agricultural output. Foodgrains production had a quantum jump from 25.92 lakh tones in 1966 to 109.8 lakh tones in 1994-95 which is more than four times.[17] The state has a very sound industrial base with the increase in registered factories, from 1168 in 1966 to 6498 in 1995 and the number of workers employed is 3.91 lakh. It produces the largest number of tractors in the country. One out of every four bicycles is manufactured here. Besides, about one-third of country's production of sanitary wares. Panipat has earned the reputation of being the weaver's city of India for its exquisite hand-tufted woolen carpets and colorful handloom products. There are 400 large and small scale units in the state. Great emphasis is being laid on dispersal of industries in rural areas.[18]

The number of Employment-Exchanges including Sub-Offices has increased from 19 in 1966 to 99 in 1995 with 6,97,965 applicants on live registers in the state. There have been 6,40,547 employees in organized sector in the state up to December, 1995, of which 4,20,761 engaged in public sector and 2,19,786 in private sector. Among the public sector employees, 37,366 are attached with Centre Government, 2,50,426 with State Government, 18,233 with Local Bodies and 1,19,736 with Quasi government agencies. Whereas among private sector employees, 1,98,411 are acted/ regular and 21,375 are non acted regular. There are 4,251 Banks in the state out of which 1,361 are Indian Scheduled Bank, 302 Cooperative Banks and 2588 Post-office Savings Banks. The deposits and credits of these Scheduled Banks have been Rs. 8930.49 crore and Rs. 4107.82 crore respectively up to March,

1996 and 14,177 Cooperative Societies having membership of 3758459. It has provided good opportunity for small and cottage industries and other activities in rural areas with a total loan advanced of Rs. 1,252 crore. Administratively the state of Haryana is divided into four Divisions. Each Division consists of certain number of Districts. These are: Ambala Division - Ambala, Panchkula, Yamuna Nagar, Kurukshetra and Kaithal; Rohtak Division - Karnal, Panipat, Sonipat and Rohtak, Gurgaon Division - Gurgaon, Mahendergarh, Rewari and Faridabad; Hisar Division - Hisar, Sirsa, Bhiwani and Jind. In all up to 31-12-1996 there were 17 Districts, 45 Sub-Divisions, 65 Tehsils, 31 Sub-Tehsils and 111 Blocks in Haryana.

Profile of District Bhiwani

The Bhiwani District derives its name from the head quarter town Bhiwani. It came in to existence as the 8th Districts of Haryana on December 22,1972 and was formally inaugurated on January 14,1973.[19] It was carved out of the erstwhile Districts of Hisar and Mahendergarh. It consisted of four subdivisions, six Tehsils, one Sub-Tehsil and eight Blocks. These include Bhiwani, Dadri, Loharu and Siwani as Sub-Division; Bhiwani, Dadri, Loharu, Siwani, Bawani Khera and Tosham as Tehsils; Badhara as Sub-Tehsil and Bhiwani, Dadri-I and II, Loharu, Siwani, Bawani Khera, Tosham and Badhara as Blocks[20]. As per 1991 Census, the number of villages in Bhiwani District was 439 out of which 433 were inhabited and 6 were uninhabited and there were six towns namely Bhiwani, Dadri, Loharu, Tosham, Bawani Khera and Siwani. The District lies between 28 19' and 29 5' North latitude and 75 28' and 76 28' East longitude[21]. It is situated along the West-Southern border of the Haryana state and is surrounded by the Districts of Hisar on North, Rohtak on North-East, Mohendergarh and Rewari on South in Haryana and Jhunjhunu and Churu on the West in Rajasthan. It shares a long boundary with Rajasthan. The District headquarter is located at about 120 km from Delhi and 240 km from Chandigarh. It is well connected with roads and railways to the main cities of the country. Though the district Bhiwani forms a part of Indo-Gangetic Alluvial Plain, yet largely it is dry and sandy. As the District lies along the Rajasthan, it is the hottest and driest District of the state. It is mostly sandy and has detached peaks of Aravalli hills, the highest of which is the Tosham hill which is 800 meters high. A sandy track stretches along the south-

Western parts of the District and sandy dunes, commonly known as 'Tibbas', can be seen in large numbers. The location of the District has influenced the climate which is hot and dry in summer and cold in winter. The maximum temperature goes up to 48 C in June and minimum 0 in January. There are frequent dust-storms in May and June. The average rainfall over the District is 377 mm. In spite of the fact that Bhiwani is not much favourably located, it has an edge over the other Districts so far as the development activities are concerned. It can proudly claim to be the dynamic District of the state.

The District has an area of 5140 sq. km and a population of 11,39,718 constituting 11.6 per cent and seven (7) per cent of the state respectively. It has been the second largest District of the Haryana. Out of the total population 9,43,150 are rurals and 1,96,568 are urbans constituting more than four-fifths (82.75 per cent) and less than one-fifth (17.25 per cent) respectively. Hence this District is a rural dominated one. Out of the total population, there are 6,06,378 males (53.2 per cent) and 5,33,340 females (46.8 per cent) in the District. The sex ratio is 880 females per 1000 males.[22] The density of population per Square km in Bhiwani District is 222 as compared to that of the state which is 372. Hence in comparison to the state, the Bhiwani District is thinly populated. The area and population of all the Tehsils of the District as per 1991 census can be seen in Table 3.2.

Table 3.2

Tehsil-wise Area and Population in District Bhiwani

Tehsil	*Area*	*Population*			*Density*
	(sq. km)	*Rural*	*Urban*	*Total*	*(Per sq. km)*
Ch. Dadri	1370.63	344555	32253	376808	275
Bhiwani	822.80	198807	121629	320436	390
Siwani	679.80	89952	11109	101061	149
Tosham	613.32	102008	8387	110395	180
Loharu	611.33	88704	9031	97735	160
B. Khera	512.25	119124	14159	133283	260
Total	5140.00	943150	196568	1139718	222

Source: Statistical Abstract of Haryana, 1995-96, p. 36.

Table 3.2 illustrates that Dadri Tehsil is the largest constituting 16.5 per cent of the District area whereas Bawani Khera Tehsil is the smallest with an area of 9 per cent. The area of the other Tehsils ranges from 9.4 per cent to 13 per cent. Dadri Tehsil is the biggest in respect of population comprising 33 per cent of the total followed by Bhiwani Tehsil with 19.5 per cent. Loharu and Siwani Tehsils are at the bottom comprising 8.6 per cent and 9 per cent of the total population respectively. The District is not evenly populated. Bhiwani Tehsil is densely populated with a density of 390 which is more than twice to that of Siwani, Loharu and Tosham Tehsil having density of 149, 160 and 180 respectively. From the density point of view, Bhiwani Tehsil is followed by Charkhi Dadri and Bawani Khera having density of population 275 and 260 respectively.

Religion-wise the population of the District can be classified as: 11,27,661 Hindus, 8,283 Muslims, 2,159 Sikhs, 156 Christians, 12 Buddhist, 1113 Jains and 334 others.[23] The strength of Scheduled Castes in the District is 2,16,162 i.e. 18.97 per cent which is quite close to their percentage (19.75) in the state. Out of the total Scheduled Castes 1,79,643 are residing in rural areas (83 per cent) and 36,519 in urban areas (17 per cent).[24] Education generally play a vital role in the socio-economic development of the people. Literacy rate in the District is quite satisfactory. The District has 4,98,103 literate persons, out of which 3,88,552 reside in rural areas and 1,09,551 in the urban areas. The literacy percentage is 43.7 as against the state's average of 45.85 which is 41.2 per cent in rural areas and 55.7 per cent in urban areas. There are 11 Colleges, 171 Senior Secondary and High Schools, 123 middle Schools and 360 Primary Schools. Besides, there are 4 professional Colleges, 4 ITIs and 2 Vocational Institutions.[25] The number of households in the District are 1,73,272 out of which 1,40,772 are in rural areas and 32,500 in urban and the number of persons per household are 7 and 6 for the respective areas. There are 3,17,482 main workers, 52,540 marginal workers and 7,69,696 non-workers in the District constituting almost 28 per cent, 5 per cent and 67 per cent respectively.[26] As per census of India (1991), a main worker is one who has worked for 183 days or more in a year in one or more than one economic activities and a person who cannot get work for 183 days in the above said economic activities is a marginal worker. The sector-wise distribution of main workers reveals that

2,19,012 people are involved in primary sector, 25,224 in secondary sector and 73,246 in tertiary sector constituting 69 per cent, 8 per cent and 23 per cent respectively. The primary sector consists of agriculture and allied activities of livestock, forestry, fishing, plantation etc. whereas the secondary sector consists of mining, household industry and construction. The tertiary sector includes of trade and commerce, transport, communication and service sector. Further the percentage of cultivators, agricultural labourers, workers in household industry and other activities of main workers is 54.8 per cent, 1.5 per cent and 30.8 per cent respectively. Hence more than two-thirds of the district's main work force is engaged in agriculture and allied activities. The Loharu Block has the highest number of main workers (29.8 per cent) whereas Dadri-I has the lowest number of main workers (25 per cent). The participation of female workers in the rural area has been quite negligible i.e. 8.9 per cent of total main work force and as such there is adequate opportunity to impart training to rural women folk to enable them to augment their income by working in small cottage industries.[27]

The total geographical area of the District is 4.61 lakh hectares of which 0.96 lakh hectares is put to non-agricultural use, uncultivable and the rest 3.65 lakh hectares is cultivable. Only 77 sq. km area is under forest in Bhiwani District. It is not only a little (4.6 per cent) as compared to the state's forestry but also thinly dispersed consisting of various kinds of herbs and shrubs. Kikar and Janti are the most popular flora of this region. According to the Agricultural census conducted in the year 1994-95, the number of operational land holdings in the District was 1,23,713 covering an area of 3.46 Lakh hectares of these 52 per cent were having an area up to 2 hectares and 29 per cent between 2 to 5 hectares and only 19 per cent were having more than 5 hectares. The District is basically agriculture dominant. Out of the total main workforce of the District 70 per cent people are engaged in agriculture and allied activities. During 1994-95, the net area sown was 3.55 lakh hectares i.e. 97.27 per cent to the total cultivable area. During 1994-95 the gross irrigated area in the District was 2.34 lakh hectares which constituted 41 per cent of the total cropped area where as the net area irrigated was 1.99 lakh hectares of which 1.11 lakh hectares[28] was irrigated under the Canals and the remaining 0.88 lakh hectares by tube wells. The Jui Canal Project, Siwani Canal Project, Loharu Canal Project and Indira Canal Project have brought a remarkable change in the rural economy of the District. The lift system adopted in these canals has made easy assess of water for irrigation to the driest part of the District. The sprinkler irrigation has become very popular in Loharu and Badhara Blocks. However, the tube wells are the main source of irrigation in these Blocks. The main food crops in Rabi are wheat, gram, barley and mustard. Bajra is the main crop of Kharif. Besides, cotton and pulses also constitute a major part of it. Of the total area sown 200 hectares was under rice, 72,500 under wheat, 1,58,400 under bajra, 1,46,900 under pulses, 1,02,500 under oil seeds and 33,500 under cotton in 1994-95. This shows that the maximum part of the sown area in the District is under Bajra (44.6 per cent) followed by pulses (41.4 per cent) and oil seeds (28.9 per cent) whereas the area under rice is microscopic. The gram and oil seeds are the major crops of the District both in respect of the sown area as well as the production comprising about thirty-six per cent and eighteen per cent of the production of the state respectively.[29] The industrial background of District is not very sound. Though there are certain big factories like Bhiwani Textile Mill, Mohta Iron and Steel Strips etc., yet the total number of registered factories in the District is 105, out of which 101 are in working order in which the number of workers employed is 11,917 constituting three per cent of the total work force of the state as per 1994-95 reports.[30] These factories are highly centralized and most of which are in Bhiwani city excluding CCI, Charkhi Dadri (now a sick unit) and few others. Almost all the villages of the District are provided with electricity, safe drinking water and metalled roads facilities. The length of metalled roads in the district is 1916 km and that of unmetalled is 118 km connecting all the Block headquarters very well whereas the length of railway line falling within the District is 145 km There are 286 Post Offices and 39 Telephone Exchanges equipped with STD/ ISD facilities available in all the Blocks[31]. The District has 993 cooperative societies having total membership of 2,56,127. There is one Central Cooperative Bank at Bhiwani having 21 Branches all over the District, 7 Primary Land Development Banks located at Bhiwani, Loharu, Bawani Khera, Dadri, Badhra, Siwani and Tosham and 178 Mini Banks. Besides, there are 38 Commercial Bank branches out of which 22 are in the urban areas and 16 in rural areas. There are 258 hospitals/dispensaries, 22 Ayurvedic, Unani and Homeopathy hospitals and 8 Family Welfare Centres in the District with 7152 Beds. According to 1992 cattle census, the livestock population was 6,54,900 as compared to 6,79,800 heads during 1988. Of the total population, the cattle constituted eighteen per cent, buffaloes thirty-eight per cent, sheep fifteen per cent, goats fourteen per cent and others fifteen per cent. The livestock density was 158 heads per sq. km as against 157 in the state. The District has a good network of veterinary institutions providing health cover to livestock population. Besides, there are 36 Veterinary Hospital, 50 Veterinary Dispensaries, 5 Artificial Semination Centres, 67 Livestock Centres, 11 Sheep Wool extraction Centres and 1 Poultry Extraction Centre and 13 Camel Breeding Centres in the district to provide a good network for animal health. There are five employment exchanges in the District. The number of educated unemployed registered with these were 58,125 as on 28-2-1996, out of which 8186 were women, 9496 Scheduled Castes, 4156 Backward Classes. The number of families identified for imparting employment under "One Family One Job" were 6425. The Tehsil-wise composition of these families were 2155 in Bhiwani, 2493 in Dadri, 695 in Bawani Khera, 582 in Tosham and 500 in Loharu.

The various steps taken by DRDA, Bhiwani for infrastructural development to IRDP beneficiaries are to establish a Hatchery unit at Bhiwani during 1979-80 to promote broiler rearing in the area to provide day old chicks to the IRDP beneficiaries establishment of a Diagnostic Lab to diagnose all types of diseases of animals; and a Semen Bank was also set up for breeding the animals of rural folks; Government Model Exotic Animal Farm was established in 1973 with cent per cent grant by Indian Dairy Cooperative Ltd., Baroda with the aim to produce good Pedigreed Jersey bullocks. As the agriculture is the main occupation of this District and a major part of rural population is engaged with it, hence it is essential to provide good infrastructural facilities to get the desired results. The various steps taken in this direction were as such: High Yielding Varieties seeds of different crops are being supplied to the farmers at subsidized rates through Agriculture Development officer (ADO) of Agriculture Department; HAFED, Mini Banks, Haryana Seed Development Corporation and Haryana Agro Industries Corporation at their door-steps. There is Government Seed Farm at Kohalawas for production of these crops besides Krishi Gyan Kendra, Bhiwani which provides necessary guidance to the farmers. There are more than 100 supply points for the supply of fertilizers owned by Government agencies as well as by be private businessmen. About 140 workers including 5 ADOs (Plant Protection) of Agriculture Department are rendering guidance to the farmers about the latest technology and plant protection measures through the use of pesticides and insecticides. Haryana Land Reclamation and Development Corporation, Forest Department, Soil Conservation Department and Haryana State Minor Irrigation and Tube well Corporation are the main agencies involved in the activities of land development.

The Dairy Development Department is sponsoring cases for Mini Dairy to the unemployed who are trained by the department keeping in view the extension services being provided by the department. There was only one milk plant at Bhiwani being run by the Haryana Dairy Development Cooperative Federation. Which has been closed now. There is no chilling plant in this District. The training programme is being undertaken through District Dairy Development Officer and Deputy-Director, Animal Husbandry. There are 6 sheep extension centres and 5 wool grading centres. The District Industries Centre, Bhiwani and the office of the Deputy Director (SISI) are providing technical assistance to the potential entrepreneurs. The District Marketing centre is also arranging the supply of raw material to help rural industrial units in marketing their products. The training to artisans is also arranged through ITIs and master craftsman under TRYSEM.

Profile of Bhiwani Block

Bhiwani Block was established in 1964. It consists of an area of 605.4 sq. km out of which 44 sq. km is under Municipal committee. It has a population of 2,74,704 as per 1991 census of which 1,47,328 are males and 1,27,368 females. The sex ratio is 865 and density is 453 persons per sq. km The rural population is 1,53,075 (55.7 per cent) of which 82,359 are males 70,716 are females. The literacy rate among rural population is 43.2 per cent i.e. 65,993 which consists of 46,992 males and 19,001 females. The strength of Scheduled Castes is 51,671 constituting nineteen per cent of total population of the Block. It consists of one Town and 53 Villages along with 65 Gram Sabhas. There are 43,067 main workers, 5,859 marginal workers and 1,04,149 non-workers constituting twenty-eight per cent, four per cent and sixty-eight per cent respectively. The main workers consist of 35,088 cultivators, 12,409 agriculture labourers and 1,084 involved in allied agricultural activities, 2,048 in cottage industries, 10,833 in trade and commerce and 9,334 in other industries. The above said figures show that the percentage of people engaged in industry, services and business (ISB) is remarkably good, Bhiwani city being a well developed market. There is hundred per cent electrification in rural areas. All the 53 villages are connected with electricity, metalled roads and safe drinking water facilities. There are 49 Post Offices and 7 Telegraph Offices in this block. There are 21 Commercial Banks including one unit of SBI, 7 Regional Rural Banks, one Land Development Bank, 4 Cooperative Banks and one Cooperative Society known as farm service society in the Block.

The total reported area in this Block is 87,000 hectares out of which 73,000 hectares is net cultivated area, 4,000 hectares is current fallows and 10,000 hectares is uncultivated and the area under forest is nil in this Block. The net area irrigated in the Block is 42,805 hectares constituting fifty-nine per cent to the total area sown. The main source of irrigation is canals covering 38,355 hectares land constituting about ninety per cent of the total irrigated area and there are 2,956 tube wells which irrigates 4,450 hectares land. In the Block 36,764 hectares area is double/multiple cropped which is thirty-four per cent of the net area sown. The area under major crops is 19,999 hectares wheat, 24,077 hectares gram, 9,807 hectares cotton, 14,513 hectares oil seeds and 21,749 hectares bajra. The above figures show that the major crops of this Block are gram, bajra, wheat and oil seeds. There are 18,000 plough animals and 49,900 buffaloes and 18,700 cows, 8,200 pigs, 25,100 goats 30,500 sheep and 6,200 poultry birds in the Block. There are 10 large scale and 1,458 small scale industries, 92 handloom units, 24 cotton spinning and weaving industries, 172 shoe making units, 92 village oil expellers, 76 blacksmith units.

Profile of Badhara Block

Badhara block came into existence in 1962. It consists of an area of 505.17 sq. km and a population of 1,09,567 as per 1991 census of which 58,048 are males and 51,519 females. The rural population is 1,09,567 and urban is nil, as the name of this Block is after Badhara village and there is no Town in this Block. The sex ration is 887 females per 1000 males and density of population is 216 persons per sq. km Out of the total population 43,438 people are literate constituting 31,468 (72 per cent) males and 11,970 (28 per cent) females. The strength of scheduled castes is 17,468 constituting 16 per cent of the total population of the Block. This Block consists of 68 villages along with 63 gram sabhas. There are 31,105 main workers, 4,948 marginal worker and 73,514 non-workers constituting twenty-eight per cent, five per cent and sixty-seven per cent respectively. The main workers consist of 25,563 males and 5,542 females. Among the main workers 22,108 are cultivators and 3,531 agricultural labourers constituting seventy-one per cent and eleven per cent respectively. Thus about four-fifths of the total work force of main workers is engaged in agricultural activities in this block. As there are a few small scale industries so a little part of population is engaged with Industry, Service and Business (ISB) sector. All the villages of this block are provided with safe-drinking water, electricity and connected with metalled roads even after the adverse climatic conditions. There are 18 Post Offices, One Telegraph Office and 6 Dispensaries, 7 Ayurvedic Dispensaries and 15 High, 9 Middle and 56 Primary schools in this Block. There are 3 Commercial Banks, 4 Regional Rural Banks, One Development Bank and 2 Cooperative Banks.

The total geographical area of the Block is 51,747 hectares of which 44,891 hectares (90.38 per cent) is under cultivation. During 1983-84, the cultivable land was 44,891 hectares of which ninety per cent was net area sown and the total cropped area was 67,204 hectares. The major sources of irrigation in this Block are tube wells and canals and the sprinkling system of irrigation is very popular. The total irrigated area was 15,400 hectares and there were 2,136 pumping sets/tube wells and 3,166 sprinkler sets. The major crops in this Block are bajra, wheat, gram and sarson covering 30,266 hectares, 10,816 hectares, 19,922 hectares and 3,355 hectares area respectively. Jawar, barley and tobacco are other crops sown in this block. According to 1982 cattle census, the total livestock population was 84,502 of which cattle constituted 21.5 per cent, buffaloes thirty-eight (38) per cent, sheep eleven (11) per cent, goats 13.5 per cent and others sixteen (16) per cent. In all 15 veterinary institutions are providing animal health cover to the livestock population. As far as the industry is concerned this Block is the poorest in the whole District and is declared by the Government of India as an industrials backward Block. There is no big or middle range industry in this Block. There are 437 small scale industries out of which 19 are that of handloom, 71 shoe making units, 16 village oil expellers, 22 blacksmith units.

Profile of Loharu Block

Loharu Block was established in 1955. It consists of an area of 608.74 sq. km and a population of 88,704 as per 1991 census of which 46,502 are males and 42,202 are females. The rural population is 79,833 and that of the urban is 8,871. The rural population is 90 per cent of the total population. The sex ration is 907 females per 1000 males and is 146 persons per sq. km The strength of scheduled castes is 17,263 which is 19.5 per cent of the total population of the Block. It consists of one town and 73 villages along with 62 gram sabhas. The occupational structure of this Block reveals that it consists of 27,708 main workers, 5,712 marginal workers and 55,284 non-workers forming thirty-one per cent, seven per cent and sixty-two per cent respectively. Out of the total main workers population 25,175 are cultivators, 2,651 agricultural labourers 260 are involved in allied agricultural activities, 201 in cottage industries, 1,364 in trade and commerce and 301 in other industries. The major work-force is engaged with agricultural and allied activities. The industry, Service and Business (ISB) sector is very poor in this Block and the bulk of the population (62 per cent) are non-workers. The infrastructure facilities are satisfactory in this Block even after this fact that the climatic are very odd. All the villages are provided with safe drinking water, electricity and metalled roads facilities. There are 29 Post Offices and one Telegraph Office equipped with STD and ISD facilities. There are three Commercial Banks, 6 Regional Rural Banks, one Land Development Bank and 2 Cooperative Banks in Loharu Block. The total reported area in this Block is 68,000 hectares of which 58,000 hectares is net cultivated area, 2,000 hectares current fallows and 1,000 hectares under forest, 7,000 hectares not available for cultivation. In this Block 45,994 hectares area is double/multiple cropped which is forty-four per cent of the net area sown (1,06,278 hectares). The area under major crops is 34,054 hectares gram, 33,962 hectares bajra, 11,562 hectares oil seeds, 7,135 hectares wheat and 587 hectares cotton. The above figures show that gram, bajra and oil seeds are the major crops of this Block constituting thirty-two per cent, thirty-two per cent and eleven per cent respectively of the net area sown. The net area irrigated is 31,369 hectares constituting 53 per cent to the total area sown. The main source of irrigation are canals and tube wells. The sprinkling system of irrigation is very popular in this Block out of the total irrigated area, 28,512 hectares (93 per cent) is irrigated by tube wells and 2,857 hectares by canals. The lift system of irrigation is popular in this Block. There are 2,569 electric motors which lift water at various sites. There are 4,700 plough animals and 35,900 dairy animals out of which 28,200 are buffaloes and 7,700 cows besides, 200 pigs, 12,300 goats, 10,700 sheep and 700 poultry birds in this Block. This Block is industrially backward declared by the Government of India and there is no major industry in this Block except a few middle range industries in Loharu city. The number of small scale industries is significant i.e. 548 of which 28 are that of handloom, 15 cotton spinning and weaving units, 79 khadi units, 110 shoe making units and 15 village oil expellers.

In brief we may conclude that the performance of a programme has a direct co-relation with the profile of that area where it is going to be implemented. The profile not only determine the viability of a particular programme but also the perception of the people to a greater extent. The state of Haryana came into existence on November 1st, 1996 as the 17th state of Indian Union. It is a small state with an area of 44,212 sq. km constituting 1.35 per cent of the Indian Union. It is on the north-western side of the Indian Union physically, it falls into the broad natural divisions-the sub-Himalayan and the Indo-Gangetic Plain which runs in south-eastern directions almost parallel to each other. No important river passes through the state. Most of the year, the climate of the state is of pronounced character. It is very hot in summer and markedly cold in winter. It has a population of 1,64,63,614 males 88,27,474 and females 76,36,174. It is densely populated as compared to the national average and three-fourths of the state population is residing in rural areas. The state's population is Hindu dominant (89 per cent). The scheduled castes constitute about one-fifth of the state's population. Whereas strength of scheduled tribes is nil. The literacy rate in the state is somewhat better (55.35 per cent) than the national average (52.21 per cent). But it is poor on the part of women who constitute only one-third of the total literate population of the state and two-thirds of the literates are residing in urban areas. Besides, the state has provided a good network for human as well as animal health.

In the short span of its existence the state has shown remarkable growth in the fields of agriculture, industry and infrastructural development. Today, it is one of the most developed states of the Indian Union. It was the first to provide electricity, pure water supply and metalled roads facilities to all its villages and towns by 1981. The state has made significant development in the fields of transport and communication. Almost all the towns are enjoying the felicities of STD/ISD. The economy of the state has increased significantly in the last three decades an it is one of the states having highest per capita income i.e. almost one and half times to that of national average. Hence the people of Haryana have good purchasing power. Less than one-third of the state's population is engaged in production and two-thirds are non-workers. Among the non-workers three-fourths are residing in rural areas. Almost sixty per cent of the population derives their livings from agriculture. The average size of land holdings is decreasing day by day and it is 2.43 hectares at present. Haryana is basically a rural dominant state and agriculture is the backbone of the state's economy though considerable network of industry has been established. Agriculture and allied sectors pay about 40 per cent of the state's gross domestic production and sixty per cent of the total main work force is attached with primary sector. The area under forests in the state is not only thinly dispersed but also poor (2.5 per cent) as compared to national average. Almost eighty per cent of the cultivable area is sown and half of it is double/multiple cropped. Haryana is beneficiary of the multi-purpose projects on Satluj and Beas. The major irrigation projects are Western Yamuna Canal, Bhakra Canal and Gurgaon Canal. The completion of Jui, Siwani and Loharu lift Irrigation Schemes and Jawaharlal Nehru Irrigation Scheme have transformed the rural economy of southern Haryana in general and District Bhiwani in particular. Canals (51 per cent) and tube wells (48 per cent) are the major source of Irrigation in the state. The state government has taken concrete steps to raise the standard of living of the farmers. It has not only written off cooperative loans of farmers but also provided other supportive facilities to them. The effects of the Green Revolution have clearly reflected in the state. Today, Haryana is not only self-sufficient in food grains production but also among the top contributors of food grains to the central pool. The state has a very sound industrial base and it produces the largest number of tractors in the country. One out of every four bicycles is produced here. Panipat, Faridabad, Gurgaon, Hisar, Ambala, Yamuna Nagar etc. have developed the advanced centres of industries and the state has a bright future in this direction.

The District Bhiwani came into existence as the 8th district of Haryana on December 22, 1972. It is situated on the south-west of the state and has a long boundary with the state of Rajasthan. Though it forms a part of Indo-Gangetic Alluvial Plain yet largely it is dry and sandy. Sandy dunes, commonly known as the 'Tibbas', can be seen in large number in the south-western parts of the district. The climate is very hot and dry in summer and cold in winter. The dust-storms are very often in May and June. In spite of the fact that Bhiwani is not favourably located, it has an edge over other district so far as the development activities are concerned. It is the second largest District in the state. More than eighty per cent of the population is residing in rural areas. The District is thinly populated (222 persons per sq. km) as compared to the state (372 persons per sq. km) and sex ratio is almost the same as that of the state. The district is Hindu dominant (99 per cent) and almost one fifth (18.97) per cent of its population is scheduled castes. The district is not evenly populated. The density in North-Eastern parts - Bhiwani, Bawani Khera and Charkhi Dadri - is more than doubled to South-Western parts - Siwani, Loharu and Tosham. The literacy rate in the District is almost the same as that of the state. The percentage of distribution of work force in the District is almost the same as is in the state and two-thirds (67.6 per cent) of the population is non-worker. Among the main workers who constitute less than one-third (27 per cent) of the total population, sixty-nine per cent are engaged in primary sector, eight per cent in secondary sector and twenty-three per cent in tertiary sector. Agriculture is the backbone of the rural economy in the district and almost eighty per cent of the land holdings are up to 5 hectares.

In spite of all the oddities the District has shown a remarkable growth in the all fronts of development. All the villages are provided with electricity, safe drinking water and metalled roads facilities. Besides, health, transport and communication network is very well established in the district. The various canal projects completed so far have brought a significant change in rural economy. The south-western parts of the district are covered by lift system of irrigation covering about sixty per cent of the net area irrigated. Besides, sprinkler system of irrigation has become very common in Lohru and Badhara Blocks. The industrial network is not sound constituting less than two per cent of the total industries in the state which are highly centralized.

Among the chosen Blocks, Bhiwani Block consists of an area of 659.45 sq. km and a population of 2,74,704 constituting 12.8 per cent and twenty-four per cent respectively of the district. The density of population is more than double to the district. It is situated on the northern part of the district and has plain area. Besides, agriculture, a significant strength of main workers is engaged in secondary and tertiary sectors due to the availability of good marketing facilities. Infrastructural development is good in this Block. The Bandhara and Loharu Blocks are situated on the South-Western part of the District. Both of them have more demographic as well as physical similarities. Loharu Block consists of an area of 608.7 sq. km and a population of 88,704 constituting 11.8 per cent respectively of the district whereas the Badhara Block has an area of 505.17 sq. km and a population of 109, 567 i.e. 9.8 per cent and 9.6 per cent of the District. Both of these Blocks are sparsely populated as compared to the average density of the district. It is 146 Loharu Block and 216 in Badhara. In these Blacks, most of the main workers (80 per cent) are engaged in agriculture and allied activities as the secondary and tertiary sectors are not so sound. Industrially these are among the most backward Blocks in the district and the climatic conditions are very odd. In spite of it, these Blocks also have good infrastructural facilities available.

Thus, the profile presents a clear demographic picture of the State, District Bhiwani and that of the selected Blocks to make the understanding more clear about the socio-economic and political milieu of the area of study.

REFERENCES

1. Lal, Muni, *Haryana - On High Road of Prosperity* (Delhi: Vikas Publishing House, 1974), pp. 17-18; Yadav, K.C., *Haryana Ka Itihas* (1803-1966) Part-3 (New Delhi: Macmillian, 1981), pp. 237-253.

2. Prakash, Buddha, *Glimpses of Haryana* (Kuruksherta University Press, 1968), p. 1.
3. *Techno-Economic Survey of Haryana* (New Delhi: National Council of Applied Economic Research, 1970), p. 1.
4. Government of India, *India 1990 - A Reference Annual* (New Delhi: Revenue and Reference Divisions, Ministry of Information and Broadcasting, Government of India, 1990), p. 76.
5. Government of India, *India 1990 - A Reference Annual, op. cit.*, p. 76.
6. Government of Haryana, Planning Department, *Statistical Abstract of Haryana 1995-96* (Chandigarh: Economics and Statistical Organization, 1977), pp. 40-42.
7. *Ibid.*, pp. 29-36.
8. *Ibid.*, p. 70.
9. *Ibid.*, pp. 27-28.
10. *Ibid.*, pp. 56-57.
11. *Ibid.*, p. 211.
12. *Ibid.*, p. 465.
13. *Ibid.*, p. 426.
14. *Ibid.*, p. 57.
15. Government of India, *India 1990 - A Reference Annual, op. cit.*, pp. 765-66.
16. Government of Haryana, Planning Department, *Statistical Abstract of Haryana 1995-96, op. cit.*, p. 273.
17. *Ibid.*, p. 419.
18. *Ibid.*, p. 375.
19. DRDA, *Annual Action Plan of IRDP, 1983-84,* District Bhiwani, p. 5.
20. Government of Haryana, Planning Department, *Statistical Abstract of Haryana 1995-96, op. cit.*, p. 22.
21. DRDA, *Annual Action Plan of IRDP, 1983-84, op. cit.*, p. 5.
22. Government of Haryana, Planning Department, *Statistical Abstracts of Haryana 1995-96, op. cit.*, pp. 40-42.

23. *Ibid.*, p. 63.
24. *Ibid.*, p. 36.
25. *Ibid.*, pp. 29-30.
26. *Ibid.*, p. 56.
27. *Ibid.*, pp. 59-60.
28. *Ibid.*, pp. 269-72.
29. *Ibid.*, p. 247.
30. *Ibid.*, p. 375.
31. *Ibid.*, p. 465.

4

Administrative Structure of IRDP

The administrative structure created for implementation of any development programme has a definite role to play in its performance. Hence after the description of Profile of the Area of Study in chapter 3, in this chapter an attempt has been made to discuss the administrative structure at various levels. In all the developing nations of Asia and Africa, state is viewed as an agency for social and economic change. A modern nation-state is distinguished from a colonial-state in the sense that while the former is a 'welfare state' engaged in activaties of social transformation, the latter is a 'police-state' trying to maintain *status quo* and maintenance of law and order. A state functions through its bureaucracy and therefore, in all the countries which are in a transitional period, passing from tradition to modernity, the bureaucracy is considered as an instrument of modernization and social change. The solution of such vital problems as removing poverty and illiteracy, and improving the living standards of the masses is not possible without an active and determined involvement of the government machinery. This makes the bureaucracy as the single most important variable influencing every type of change-social, economic, political or technological. In a developing country like India, administrators are prime moves and energies in the process of modernization of the country under their changed role in the 'welfare-state'. It is not only an instrument for the maintenance of law and order and collection of revenue, but the most important instrument for the welfare and well-being of the masses. Further in all developing nations, it is the only trustworthy, stable and continuous organization for carrying out goal-oriented development plan[1]. However, it has been noticed that the bureaucracy in all the developing nations including India has been finding it difficult to generate the required level of confidence in the people and to elicit their active support and cooperation in the process of social transformation[2]. The Bureaucracy in India has been the victim of its colonial past. The British called the Indian Civil Service as the 'steel frame' within which was prescribed the entire policy and functioning of government.[3] Changes were often introduced in an ad hoc manner and these were more marked at the central level than the lower levels of the government. At the State, District and Block levels, the old bureaucratic setup remained almost the same in nature with the result that there existed dual forms of government at the top and lower levels. While the central government was looked upon as an agency for development and change, the principle of a 'police-state' continued to govern the functioning of the state structure at the various levels and common man still took the state as government as was the tendency during colonial times.[4]

The nation has adopted various programmes of rural development started from Community Development Programme in 1952 to Integrated Rural Development Programme in 1978-79 one after another. However, the administrative setup remained almost the same with certain minor changes. The Government of India has adopted various models of development in the last four decades but not much has been achieved so far. Professor Rajini Kothari has cautioned against these frequent changes and said "when we take a different model for development, we must carefully diagnose the ills that we have confronted all the years for development. We are always enamoured of the models emulated in the west without understanding the ground realities.[5] Paul Appleby, the American Expert on Public Administration, had stated in his report on Indian Administration that when a new programme is undertaken, it is better to implement it through an existing organization by suitably strengthening it rather than starting as new administrative setup altogether. It was this approach which we seem to have followed in the Indian experiment. Thus, the Community Development Block administration was essentially built within the framework of traditional District administration though the functionaries like Block Development Officer (BDO) and the Village Level Workers (VLW) were a new creation. Thus, these new organizations, whether administrative agencies or registered societies, consist of the representatives of various departments and do not constitute the establishment of altogether a new administrative structure. They are rather adaptation of the existing administrative structure to new tasks and programme.[6] Administrative and organizational agencies working entirely outside the framework of normal administration and altogether cut-off and aloof from it may not be able to deliver the goals.[7]

The crux of the problem of development is the failure of political and economic system to fulfill the basic needs of the people especially in rural areas despite our achievement in the fields of agriculture, industry, technology, science, education and other areas. Reality is that vast majority of the Indian populace lives in poverty land is unable to get even the basic amenities like food, protected water supply, health facilities, adequate clothing and shelter. The gap between the rich and the poor is increasing enormously. Like-wise the facilities available in urban areas are not available in rural areas. More specifically barring a few, majority of the villages are facing in numerable problems one way or other and the life in the rural areas is real struggle against the oddities.[8] The problem of how to maximize the effectiveness of an administrative system so that it contributes to growth in the direction of development is a problem of how to string then rational and creative forces in the administrative system. Administrator with development responsibilities must be familiar with different forms of rationality needed for different areas from development administration. With the increase of pressure of new development programmes on the existing administrative structure, there is need of training of civil servants for new development tasks and responsibilities.[9] The administrative structure which is engaged in the implementation of various programmes of socio-economic change has been given the name development administration. Caiden views development influenced change towards progressive political, economic and social objectives.[10] The term 'Development Administration' has been used to focus attention on administration in the sense of 'getting results' or 'getting things done through organization' as distinguished from the use of 'administration' to refer to specialized staff services or administrative or managerial techniques and processes.[11] An economic interpretation of Development Administration has been made by John D. Montgomery who defined it as carrying out planned change in economy (in agriculture or industry, or the capital infrastructure supporting either of these) and to a lesser extent, in the social services of the state (especially education and public health)[12]. Of course, he maintains that 'politics' remains and important aspect of development administration. If the citizens are enlightened, vigilant and enterprising, the development process is likely to be quicker and the goals of development more easily achievable. The administrative machinery becomes an effective tool of change in the process.[13]

India has presented before the world an example of a nation providing to its rural masses a 'well penetrated and development oriented' administrative system. Important structural changes were introduced in Indian Administration particularly after 1950, with a view to meet the new challenges thrown by the need to modernize the country. First, the goals of administration were expanded so as to make it a 'welfare-administration'. Secondly, the pattern of administrative organization was transformed in 1952 when, with the commencement of the scheme of Community Development Blocks which functioned under one coordinating officer who was designated as the Block Development Officer (BDO). And lastly, changes in the norms and ethos of the administrative personnel were introduced and the officials were made aware of the need to adopt a democratic approach to administration.[14] Community Development Administration was a new step forward towards the building up of an effective and firmly based local government system in the rural areas which had remained 'relatively undeveloped' during the British Regime.[15] It was through the Community Development organization that the government reached down to the villages "not merely as policeman and tax-collector but as an agent for the improvement of agriculture and transformation of rural society. The little finger became the whole hand and the government was everywhere and inescapable.[16] But the bureaucracy failed to inspire the people's cooperation in Community Development Programme due to its rigid approach, conservatism and lack of development attitudes. The introduction of Panchayati Raj System in many states in the late fifties and early sixties was yet another important structural modification in Indian Administration. It was designed to change the entire tone of rural administration which was till then more authoritarian and official oriented than begin democratic and people oriented.

This change warranted that the administration should establish cordial relations with the citizens and also try to build a good image of its own in the minds of the rural poor. Though these change brought people closer to administration, they were minor ones as the people belong to traditionally dominant castes only are approaching the adminsitration.[17] In India, like other countries, the higher civil service is a comparatively better salaried class than the lower level. Their social background and vision are centred round the big cities. Socialistic goals and slogans of equality raised by the politicians are only of academic interest to them. In certain cases the civil service, may even sabotage socialist programme at the stage of implementation, if not at the policy formulation level it self.[18] Rigidity, insecurity and frustration among officials are part and parcel of bureaucratic culture in development administration. In most of the cases lower level bureaucracy is found always busy with the completing paper targets without any feed back from the rural areas. Most of the time fictitious reports are prepared and presented just to demonstrate wonderful results. The deterioration in standard of efficiency was mainly due to the bad temperament and negative attitudes of officers occupying higher levels.[19] The traditional service structure in the government of India is based on what is called as career staffing. While such a staffing system guarantees a certain degree of continuity, members of these services have no commitment to the success of a specific programme.[20] It was expected that during the course of time the attitude of the bureaucracy would change and in course of time they would be quite responsive to development. However, the attitude of bureaucrats in due country have not been changed to the desired extent. The success of rural development programme, to a large measure, depends on the involvement and participation of the beneficiaries groups in their implementation. For this purpose, an appropriate relationship between the beneficiary group and the organizational structure should be developed. The effective implementation of integrated programme calls for better planning at the district level and below, closer monitoring and a tighter organizational setup to ensure optimum use of resources and reaching the benefits to those for whom they are meant. All this requires a high level of competence, dynamism and devotion on the part of the field-level functionaries, and intelligent and imaginative supervision and support from the higher level of administration.[21] Adequate administrative efforts and organizational structures are as relevant, or even more, than the financial disbursements and the programmes themselves, if they have to have any success. The Economic-Survey of Government of India (1994-95) has observed simply increasing budgetary allocations for social sector and poverty programmes is not enough. The emphasis must now shift to revamping delivery system and administrative structure for all these programmes to make them accountable and responsive to the beneficiaries they are intended to serve. Leakages and malpractices must be curbed.[22]

The organizational setup of Integrated Rural Development Programme is almost the same as that of Community Development Programme with certain changes at the district level. The establishment of Small Farmer development Agency and District Rural Development Agencies during the 4th and 5th plans at the district level are major ones in this direction to make the agencies, responsible for implementation of rural development programmes, and to make it more and more development oriented. The description of the Administrative setup of IRDP and allied Programmes of poverty alleviation and employment generation is rural area has been given in this chapter.

Central Level Administrative Structure

The Ministry of Rural Development, Government of India, New Delhi has the overall responsibility of policy formulation, planning, monitoring, evaluation of the programmes of poverty alleviation and release of central share of funds. It is headed by a Minister of Rural Development. The Minister is assisted by a Secretary to the government of India. In addition, there is an Additional Secretary, Six Joint Secretaries and other supporting administrative as well as technical staff. The Ministry is divided into seven wings viz., Administration, Rural Employment, Integrated Rural Development, Land Reforms, Finance, Monitoring and Technology Mission. Each of these wings is headed by a Joint Secretary. The Ministry also runs the following institutions viz., National Institute of Rural development (NIRD), Council for Advancement of People's Action and Rural Technology (CAPART) and Directorate of Marketing and Inspection (DMI) under its administrative control. The administrative structure of the Ministry and its attached Institutions can be seen in Chart 4.1.

Chart 4.1
Ministry of Rural Development

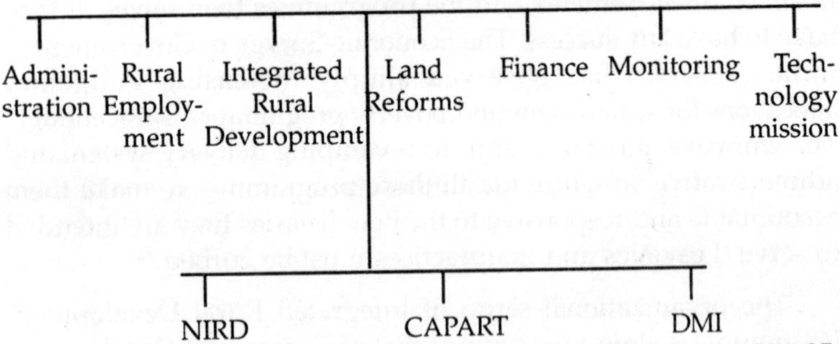

Source: Ministry of Rural Development, Annual Report, 1994-95, pp. 78-79.

Due to creation of six new Departments in the Central Ministries during March, 1995, the nomenclature of the Ministry of Rural Development has been changed and this Ministry has now come to be known as Ministry of Rural Areas and Employment.[23] This Ministry has now two Departments viz. Department of Rural Development and Department of Rural Employment and Poverty Alleviation each headed by a Secretary to the Government of India. Integrated Rural Development Programme and other programmes of poverty alleviation and employment generation are now under the Department of Rural Employment and Poverty Alleviation. Government circulars constitute the most important means employed by the Ministry for fulfilling its responsibilities. Since the Inception of IRDP in 1978-79, the Ministry has issued a number of circulars through which it has sought to revise, clarify and supplement the original guidelines and instructions incorporated in its manual on IRDP. A perusal of these circulars would show that most of them have been issued in response to the feed back comments and suggestions received by the ministry from time to time. This shows that the ministry has been sensitive, open and responsive in its approach to planning and implementation of IRDP.[24]

Central Level Coordination Committee

The Ministry of Rural Development is assisted by a Central Level Coordination Committee (CLCC). This committee has been constituted to review Integrated Rural Development Programme (IRDP), Training of Rural Youth for Self-Employment (TRYSEM), Development of Women and Children in Rural Area (DWCRA) and other programmes of rural poverty alleviation and employment generation at the central level. The detailed structure of CLCC is given in Appendix 2.

The functions of Central Level Coordination Committee (CLCC) include:

- Framing and revision of guidelines for the IRDP and allied programmes.
- To ensure effective implementation of the programmes.
- To review preparation of Block Plans, District Plans, Annual Action Plans and Credit Plans etc.
- To review linkages for supporting services for the IRDP beneficiaries.
- To consider changes in administrative setup under IRDP and for other rural development programme.
- To review progress of these programmes in physical, financial and qualitative terms.
- To consider concurrent evaluation reports.
- To provide a forum for a continuous dialogue with the State Governments: and
- To consider proposals for strengthening of infrastructure of training institutions, establishment of new training institutions, modification in the norms prescribed for grant of stipend and in the pattern of training institutions etc. Under Training of Rural Youths for Self-Employment (TRYSEM)[25].

This structure and its modus operand seem to be appropriate for meeting the policy and planning needs of Integrated Rural Development Programme (IRDP) at the national level. The Ministry of Rural Development has prescribed that programmes like Integrated Rural Development (IRDP), National Rural Employment Programme (NREP), Rural Landless Employment Guarantee programme (RLEGP), Drought Prone Areas Programme (DPAP) etc. at the state level should be looked after by a single department having an overall control over the development administration right up to the Block and field levels so that the inter-sectoral coordination with other departments, operational aspects of implementation, review, monitoring etc. are adequately taken care of[26].

State Level Administrative Structure

The Department of Rural Development or any other Department to which the subject of Rural Development has been allocated should be responsible for planning, implementation, monitoring and evaluation of the programme. The nomenclature of the Department and the Ministry has been changed from time to time. Earlier this task was given to a 'Special Project Cell-Agriculture' established under the Ministry of Agriculture, Haryana, which kept it up to 1984-85. Later on in 1984-85, this project-cell was converted into a Directorate and named as Directorate of Development under the Ministry of Development, Haryana, headed by a Director and a Commissioner-cum-Financial Secretary respectively and given the charge of Rural Development. Again in 1990-91, a separate Directorate of Rural Development was established under the Ministry of Development and Panchayat, headed by a Director-cum-Joint Secretary, Rural Development and a Commissioner, Development and Panchayat respectively, which are responsible for all types of above-said activities of Integrated Rural development Programme (IRDP) at the state level. Thus, the Commissioner, Development and Panchayats, is at the top of administrative hierarchy and the overall in-charge of all the rural development programmes including IRDP in the state. He takes help of various staff members provided for this purpose. Below it, there is Directorate of Rural Development, headed by Director-cum-Joint Secretary, who with the help of various staff members is actually responsible for planning, implementation, monitoring and evaluation of rural development programmes in the state. Besides, Haryana Institute of Rural Development (HIRD), Nilokheri helps in training of personnel and evaluation of the programme. The composition of administrative machinery of IRDP at the state level has been shown in Chart 4.2.

A State Level Coordination Committee (SLCC) has also been instituted to assist the Ministry in discharging its responsibilities. The actual and perspective composition of the SLCC in the state is given in Appendix 3 and 4.

The functions of State Level Coordination Committee (SLCC) include:

- To provide leadership and guidance to the District Rural Development Agencies (DRDAs) in the planning, implementation and monitoring of the programme.
- To secure inter-departmental co-ordination between various implementing agencies of programme like Operation Flood, Operation Blackboard, Applied Nutrition Programmes etc. And to ensure development of strong forward and backward linkages for the programmes.
- To consider needs and changes in the administrative setup for the implementation of the programme and approve the establishment pattern and sanction the posts accordingly.
- Fix norms for office expenses, equipment, vehicles, hiring of accommodation etc. where necessary and to review the expenditure on these items to ensure that it remains with in the prescribed limits.
- To review the physical targets and achievements of the districts keeping in view the objective conditions attracting the provision and operation of viable schemes and modify the targets accordingly, keeping in view the overall objectives.
- To monitor and evaluate the implementation of the programme with reference to the objectives of the programme.
- To review implementation of IRDP and allied programmes by voluntary agencies and other Non-Government Organizations.
- To provide a forum for a meaningful dialogue between the policy makers at the state level and the implementors at the field level. The SLCC normally meets quarterly.

District Level Administrative Structure

At the district level, District Rural Development Agency (DRDA) is responsible for planning, implementing, coordinating, supervising and monitoring of all rural development programmes including IRDP. This agency is a registered society under the Registration of Societies Act, 1860. It is generally chaired by the Collector/Deputy-Commissioner/Sabhapati of Zila Parishad depending upon the practice prevailing in the state. In Haryana, Deputy-Commissioner is the chairman of the District Rural Development Agencies (DRDA), besides him there is a full-time Chief Executive Officer (CEO) of the DRDA. This post is held by Additional deputy-Commissioner (ADC) and is known as CEO-cum-ADC, DRDA. Besides, there is a Governing Body and an Executive Committee in each District Rural Development Agency (DRDA) to assist it in formulation and approval of annual action plans. The detailed composition, powers and functions of these agencies are given below. The composition of District Rural Development Agency (DRDA) as desired by the Government of India and as adopted by the State of Haryana has been given in Charts 4.3 and 4.4.

The staffing pattern of District Rural Development Agencies (DRDA) has been given in charts 4.3 and 4.4.

In addition, District Bhiwani has also been provided the posts of– Stenographer (1), Computer Assistant (1), Daftri and Class IV (3).

In the state IRDP and Allied Programmes are implemented by IRDP staff at District Headquarters. The District is divided into Blocks and the Assistant Project Officers (APO) look after one or more Blocks for planning and implementation of the programmes. However, also take help of Block level staff i.e. VLW, Extension Officers, BDO etc. in survey of Below Poverty Line (BPL) families, identification of beneficiaries, purchasing of assets, organization of camps and supervision of IRDP beneficiaries and recovery of loans.

Functions of District Rural Development Agency (DRDA)

The DRDA is the overall in-charge of the planning, implementation, monitoring and evaluation of the programme in the District. The main functions of District Rural Development Agency are as follows:

- To keep the District and Block level agencies informed of the basic parameters and the requirements of the programme and tasks to be performed by all these agencies.
- To coordinate and oversee the surveys, preparation of Perspective Plans and Annual Plans of the Blocks and finally prepare a District Plan.

- To monitor and evaluate the programme implementation by Government and non-Government agencies to ensure its effectiveness.
- To secure inter-sectoral and inter-departmental coordination and cooperation.
- To give publicity to the achievements made under the programme and disseminate knowledge and build up awareness about the programme.
- To send periodical returns to the state government in the prescribed formats.

Governing Body

The Governing body of DRDA includes Deputy Commissioner as Chairman and all the MLAs, MPs, the officials of all the concerned departments and financial institutions of the district as members and ADC-cum-Chief Executive Officer as member secretary. The detailed composition of Governing Body[27] both illustrative as well as actual is given in Appendix 5 and 6. The Governing Body normally meets once in three months but emergency meetings can be called, if required at a short notice. The functions of the Governing Body include:

- To coordinate and oversee the survey, preparation of plans and annual action plans of the Blocks and to finally prepare the District plan.
- To provide leadership and guidance to DRDA in the planning, implementation and monitoring of the programme.
- To secure inter-departmental coordination and linkages for the programme.
- To evaluate and monitor the programme so as to ensure its proper implementation.
- To approve the expenditure of the staff and the programmes of the DRDA.
- To give publicity to the achievements made under the programmes and disseminate knowledge and build up awareness about the programmes.

Executive Committee

The chairman of the district Rural Development Agency (DRDA) is empowered to form an Executive Committee to assist

Chart-4.2
Administration Structure of Rural Development at State Level

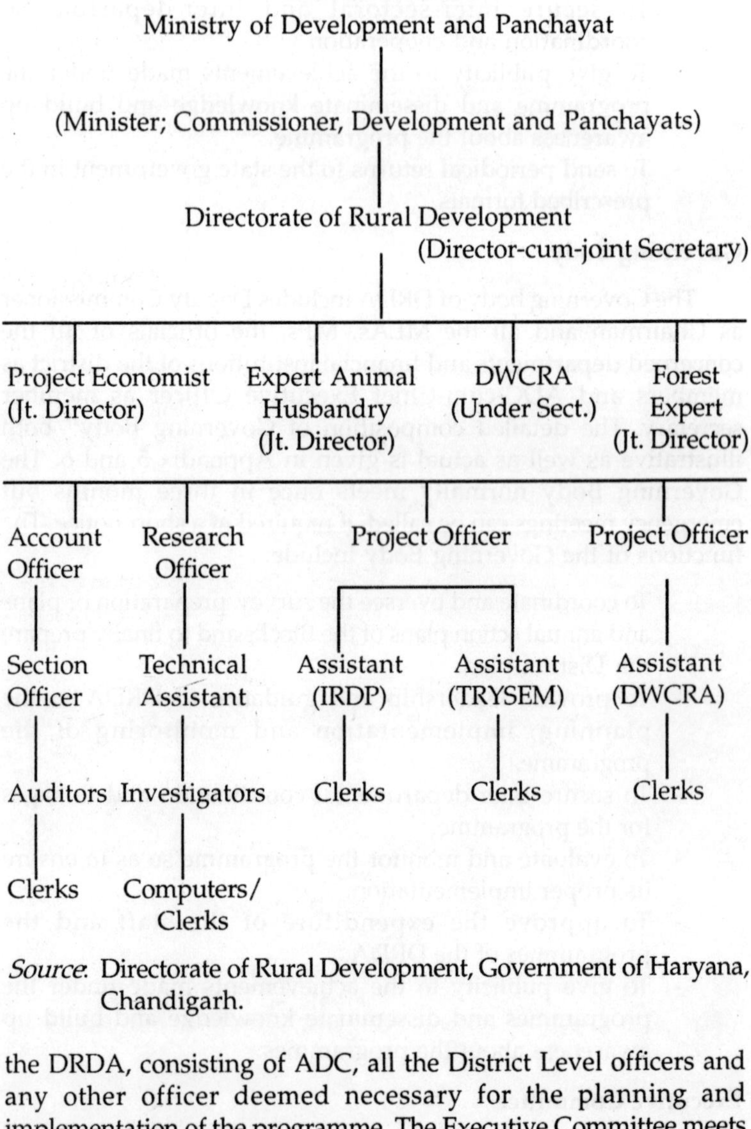

Source: Directorate of Rural Development, Government of Haryana, Chandigarh.

the DRDA, consisting of ADC, all the District Level officers and any other officer deemed necessary for the planning and implementation of the programme. The Executive Committee meets once in a month.

Duties and Powers of the Executive Committee

The duties and powers of the Executive Committee are as follows:

- To perform all the duties, functions and exercise powers required for achieving the objectives of the society.
- To assess and evaluate the working of the Agency once in a month and give necessary directions as are considered relevant for proper implementation of the programmes.
- To take necessary steps to maintain financial discipline; and
- To ensure that the staff in the DRDA is according to the requirements.

Like Governing Body, the Deputy Commissioner is also the chairman of the Action/Executive Committee and presides over all the meetings of the committee. The plan known as Annual Action Plan is formulated by the Planning Committee[28] of DRDA consisting of an Economist/Statistician, a Credit Planning Officer, and a Small and Cottage Industries Officer with the help of other concerned officials if required under the supervision of Chief-Executive Officer, District Rural Development Agency (DRDA).

Restructure of District Rural Development Agency (DRDA)

Consequent upon the Seventy Third Amendment of the Constitution and the formation of newly elected Panchayati Raj Institutions, there was a need for closer link and effective coordination between Zila Parishad and the District Rural Development Agency (DRDA). Accordingly the Central Government after taking into consideration the resolution unanimously adopted both in the Conference of Panchayati Raj Ministers and All India Panchayat Adhyakshas Sammelan decided to bring some changes in the existing structure of the District Rural Development Agencies (DRDAs)[29].

The District Rural Development Agencies (DRDAs) would now function under the overall supervision, control and guidance of the Zila Parishad, and provide executive and technical support to the Zila Parishad in discharging its functions. Chairman, Zila parishad would be the ex-officio chairman of the Governing Body of the DRDA, instead of the Deputy-Commissioner. The Panchayati Raj Institutions will implement the anti-poverty programme with

Chart-4.3

Staffing Pattern for DRDA as recommended by the Government of India

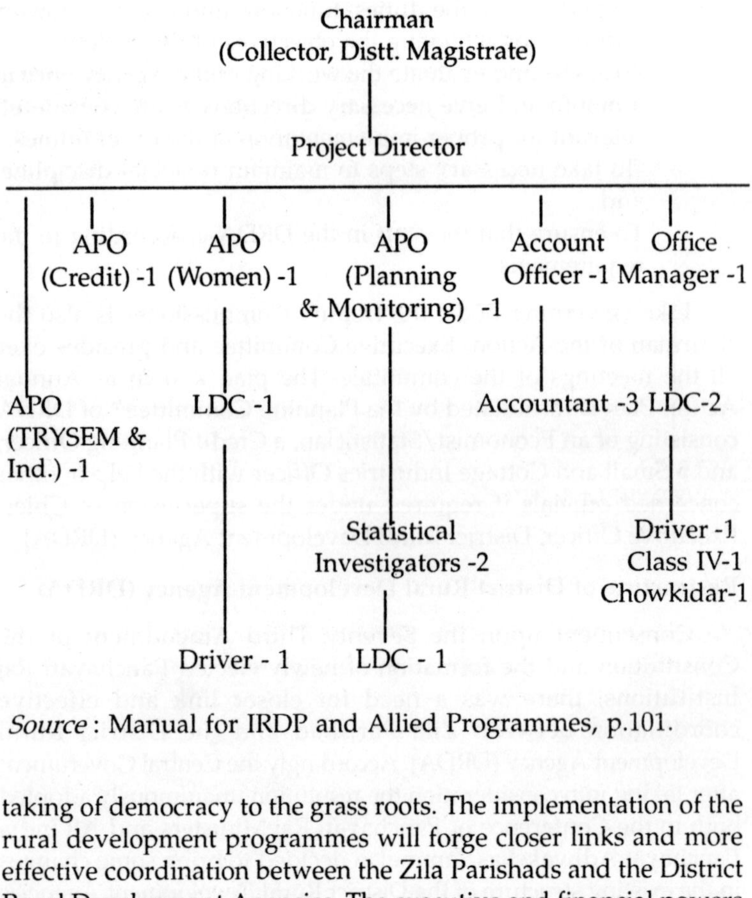

Source : Manual for IRDP and Allied Programmes, p.101.

taking of democracy to the grass roots. The implementation of the rural development programmes will forge closer links and more effective coordination between the Zila Parishads and the District Rural Development Agencies. The executive and financial powers would however, vest in the District Collector to be designated as Chief Executive Officer or Executive Director. The changes being brought about in the existing structure of the DRDAs is to make them more representatives. The Governing Body of the DRDA would consist of all MPs and MLAs of the District and District level officers of various development departments. Provisions had also been made for including Ex-MPs and Ex-MLAs, one third of Panchayat Samitis' Chairmen and Chairmen of standing

Chart-4.4
Staffing Pattern for DRDA in Haryana

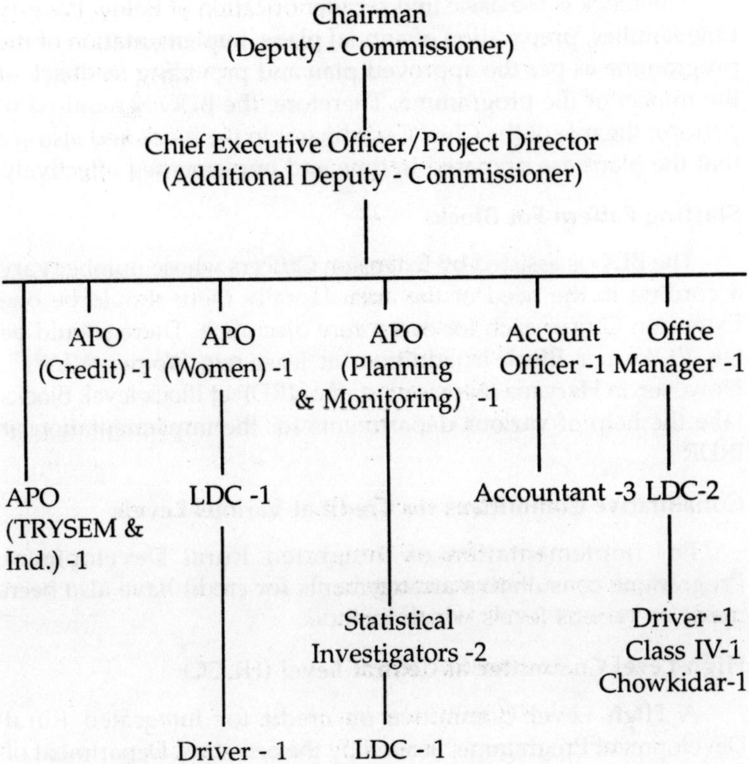

Source: 1. Department of Rural Development, Government of Haryana, Chandigarh.
2. Guidelines of Government of India, Department of Rural Development, Circular No. S 11011/43/81 - IRD-2, dt. 10.3.1981, New Delhi.

Committees of the Zila Parishad as members of the Governing Body[30]. The Governing Body of the DRDA will provide policy direction, approve the national plan as well as all schemes, both in physical and financial terms and also review the implementation of the Government of India. However, Deputy-Commissioner still continue to be the Chairman of the Governing Body of District

Rural Development Agency (DRDA).

Block Level Administrative Structure

The Block is the basic unit for identification of Below Poverty Line families, preparation of annual plans, implementation of the programme as per the approved plan and providing feedback of the impact of the programme. Therefore, the BDO is required to perform the role of the Chief Coordinator in the Block and also see that the plans are prepared in time and implemented effectively.

Staffing Pattern For Block

The BDO is assisted by Extension Officers whose number vary according to the need of the area. Usually there should be one Extension Officer each for every core discipline. There should be ten VLWs per Block in addition, at least two Women VLWs[31]. However, in Haryana there is no staff of IRDP at Block level. Blocks take the help of various departments for the implementation of IRDP.

Consultative Committees for Credit at Various Levels

For implementation of Integrated Rural Development Programme consultative arrangements for credit have also been made at various levels which include:

High Level Committee at Central Level (HLCC)

A High Level Committee on credit for Integrated Rural Development Programme, headed by the Secretary, Department of Rural Development, Government of India and including senior representatives from the Government of India, State Government, Commercial Banks, National Bank for Agriculture and Rural Development (NABARD) and Reserve Bank of India (RBI) has been constituted to consider the various problems arising from time to time in the course of implementation of the programme and review the credit arrangements to recommend changes and improvements as and when necessary. This committee meets regularly.

State Level Banker's Committee (SLBC)

State Level Banker's Committee (SLBCs) has been setup as inter-institutional form for coordination and joint implementation of development programmes. The meeting of this committee are convend by the designated convener Bank, which is usually the Bank with substantial lead responsibility in the state. In Haryana, this responsibility is owned by Punjab National Bank (PNB). The agenda items discussed by the SLCC relate mainly to branch expansion, implementation of Annual Action Plan, support from government agencies, inter-Bank differences, problems raised at District Consultative Committee which require attention at State level etc.

District Level Consultative Committee (DLCC)

At the District level a District Level Consultative Committee (DLCC) has been constituted under the chairmanship of the Deputy-Commissioner. All the Banks and the District level officers of the government, National Bank of Agriculture and Rural Development (NABARD), District Rural Development Agency (DRDA) and District Industries Centre (DIC) are represented in this committee. This forum is utilized for allocating share of credit disbursement to various Banks, monitoring and reviewing the overall progress in physical and financial terms, ironing out inter-agency differences and to prepare items for consideration of State Level Committee. The Lead Bank i.e. Punjab National Bank (PNB), a Bank with maximum number of branches and credit, functions as a coordinator between various Banks of the District.

Block Level Consultative Committee (BLCC)

This committee has been constituted in each Block. The composition of Block level Consultative Committee (BLCC) is given as under.

The main functions of BLCC can be mentioned here:

- Acceptance of branch wise, scheme-wise targets.
- Selection of clusters of villages and allocation of villages to various Banks.
- Fixing dates for credit camps.
- Monitoring the progress of sanction-number of applications sponsored by BDO to each branch, numbers rejected, reasons of rejection etc.
- Fix up dates for meetings of Purchase Committees for assets procurement.
- Monitoring progress of IRDP recoveries and fix dates for

recovery camps etc.:

- Review of implementation of schemes, conduct sample checks of verification of assets. The BLCC should hold meeting once every month.

Chairman
Sub-Divisional Officer (c)

Convener
Block Development Officer

Members

Branch Mangers of all Commercial Banks
Chairman/Secretary of the Primary Land Development Bank,
District Cooperative Bank
Tehsildar
APO (credit)

An Evaluation of Administrative Structure of IRDP

The foregoing description indicates that there exist many weaknesses in the organizational setup presently in existence for the implementation of poverty alleviation programmes in the State of Haryana in general and District Bhiwani in particular. The short comings as observed at various levels may briefly be discussed here so that a picture of the organizational weaknesses may emerge at various level.

State Level

Over the years, many new Rural Development Programmes have been launched by the Government but the staffing pattern by and large remained the same as it was during the initial stages when Community Development Programme was started. There has not been any proportionate increase in the staffing strength especially on planning and monitoring side as would be evident from the organizational chart (see chart 4.2). The existing staff can only perform routine type of functions such as general administrations, compilation of reports and returns, and financial control. Haryana Institute of Rural Development (HIRD), Nilokheri, has not proved effective in the organization of training programmes and motivation camps for IRDP personnel and concurrent evaluation of programmes. The kind of strong setup recommended by Government of India for the effective implementation of poverty alleviation programmes has not been followed despite Government of India's offer to share the burden of expenditure on additional posts. Besides, the lack of dedication toward programmes seems to be very clear among the members of the staff.

District Level

The weakness in the administrative structure at the district level as observed may be highlighted here. First, the District Rural Development Agency was setup for the implementation of Integrated Rural Development Programme. Many new programmes like National Rural Employment Programme, Rural Landless Employment Guarantee Programme, Jawahar Rojgar Yojana etc. were also entrusted to District Rural Development Agencies for implementation without providing any additional staff. Though the staff in District Rural Development Agency, Bhiwani is more than the guideline of Government of India, lack of interest and spirit towards work among officials is one of its major features. Most of the time, it has been observed that either there were few officials in office or otherwise they were gossiping. Most of them seemed to be unskilled and incompetent in their work. It has been observed that it is very difficult for the concerned Assistant Project Officers to get work done from their subordinates. Secondly, it was observed that the effectiveness and efficiency of DRDA is determined to a large extent by Chief Executive Officer-Cum-Additional Deputy-Commissioner. As he is from IAS cadre and have no specific technical knowledge about the programme and the frequent transfers of CEO-Cum-ADC has adversely affected the performance of DRDA in District Bhiwani. Thirdly, the post of Project Economist is laying vacant since long in DRDA, Bhiwani and is held by Assistant Project Officer (Credit). Hence no proper statistics was maintained and the data are highly contradictory in many cases. Fourthly, the Computer Assistant seems uninterested towards research programme and remains always busy in adjusting data. Similar is the situation with that of statistical investigators, who are in the habit of forgetting things and we have tough time with them to collect relevant data. Fifthly, the post of Assistant Project Officer (Recovery) is still held by another Assistant Project Officer who has to work besides his own, which has affected the monitoring as well as recovery process.

Block Level

There is no staff of IRDP at Block level in Haryana and also in District Bhiwani. The Block officials who are engaged with the process of implementation of Integrated Rural Development Programme at various stages take only as much interest as is essential to fulfill the formalities. They do not take sincere step in dealing with IRDP as they consider it additional burden on them. Lack of Block Level staff of IRDP is one of the major cause of increase in project expenditure as the concerned APO has to visit to the farthest villages which take a lot of time and resources and is a major hurdle in development of cordial relations between the beneficiaries and concerned officials, which is needed for the effective implementation of the programme and its pragmatic out put. It has also adversely affected the functioning of the DRDA, as and when the APOs went to the field, their subordinates slip away from office and to their other work. Most of them come for one hour in the morning and one hour in the evening.

Even after clear cut directions and guidelines from Government of India no fundamental change has been brought at State Level to cope with such a magnitude problem of rural development and for effective implementation of poverty alleviation and employment generation programmes in rural areas like IRDP. Though it is the subject of state to implement programme of rural development, it has remained as post office to pass information from center to DRDAs and vice-versa. All the major decisions regarding the policy formulation, implementation and evaluation of these programmes have been taken by the Central Government and the programmes of rural development have become highly centralized. At the District level, there is a District Rural Development Agency, a registered society under the 'Registration of Society Act 1860' but it is still far to ensure active participation of the people for whom the programme is meant. Though certain significant steps have been taken by restructuring DRDAs, it has still remained on paper and needs to strengthen the programme at the field level. The performance and role of Block officials regarding IRDP is far from satisfactory and requires fundamental change.

We are inclined to conclude that in all the developing nations of Asia and Africa, state is viewed as an agency for social and economic change. The modern state has become a 'welfare-state' engaged in activities of socio-economic transformation. As the state functions through its bureaucracy which is considered as an instrument of modernization and social change, the solution of vital problems of rural development depends to a large extent on the mode of functioning of the bureaucracy. But the Bureaucracy in all the developing nations including India has been finding it difficult to generate the required level of confidence in the people and to elicit their active support and cooperation in the process of social transformation.

In India, it has been the victim of its colonial past, though changes were introduced but in an ad hoc manner and these were more marked at the central level than the lower levels of the government. While the central government was looked upon as an agency of development and change, the principle of a 'police-state' continued to govern the functioning of the state structure at the various levels and common man still took the state as government as was the tendency during colonial times The nation has adopted various programmes of rural development started from CDP in 1952 to Integrated Rural Development Programme in 1978-79 one after another but the administrative setup at the state, District and Block levels by and large remained same with certain changes such as creation of DRDAs, Panchayati Raj Institutions and Block Development Offices. The problem is of how to maximize the effectiveness of an administrative system so that it contributes to the growth in the direction of development and how to strengthen rational and creative forces in the administrative system. Administrators with development responsibilities must be familiar with different from of rationality needed for different areas for development administration. Hence the administrative structure engaged in the implementation of various programmes of socio-economic change has been given the name development administration. It was expected that during the course of time the attitude of the bureaucracy would change and in course of time they would be quite responsive to development. However, the attitudes of bureaucrats in our country have not been changed to the desired extent. In India, there seems no difference between the regular bureaucracy and personnel engaged in development activities as far as their functioning and service conditions are concerned.

The administrative structure of Integrated Rural Development Programme and allied programmes of poverty alleviation and employment generation at various levels may be briefly mentioned here. The Ministry of Rural Development, Government of India, New Delhi has the overall responsibility of policy formulation, planning, monitoring, evaluation of the programmes of poverty alleviation and release of central share of funds. It is headed by the Minister of Rural Development, who is assisted by the Secretary. Besides, there is an Additional Secretary, Six Joint secretaries and other administrative as well as technical staff. National Institutes of Rural Development (NIRD), Council for Advancement of People's Action and Rural Technology (CAPART) and Directorate of Marketing and Inspection (DMI) are other technical institutions under the Control of the Ministry. In addition to the Minister In-charge, the Commissioner, Development and Panchayats is at the top of administrative hierarchy and is the overall In-charge of all the rural development programmes including Integrated Rural Development Programme in the state. Below it, there is the Directorate of Rural Development, headed by Director -cum-Joint Secretary, who with the help of various staff members is actually responsible for planning, implementation, monitoring and evaluation of the programme. Besides, Haryana Institute of Rural Development (HIRD), Nilokheri helps in training of personnel and evaluation of the programme. A State Level Coordination Committee has been instituted to assist the Ministry in discharging its responsibilities. At the District level, DRDA is responsible for planning, implementing, and monitoring of all rural development programmes including IRDP. In Haryana, Deputy Commissioner is the chairman of DRDA. Besides him, there is a full time Chief Executive Officer of the DRDA and this post is held by Additional Deputy Commissioner. To help the ADC in formulation of annual action plan, a planning committee has been constituted which consists of an Economist, a Credit Planning Officer and Small and Cottage Industries Officer.

REFERENCES

1. Ghildial, A.K., "From Steel Frame to Open Structure: Bureaucracy and Social Change in India", *The Administrator,* Vol. 28, No. 1, January-March, 1983, p. 33.

2 *Ibid.,* pp. 33-34.

3 *Ibid.,* p. 34.

4 *Ibid.,* p. 35.

5 Kothari, Rajni, *Democratic Polity and Social Change in India: Crises and Opportunities* (New Delhi: Allied Publications, 1976).

6 Dubhashi, P.R., "Approaches to Integrated Rural Development in India: Administrative and Organizational Issues", *The Administrative Change,* Vol. 6, No. 1-2, July, 1978-June, 1979, p. 120.

7 *Ibid.,* p. 121.

8 Palanithurai, G., *Indian Polity: Myth and Reality* (Delhi: Kanishka Publication, 1993), p. 128.

9 Ahmad, R. Furqun, "Development Administration: Need for New Training Pattern", *Indian Journal of Politics,* Vol. 29, No. 1-2, 1995, pp. 153-154.

10 Caiden, Gerald E., *Dynamics of Public Administration: Guidelines to Current Transformation in Theory and Practice* (New York: Hort, Rinehart and Winston, 1971), p. 267.

11 Gross, Bertram M., "Space - Time and Post Industrial Society", in James J. Heaphy (ed.), *Spatial Dimensions of Development Administration* (Durham, N.C.: Duke University Press, 1971), p. 217.

12 Montgomery, John D., "A Royal Invitation: Variations of Three Classic Themes", in Montgomery and William J. Siffin (ed.), *Approach to Development: Politics, Administration and Change* (New York: McGraw-Hill, 1966), p. 259.

13 Pai Panandikar, V.A. (ed.), *Development Administration in India* (New Delhi: Macmillan, 1974), p. 203.

14 Puranik, S.N., "The Villagers' Perception of the Administrative System: An Empirical Analysis", *Administrative Change,* Vol. 5, July-December, 1977, p. 12.

15 Hanson, A.H. and Douglas, J., *India's Democracy* (New Delhi: Vikas Publication House, 1974), p. 181.

16 Morris-Jones, W.H, *The Government and Politics of India* (Bombay: B.I. Publication, 1974), p. 18.

17 Puranik, S.N., "The Villagers' Perception of the Administrative System: An Empirical Analysis", *op. cit.,* p. 25.

18 Valson, E.H., "Development Bureaucracy: A Tentative Model', *op. cit.,* p. 39.

19 Hargopal, G. and Murli Manohar, K., "Some Aspects of Morale in the Rank and File of Indian Bureaucracy", *Indian Journal of Public Administration,* October-December, 1976, p. 724.

20 Pai Panandikar, V.A., "Development Administration: An Approach", *Indian Journal of Public Administration,* January-march, 1964, p. 41.

21 Maheshwari, S.R., *Rural Development in India* (New Delhi: Sage Publications, 1985), pp. 121-122.

22 Sunderam, I. Satya, "Eighth Plan-mid-Term Appraisal", *Third Concept,* Vol. 9, No. 108, February, 1996, p. 35.

23 Government of India, Ministry of Rural Development, *Annual Report, 1994-95,* New Delhi, 1995.

24. NIRD, Proceedings of the National Workshop held at NIRD, *Administrative Arrangements for Rural Development: A perspective* (Hyderabad: NIRD, 1985), p. 329.

25 Government of India, Department of Rural Development, *Manual for IRDP, and Allied Programmes, 1991, op. cit.,* p. 16.

26 NIRD, *Administrative Arrangements for Rural Development: A Perspective, op. cit.,* p. 277.

27 Government of India, Ministry of Rural Development, *Circular No. S. 11011/18/82-IRD-III, dated 9-11-83,* New Delhi.

28 Government of India, Ministry of Rural Development, *Circular No. S-11011/130/81-IRD-I, dated 24-9-1982,* New Delhi.

29 Government of India, Ministry of Rural Areas and Employment, *Circular No.: R. 20016/2/95-IRD-I, dated 6-11-1995,* New Delhi.

30 *The Tribune,* Chandigarh, November 10, 1995.

31. Government of India, Department of Rural Development, *Manual for IRDP and Allied Programmes, 1991, op. cit.,* p. 19.

5

IRDP: The Process of Implementation

After describing the administrative structure of IRDP at various levels in preceding chapter, an attempt has been made to examine the process of implementation of IRDP in this chapter. The process of implementation of IRDP includes: (a) the survey for identification of Below Poverty Line families, (b) formulation and approval of annual action plans, (c) organization of credit camps, (d) processing of loan applications, (e) disbursement of loans, (f) purchasing of assets, (g) monitoring, (h) recovery of loans. Besides, funding pattern and financial procedure have also been discussed.

The Operational Mechanism of IRDP

In every Block three thousand estimated households are supposed to be below the poverty line (a family having total income of Rs. 6400/- per annum for the Seventh Plan and that of Rs. 11,000/- or below per annum for the Eighth plan has been considered to be below poverty line as per the guideline of Planning Commission).[1] These are to be identified during the entire Five Year Plan. Every year at the rate of 600 such families are to be given loan assistance and subsidy to acquire productive assets. This will ensure a regular stream of income to the family. The projects under IRDP are formulated and implemented by DRDA - a registered body under the Societies Registration Act (1860). This agency is headed by the Deputy Commissioner/Collector. It has a wing with the functional heads of various departments at the District level including a Project Director, an IAS Officer, now known as Chief Executive Officer. In Haryana, this post is held by ADCs. This wing also a planning team consisting of an Economist, a Credit Planning Officer and a Rural Industries Officer.[2] The Programme is implemented by DRDA with the help of the Block development machinery. The latter is incharge of the task of identification of families, preparation of Bankable schemes for Beneficiaries and monitoring the implementation of the programme. The field level functionaries at the Block level are expected to play a liaison role with the Banks and other institutions for mobilizing credit, supply of inputs, organization of marketing facilities etc., and take follow-up action at periodical intervals for ensuring supply of raw materials etc. They are also expected to assists the financing institutions in recovery of loans from the Beneficiaries[3]. At the village level where the people below poverty line are identified, viable projects are given to them and a well coordinated linkage with the infrastructure is provided by the Village level Workers/Gram Sachiv. The Village Level Worker (VLW) is linked with the Block development machinery. In respect of the projects to be identified, roughly two-thirds of them are to be from agricultural and allied sectors and one-third from rural industries, services and business sectors. This proportion can vary from area to area on the basis of actual conditions. Diversification of agriculture through animal husbandry, dairying, forestry, fishery, sericulture etc. was also made an integral par of the programme. Since the majority of the poor people were landless and marginal farmers, a significant proportion of the activities for their benefit was sought in the non-farm sector. The Industries, Services and Business (ISB) Component was built into the IRDP programme in 1979 with the objective of maximizing employment opportunities in the Secondary and Tertiary sectors.[4]

In Haryana the Integrated Rural Development Programme is implemented at the District level by the IRDP wing of DRDA. These officials take help of Block Officials in the process of survey, identification of beneficiaries, organizing credit camps, monitoring and recovery of loans as no separate staff has been provided at Block level in the state.

The Steps in the Process of Implementation of IRDP

The first step in the process of implementation of IRDP is the survey for identification of families which are below poverty line. A household survey at the village level is conducted with the help of Gram Sachiv/VLW, teachers, patwari etc. Training and motivation camps of Sarpanchas/pardhans, VLWs and other functionaries, associated with identification of Beneficiaries are organized by DRDA. Survey forms and other stationery items are distributed in these camps. The families whose annual income was Rs. 11,000/- per annum or less during the Eighth Five Year Plan, are searched out and a detailed list of these families is made. After the survey, the procedure adopted for the selection of Beneficiaries includes:

- The priority list of the poorest of the poor families is prepared by the BDO giving special emphasis to out lying hamlets, women headed household and nomadic families.
- The list is then placed for approval in the meeting of Gram Sabha convened by the BDO after sufficient advance publicity. The meetings of the Gram Sahba as far as possible are arranged on non-Banking days to enable the Bank Officials to participate in them.
- The Village Assembly is attended by local people, Non-Officials, Block Officers, Bank officer, prominent voluntary action groups etc.
- The list of selected persons is displaced on Notice-Board of village pancahyat and Block office by giving sufficient time for filling objections.[5]

The Expert Committee on IRDP headed by Sh. D R Mehta, Deputy Governor, RBI in September, 1993 recommended that the Below Poverty Line list drawn by BDO should be approved by Panchayats. In the meeting convened for this purpose Panchayat should invite Bank officials, teachers, village postmaster, representatives of grass root Non-Government Organizations and prominent village elders. The Panchayat should display at public places an approved list of such people and place it before gram sabha after 15 days. The date on which gram sabha considers the list, it should be widely published.[6] The Government of India has accepted this recommendation[7] and circulated to those who are responsible for the implementation of IRDP. After 73rd Constitutional Amendment for proper identification of the Beneficiaries and to ensure the maximum participation of Panchayati Raj Institutions in poverty elimination programmes, the Ministry of Rural Development directed that the Gram Sabha presided over by the Sarpanch should identify the families below poverty line and sent its list to the BDO or DRDA for approval.[8] Any objection regarding the list is tendered by the Block Development and Panchayats Officer or by the SDM, if necessary. Through the above procedure these lists are compiled at Block level and later on at District level. This gives a clear picture to the District Planning Committee village-wise and Block-wise which helps them in proper planning. However, for giving the benefits of development to the needy people (target group) it is essential that a sincere and unbiased/impartial survey should be conducted. In Haryana, this type of survey were conducted only twice and the third is in continuation since 1997-98. The number of households below poverty line for 8th Plan in Bhiwani District were 48,231 out of which 17,103 were from scheduled castes.

The second step in the process of implementation of IRDP is the formulation of Perspective as well as Annual Action Plans. For meaningful implementation of IRDP, proper planning, project identification and Beneficiary selection are very essential. Since IRDP envisages transfer of income generating assets to the Beneficiary, it is very important that proper planning should be done before implementation of the programme. Proper identification of income-generating activities cannot be done without comprehensive annual planning as well as perspective planning. Before preparing the annual action plan, the perspective Block plans have to be formulated which are aggregated and coordinated at the District level in to the Perspective District Plans. The perspective plans consist of the following information:

- An inventory of local resources which includes: demographic trends and human resources; area and location specific resource data; economic activities with details of institutions engaged in these activities; and social and institutional infrastructure including the status of voluntary action groups.
- Information about the on going programmes both under-plan and non-plan schemes containing an analysis of the potential of these programmes in terms of offering opportunities for economically viable activities either through creation of direct employment opportunities or through provisions of backward-forward linkages and infrastructural support.

- Assessment of likely activities under the programme of the development departments in the next few years.
- Impact of the previous plans activities of Integrated Rural Development Programme on the economic environment and the quality of life of the poor people.[9] However, in practice it has not been fully followed in Haryana. On the basis of the perspective plan and the allocation of funds from Government of India, an Annual Action Plan is formulated at the District level by the Planning Committee of DRDA. It includes the following information:
- The economic profile of the Block/District spelling out the thrust areas proposed to be adopted.
- The profile of the Beneficiary families categorizing them according to their aptitudes and choices for the remunerative projects and the projects actually proposed for them.
- The spatial distribution and the time-scheduling of Beneficiaries over the years assigning reasons for such distributions.
- The areas of coordination with other departments and the extent of the involvement of other agencies and departments.
- Sources and mechanism for procurement of raw materials and disposal of finished goods.
- Linkage with the Droughts Prone Area Programme, Desert Development Programme, Jawahar Rojgar Yojana, Land Reforms, SC Component, Tribal Development Plans and the infrastructural support drawn from these programmes.
- An overall assessment of the impact of the proposed activities on the income of the assisted families and the economy of the area.
- A list of the Beneficiaries proposed to be benefited in the year. This annual action plan is prepared by the month of February of the preceding year. Selection of Projects for identified families is made keeping in view their needs, aptitudes and local resource profile.

In Bhiwani District, the activities which have been identified for assistance under IRDP include:

- Agriculture sector consisting of minor irrigation, bullock pairs, camel, bullocks/camel cart, mule cart etc.

- Animal Husbandry sector consisting of milch animal (3 buffaloes, sheep (20+1), cross breed cows (2 Nos.), poultry, piggery and fishery.
- Industry, Service and Business (ISB) sector (Secondary Sector) consisting of large varieties of activities.

The ultimate selection of schemes has been made under ISB sector in consolation with the General Manager, District Industries Centre, Bhiwani and Assistant Project Officer of DRDA. The schemes recommended by the District Industries Centre for the District were handloom weaving, carpentry, blacksmithy, duri/ tatpati making, atta chakki, shoe making, watch repair, kiryana shop, tailoring shop, bakery unit, tea stall, barber shop, welding and general repair shop, radio and TV repairing, pesticides shop, vegetable and milk vendor, watch repairing etc.

- Tertiary sector consisting camel and camel cart, bullocks and bullocks cart, mule and mule cart, horse and horse cart and motor-cycle and milk canes, rickshaw etc.

The governing Body of DRDA approves the Annual Action Plan. A copy of the approved plan is sent to the Department of Rural Development of the state to enable it to see that the plan conforms to the guidelines. While approving the plan for the year, the governing body undertakes a critical analysis of the previous year plan, its implementation and its impact on the economy of the beneficiary families on the one hand and that of the overall economy of the area on the other hand. While approving the plan the following things are taken in to consideration: Whether the activities chosen for the Beneficiaries are justified by local economic profile; the back up support for the Beneficiary; the forward linkages particularly marketing support is available to the Beneficiary as and when the assets generate marketable goods and services; the distribution of activities with regard to sound economic principles; and the family approach has been followed in proposing the assistance.

The third step of the process of implementation of IRDP is the Organization of Credit Camps. A credit camp is organized in each village taken up in action plan on a particular date decided by the Executive Committee of District Rural Development Agency, to collect, complete loan application forms of all the desirous and eligible IRDP Beneficiaries on the spot and to verify them. To ensure the maximum presence of concerned Officials and Beneficiaries in the credit camp, it has been given full publicity. The credit camp is attended by the representative of District Rural Development Agency, particularly the Assistant Project officer (credit) or the APO of the concerned Block, Patwari, Village Secretary, Manager of concerned Bank, representative of District Development Manager, National Bank of Agriculture and Rural Development, Local Panchayat through Sarpanch, Local level's representatives of Animal Husbandry, Agriculture, Industry Department and Beneficiaries of the programme and any other person on the direction of chairman, District Rural Development Agency. The credit camps are organized to save the time and resources of both the Beneficiaries as well as that of the agencies involved in implementation process of Integrated Rural Development Programme. After filling the loan application forms of the Beneficiaries, their identification is made by the Village Panchayat Secretary and Patwari on the concerned loan application form. The APO concerned ensures that the selected Beneficiaries should be from Survey List only. He should also ensure that none of the beneficiaries should be benefited in previous year. The presence of concerned Bank representative is essential to ensure whether the identified Beneficiary is a Bank defaulter or not. He also have to collect the loan application forms of identified Beneficiaries on the spot to avoid unnecessary delay in disbursement of loans. While finalizing loan application forms of Beneficiaries, the concerned officials have to ensure that out of the total Beneficiaries forty (40) per cent should be of women, fifty (50) per cent should be of SC/ ST families and at least three (3) per cent of the beneficiaries should be from the category of physically handicapped persons. The category-wise coverage of Beneficiaries in District Bhiwani and State of Haryana has been given in Chapter-6.

Fourth step of the process of implementation of IRDP is the Processing of loan application forms. After completion of loan application forms of the identified Beneficiaries in all respects, these application forms are submitted to the representative of concerned Bank for further verification. The Bank Officials can not take more than 15 days to complete this process according to Reserve Bank of India's instructions. In Bhiwani District, the application forms of the proposed Beneficiaries are collected by the concerned APO or by the Representative of District Rural Development Agency and these application forms are sponsored to the concerned Bank after enclosing all the required documents (No Objection Certificate and receipt of subsidy) and completing his own official record. The Lead-Bank acts as the coordinator between the Government and Banks. In Bhiwani District the Punjab National Bank acts as the lead Bank. While sanctioning projects, the Bank Manager has to ensure that the project and the unit cost, the terms of the loan and repayment schedules should be in accordance with the guidelines laid down by the Reserve Bank of India and National Bank of Agriculture and Rural Development. In order to ensure sufficient and quick inflow of financial credit to the weaker sections of the society, the Government of Haryana, vide C.S. office order No. 1/1/6/82, SII, dated 30-7-82 has designated all the Additional Deputy Commissioner-cum Chief Executive Officer of District Rural Development Agencies to function as Joint-Director, Institutional Finance and Credit Control. It is a significant step towards stepping up and coordinating the flow of institutional credit from Commercial Banks/Rural Regional Banks and other financial institutions for the economic benefit of weaker sections of the society.[10] In a zonal meeting of Bankers, it was found that the average time taken for sanction was 30 to 60 days and for disbursement of loan after release of subsidy was 30 to 45 days.[11]

The fifth step of the Implementation of IRDP is the Fixation of Unit Cost to avoid under-financing of IRDP projects and purchase of substandard assets and consequent low incremental income. Unit Cost Committees for the farm sector have been constituted in the various Regional Offices of National Bank of Agriculture and Rural Development. The unit cost of investment under various activities is reviewed every year by the 'State Level Committee on Unit Cost' setup for this purpose and updated wherever it finds necessary. The Regional offices of National Bank of Agriculture and Rural Development have been delegated powers to revise unit cost, where the cost of escalation is within twenty (2) per cent of the unit cost approved earlier. After the approval of the unit cost, these are communicated to the State Government, Bank and District Rural Development Agencies.[12] With regard to the loans for various purposes falling under Industry, Service and Business Sector of IRDP, the responsibility of fixing the unit cost and other techno-

Table 5.1
The unit cost of various assets (1991-92) in Bhiwani District

Sl. No.	*Sector*	*Activity*	*Unit Cost (loan + subsidy)*
(A)	Agriculture		
01.		Plough Camel	4500
02.		P. Bullocks (2)	4800
03.		Mushroom	11800
(B)	Animal Husbandry		
04.		Piggery	7900
05.		Milch Cattle(2)	11000
06.		Sheep(20+1)	8500
07.		Cross Breed Cow(2)	14000
08.		Broiler	15000
(c)	Secondary (Industry, Service and Business)		
(i)	Industry		
09.		Amber Charkha	4500
10.		Atta Chakki	12000
11.		Beed Making	7500
12.		Ban Making	6000
13.		Mudha Making	3000
14.		Black Smith	12000
15.		Carpentary	12000
16.		Dari Making	4500
17.		Embriodary	5000
18.		Handloom	12000
19.		Chuna Bhati	15000
20.		Tailoring	3000
21.		Shoe unit	9000
22.		Steel gate grill	18000
23.		Wax candle	10000
24.		Bakery	9000

(contd.)

S.No.	*Sector*	*Activity*	*Unit Cost (loan + subsidy)*
25.		Chalk Making	3000
26.		Cotton grinding	16000
27.		Sheet trunk making	12000
(ii) Service			
28.		Cycle repair	6000
29.		Motor cycle/ Tractor repair	15000
30.		TV/Radio repair	12000
31.		Watch Repair	5000
32.		Motor Winding	8000
33.		Welding and Tyre Puncher	10000
34.		Barbar Shop	5000
(iii) Business			
35.		Beverage/Pan Shop	5000
36.		Kiryana	7500
37.		Tea Stall/Sweet/ Veg. Shop	5000
38.		Egg Card	6000
(D) Tertiary			
39.		Camel and C Cart (2 & 4 Tyres)	4500/12500
40.		Donkey Unit	3000
41.		Mule & Mule Cart	12000
42.		Rickshaw/Milk Cane	3000

Source: *Annual Action Plan* (1991-92), DRDA, Bhiwani.

ecnomic parameters had been left to the Financing Banks/DRDA/ District Level Consultative Committee set up under the 'Lead Bank' Scheme. The DRDA can also recommend the unit cost for different items under Industry, Service and Business Sector in the District for ratification by District Level Consultative Committee. With a view to achieve uniformity, project profile are prepared for major activities in each district, indicting therein unit cost, repayment period, moratorium period etc. NABARD has cleared that unit cost approved by them are average and not the maximum or minimum ones. The cost of each item of investment needs to be determined by the Financing Bank in each individual case with reference to the realistic cost estimates at the time of appraisal of individual loan proposals. Variation of up to 15 per cent at the Branch level are acceptable for purpose of refinance by NABARD. The per unit cost can be seen in Table 5.1.

The sixth step of the implementation Process of IRDP is the Disbursement of Loans after verifying various aspects such a No Objection Certificate, Receipt of Subsidy, the Bank record of Beneficiaries etc. The Bank sanctions the loans as per the unit cost of the concerned project and the IRDP wing of DRDA releases the subsidy. The Pattern of Subsidy given under IRDP may be seen in Table 5.2.

Table 5.2
The Pattern of Subsidy

S. No.	*Individual/Family*	*Percent of Subsidy*
(a)	Small Farmers	25 per cent or Subject to a ceiling of Rs. 3000/- in non-DPAP/DDP area
(b)	Marginal Farmers/ Agricultural Labourers/ Non-Agricultural Labourers And Rural Artisans.	33.33 per cent or Rs.4000/ in DPAP/DDP areas.
(c)	SC/ST Families/ Physically handicapped Persons	50 per cent or Rs. 5000/- per family in all rural areas.

Source: Manual for IRDP and Allied Programmes, 1991, p. 32.

The same pattern of subsidy is adopted for all sectors i.e. Agriculture, Animal Husbandry, Industry, Service and Business (ISB) and Tertiary Sectros.[13] As per Government of India's latest directions, the limit of subsidy has been increased to Rs. 6000/- or fifty (50) per cent of the project cost whichever is less in case of SC/ST and handicapped cases. Whereas Rs. 5000/- or 33.3 per cent in case of marginal farmers/agriculture labourers and twenty-five (25) per cent or Rs. 4000/- in case of small farmers whichever is less. In case of community minor irrigation schemes, it shall be fifty (50) per cent without any ceiling on project cost.[14] It is normally the responsibility of District Rural Development Agencies to make assets available to the Beneficiaries, of standard quality, at economic prices and to the satisfaction of Beneficiary. In order to ensure this, Purchasing Committees have been constituted in all the District Rural Development Agencies (DRDAs) consisting of the Beneficiary, a representative each of DRDA/Assistant Project Officer (APO) credit, the Financing Institution, the concerned department and a Public representative of SC/ST.[15] In order to give greater choice to beneficiaries in purchasing assets, arrangements for purchase committee have been revised from 1991-92. Earlier an experiment to introduce the Cash Disbursement System was tried in fifty (50) Blocks. The High Level Committee on Credit Support for IRDP of RBI studied system for Disbursement of loan and subsidy in cash under IRDP in selected Blocks and observed that the degree of success depends to a large extent on the location of the Block, availability of infrastructure facilities, backward-forward linkages in the block, pre-disbursement counselling as also post-disbursement follow up and supervision including visits for verification of utilization of assistance by the implementing agency. Full utilization of assistance by more than ninety (90) per cent of the Beneficiaries surveyed was observed in some Blocks having the above facilities while the Blocks which were not developed or where supervision/monitoring of assistance to the Beneficiaries were lacking, misutilization of assistance was observed to the tune of fifty four (54) per cent of the Beneficiaries covered. As the results were mixed, hence RBI recommended that this experiment be extended with some safeguards to other Blocks which has now been extended to at least (50 percent) half the number of Blocks in every District. The Blocks to be covered under Cash Disbursement Scheme are selected by District Level

Consultative Committee (DLCC). In this scheme the Beneficiary has to submit the bill of assets purchased in case of its being of standard Brand or Mark, or a utilization certificate from the concerned official in case of its opposite position within one month of disbursement of the loan.[16] Later on the RBI on the Topic 'IRDP-Streamlising the Arrangement for Flow of Credit and Supply of Inputs and Outputs to Beneficiaries' advised to All India Scheduled Commercial Banks not to insist on standard type, brand names etc. in respect of purchase of camel/bullock cart under Cash Disbursement Scheme.[17] In case of livestock the health certificate for the animal is given free of cost by the veterinary doctor of that area and simultaneously the insurance is essential of the asset purchased in Cash Disbursement Blocks.[18] The Haryana Government has directed all the veterinary doctors to ensure that the health certificate for animals should be provided free of cost.[19] First of all the Cash Disbursement Scheme was initiated in Bhiwani and Bawani Khera Blocks of the Bhiwani District after the recommendation of District Level Consultative Committee on 29-4-1991. It was later on extended to other five Blocks out of nine of the District as per the direction of the Ministry of Rural Development.[20] In Bhiwani District the Cash Disbursement Scheme has been adopted in Bhiwani, Dardi-I, Dadri-II, Bawani Khera and Tosham Blocks. In Loharu, Siwani, Badhara and Kairu Blocks, the loan is not given in cash form, but is given in the form of assets which are purchased by the Purchasing Committee. The Bank will either open a saving Bank account in the Beneficiary's name or may give the amount in cash and the Beneficiary in turn will furnish a receipt of the item purchased to the Bank. Under ISB sector, when the number of sundry items are to be purchased, disbursement up to Rs. 10,000/- will be made in cash. The Reserve Bank of India's Rural Planning and Credit Department has also circulated the guidelines to all the Indian Commercial Banks vide letter No. RPCD: SP: BC ; 80/09/01-06/95-96 on 5th January, 1996 regarding it.[21] This can be done within one lump-sum or in stages depending upon the items to be purchased. The Beneficiary will be at liberty to negotiate and settle the price of asset purchased and will also get the satisfaction that he has purchased goods of his own choice. The Beneficiary need not to produce cash memo, invoice, vouchers etc. to the Bank. Utilization certificate given by him to the Bank fulfills the requirements of the Bank. However, the follow-up visit would be done by the Bank field staff within one month to ensure that the money has been utilized for the purpose for which it was advanced.

The Government of India has directed the concerned Institutions that the Loan Disbursement System should be made in an open manner in the presence of a small committee of non-Officials so as to ensure greater transparency and to minimize the bottleneck in disbursement system.[22] This process has been adopted both at the State as well, District levels to check the misutilization or transfer of the assets, marking is done. This is also necessary in the eventuality of filing insurance claims and physical verification of the assets etc. Insurance cover is available for livestock assets, given under the programme by General Insurance Corporation on the terms and conditions of Master Policy and Long Term Master Policy Agreement. Master Insurance Policy is implemented under IRDP for three years at the concessional rate of premium as applicable from time to time. The premium of insurance is charged in the shape of Beneficiary 1.25 per cent which ever is applicable and to DRDA one per cent in all other cases. A Group Life Insurance Scheme for IRDP Beneficiaries aged not less than 18 years and not more than 60 years has been introduced w.e.f. 1-4-1988. The period of insurance cover will commence from the date on which the asset is disbursed to the Beneficiary. The scheme is implemented through the DRDA. The sum assured will be Rs. 5000/- with double benefit in the case of accidental death.[23] The DRDA has to process the claim receipt within 6 months of the death of the insured Beneficiary and the Life Insurance Corporation has to settle the claim within a fortnight of receipt of claim papers including death certificate.

The seventh step of the process of implementation of IRDP is known as Monitoring. It is a process or a strategy to keep a close watch on the implementation of a project so as to ensure the timely completion of its various components within the sanctioned outlay and time frame. It also entails assessing difficulties and bottlenecks which arises in the execution of projects and taking corrective action whenever necessary. It also observes whether the stated objectives of the project were being achieved. The important objective of the Monitoring strategy is to prevent the misuse of the Government/public money. It has to be a built-in system as a part of the project itself. Monitoring of programmes are carried out by the implementation agency itself. The Department of Rural Development, Government of India, has taken various steps to develop monitoring system at various levels. Monitoring cell as the State Level was established.[24] The Central Government is providing the necessary guidance to the Government of the States, DRDAs and Block agencies in establishing their own mechanisms of monitoring. The monitoring system evolved for IRDP is a traditional type i.e. concentrating mostly on financial expenditure and attainment of physical targets rather than addressing itself to the achievement of the programme objectives. The monitoring process starts with the first visit of concerned Bank representative to the Beneficiary after one month of submission of receipt of purchase of assets or utilization certificate. After this various visits are made by the concerned Assistant Project Officer/APO Monitoring, Bank Official, VLW, Patwari etc. Besides, arrangements have been made for qualitative monitoring of the programme implementation. For effective and qualitative monitoring of IRDP at DRDA and State levels, the Government of India has suggested two types of schedules. Further, the Government of India has also indicated monthly targets for conducting qualitative monitoring[25] by the Inspecting Officer which can be seen in Table 5.3.

Table 5.3
Targets of Monitoring

S. No.	*Officials*	*Visits*
1.	District Magistrate/Chairman, DRDA	10 per month
2.	District Development and Panchayat Officer	20 per month
3.	APO (Monitoring)	40 per month
4.	Sub Divisional Magistrates	20 per month
5.	Block Development and Panchayat Officers	20 per month
6.	Agriculture Development Officers	20 per month

Source: *Manual for IRDP and Allied Programmes,* 1991, p. 56.

On the basis of the monitoring done by the Inspecting Officers, the quarterly consolidated report is prepared at DRDA level for circulation among the Block Development and Panchayat Officers.

Eighth is the most important step of the process of implementation of IRDP. This step relates to the system of Recovery. The Beneficiary has to repay the amount of loan to the concerned Bank within a period of five years in yearly installments. The loan amount would be equal to the total project cost minus the amount of subsidy admissible to the beneficiary. The Bank charges interest[26] form the Beneficiary at the rates announced by Reserve Bank of India on 22nd September, 1990 which may be seen in Table 5.4.

Table 5.4
Bank Interest Rates

S.No.	*Amount in Rs.*	*Rate of Interest (%)*
1.	Up to 7,500	10.0
2.	7,500 - 15,000	11.5
3.	15,000 - 25,000	12.0
4.	25,000 - 50,000	14.0
5.	50,000 - 2 Lakh	15.0
6.	Over 2 Lakh	16.0

Source: Manual for IRDP and Allied Programmes, 1991, p. 43.

The routine work of recovery is done by the officials of concerned Bank. The Expert Committee of Reserve Bank of India on IRDP recommended to the Government of India in its Interim Report for improving recovery of loans by considering linkage of certain percentages of subsidy allocation to recovery programme. Special recovery officers may be appointed by the concerned state government. Enactment of Modified Bill on the recommendation of Talwar Committee may be expedited by the state government. Loan waivers may not be declared. DRDAs, voluntary organizations and SHOs may help Bankers in matters of recovery. Utilization Reporters-cum-Recovery facilitators may be appointed on Commission basis. These recommendations have been accepted by the Ministry of Rural Development and directed the State Government to take necessary step in this direction.[27] However, in case of default the Bank may take the help of Block Development Office staff or local police. After seeing poor recovery in IRDP, the Government of Haryana, in its State Level Consultative Committee meeting has adopted a resolution to appoint an APO (Recovery) in each DRDA to ensure better recovery. Though in practice, this post is held simultaneously by another existing APO with his own work. For checking the misutilization of loans or subsidies amount, the Government of Haryana has directed to all the Superintendents of Police to cooperate with Banking Institutions in recovery of lans or subsidies from the defaulters. Registration of FIR under Indian Penal Code section 406 can be done against misutilization of loans or subsidies amount.[28] To check the intensity of loan defaulters and to ensure good recovery of loans the 'Back End Subsidy Policy' has been started since 1996. In this scheme the Bank disbursed the full project cost including subsidy to the Beneficiary as loan right at the beginning. The subsidy will be deposited in the name of the Beneficiary in the Bank with the stipulation that the money so deposited will be adjusted towards the last few installments of repayment. The lock-up in period of the fixed deposited subsidy will be three to five years. If a Beneficiary makes all the repayment before three years, he is not entitled for claim of subsidy i.e. to prevent abuse of the credit facility by non-entitled persons. Premature repayments will not be entertained. In case of misutilization or any other malpractice the subsidy would be forfeited after giving due opportunity to the Beneficiary. While implementing this policy the Bank officials have to ensure that the changed system does not impose any (financial) additional interest burden on the Beneficiary.[29]

It is worthwhile to mention here the Funding Pattern and Financial Procedure for IRDP. During the 6th Plan period, funds were allocated to the states on a uniform basis according to the number of Blocks. Allocations are now being made in relation to the incidence of poverty in the states. Funds developed to Districts are based on a formula evolved by the State Government and approved by the Government of India. Further devolution to the Blocks is made by the Governing Body of DRDA based on the level of poverty, opportunities available and Banking infra-structure facilities. The economic activities under the programme are financed through a package of subsidy and credit. Funds for the expenditure on subsidy and other items related to the administrative and infrastructure are provided in the budget of the Centre and the States. The items of expenditure charged to the budgetary provision include: Subsidy for the economic activities, Programme infrastructure and Administrative infrastructure.

Besides, the amount of subsidy for economic activities which varies from twenty-five (25) per cent to fifty (50) per cent, the programme implementing agency can spent ten (10) to fifteen (15) per cent on administrative infrastructure of the total budget[30]. Ten per cent of the allocations the development of programme infrastructure that may be in the form of establishing Training Centre, Breeding Centre etc. for filling up the gaps to ensure output-input linkages for IRDP Beneficiaries.[31] The Government has increased the ceiling for programme infrastructure under IRDP from ten (10) to twenty-five (25) per cent in North-Eastern States including Sikkim and tan (10) to twenty (20) per cent in other parts of the country so that the projects can support adequate forward and backward linkages.[32] Besides, the programme implementation agency can spent Rs. 1500/- for organizing Training Programme for IRDP Beneficiaries for one day, once in a year in each Block. The cost is born by DRDA and Lead Bank alternatively.[33] To avoid the bunching of loan applications at the end of financial year, the allocation is utilized during the year as: First quarter (April-June), 15 per cent; Second quarter (July-September), 25 per cent; Third quarter (October-December), 35 per cent; and Fourth quarter (January-March), 25 per cent. In case if there is short fall in utilization of funds, the allocation may be reduced proportionately and funds will be deducted from the release of second instalment of central share. The funds are released to DRDAs on the basis of following guidelines: The expenditure should be equally shared by the Centre and States. For Union Territories the entire expenditure is met by Government of India. Expenditure should not be repugnant to the objectives and the needs of the programme. The funds are released into who installments by the Centre and in case of cold snow bound Districts where the working period is limited to a few months, the entire central share of assistance can be released in one installment. These releases should be matched with the releases of the State.

Briefly we may conclude that the Integrated Rural Development Programme is implemented at the District level by the District Rural Development Agency with the help of Block level functionaries of various departments. The process of implementation of IRDP consists of survey for identification of Below Poverty Line families, formulation and approval of annual action plans, organization of credit camps, processing of loan applications, disbursement of loans, purchasing of assets, monitoring and recovery of loans. On the directions of state government, the DRDA conducted a house hold survey for identification of Below Poverty Line families with the help of village level functionaries of various departments. After 73rd Constitutional Amendment, Panchayati Raj Institutions have to play a concrete role in proper identification of families below the poverty line. The lists so prepared are widely publicized and sent to Block Development Officer or DRDA for approval which are later on consolidated at District level to have a clear picture. On the basis of this BPL list and the financial allocations, the DRDA prepares perspective as well as annual action plans with the help of its planning team. This annual action plan is approved by the Governing Body of DRDA and its copies are sent to the state government for further information and necessary action. The DRDA organizes credit camps on the basis of annual action plans for filling loan application forms from all desirous and eligible persons. These credit camps are organized to save time and resources of the Beneficiaries as well as that of the staff concerned. After completion of loan applications of the identified Beneficiaries in all respects, these are submitted to the representative of concerned Bank for further verification. The Bank is bound to complete this process within 15 days as per guidelines of Reserve Bank of India. After seeing the various aspects like No Objection Certificate, receipt of subsidy amount, unit cost of project etc., the Bank Official sanctions the loan. The unit cost of various activities identified for IRDP assistance is determined by the 'State Level Committee on Unit Cost' setup for the purpose which communicates it to the State Government, Banks and District Rural Development Agencies. The unit costs so decided are average ones with an escalation of twenty per cent which can further revised by District Level Consultive Committee with the help of 'Lead Bank'.

It is normally the responsibility of DRDA to make assets available to the Beneficiaries, of standard quality, at economic prices and to the satisfaction of Beneficiaries. In order to ensure it, Purchase Committee have been constituted in all the DRDAs for purchasing the assets. For giving greater choice to Beneficiaries in purchasing assets, arrangements for Purchase Committee have been revised from 1991-92 and Cash Disbursement System has been introduced and extended to at least 50 per cent of the total Blocks.

In these Blocks, the Bank makes available the whole amount of unit cost to the Beneficiary in advance and the Beneficiary is supposed to submit the utilization certificate/cash memo within a month of receiving the loan. The follow-up action is started simultaneously by the Bank, IRDP staff and concerned department to put the asset in income generation position and to check its misutilization. For effective and qualitative monitoring of IRDP at DRDA and State Levels, the Government of India has suggested two types of schedules. Further the Government of India has also fixed monthly targets for conducting qualitative monitoring by the Inspecting Officer who pays a number of visits to the Beneficiaries. On the basis of the monitoring done by the Inspecting Officers, the quarterly consolidated report is prepared at DRDA level for circulation among the Block Development and Panchayats Officers.

The Beneficiary has to repay the amount of loan with interest to concerned Bank within a period of five years in yearly installments. The Reserve Bank of India's Expert Committee on improving recovery of loans under IRDP has suggested for a linkage of certain percentage of subsidy allocation to recovery programme. Besides taking some concrete steps at administrative level, the 'Back End Subsidy Policy' has been introduced since 1996. In this the Bank disbursed the full project cost including the subsidy amount as loan to the Beneficiary at the beginning. However, the subsidy is deposit in his account in the Bank with a lock-up period of three to five years. It is adjusted towards the last few instalments of repayment. The central government allocates funds to the DRDAs in two installments for normal areas. During 6th Plan period the funds were allocated to the states on a uniform basis according to the number of Blocks. But at present allocations are made on the basis of the percentage of poverty. The DRDA can spend ten to fifteen per cent of the total budget on administrative infrastructure and ten per cent on development of programme infrastructure and rest on giving subsidy to the Beneficiaries.

REFERENCES

1. Government of India, Department of Rural Development, *D.O. Letter No. M. 19010/1/93-REJ-IV, dated 1.7.1993,* New Delhi.
2. Government of India, Ministry of Rural Development, *Circular No. S. 11011/130/81-IRD. I dated 24-9-1982,* New Delhi.

3. Government of India, Ministry of Rural development, *D.O. No. 14012/4/82-IRD-III, dated 26-8-1982,* New Delhi.

4. Subramaniam, R., (ed.), *Rural Development, op. cit.,* p.34.

5. Government of India, Department of Rural Development, *Manual for IRDP and Allied Programmes, 1991, op. cit.,* p. 22.

6. Reserve Bank of India, *RPCD No. SP. BC/115/09-01-01-1994-95, dated 7-2-1995,* Mumbai.

7. Government of India, Ministry of Rural Areas and Employment, *No.1 12011/1/95-IRD credit, dated 12-2-1996, Department of Rural Employment and Poverty Alleviation,* New Delhi.

8. Government of India, Ministry of Rural Areas and Employment, *D.O. No. 28012/16/91-IRD-III, (Vol. II), dated 23-1-1995,* New Delhi.

9. Government of India, Department of Rural Development, *Manual for IRDP and Allied Programme, 1991, op. cit.,* p. 23.

10. The Financial Commissioner and Secretary to Government of Haryana, Memo. No.6/2/82-RD-INST, FIN, And C.C., dated 11-11-1982, Institutional Finance and Credit Control Department, Chandigarh.

11. Punjab National Bank, Zonal Office, *Ref, No. DGM : DEV : 77/53, dated 29-7-1994,* Chandigarh.

12. Government of India, Department of Rural Development, *Manual for IRDP and Allied Programme, 1991, op. cit.,* p. 24.

13. *Ibid.,* p. 32.

14. Government of India, Ministry of Rural Areas and Employment, *Circular No. 1 12011/1/95, IRD credit, dated 1-1-1996,* New Delhi.

15. Government of India, Ministry of Rural Development, *Circular No. 14013/1/83-IRD-II, dt. 30th August, 1984,* New Delhi.

16. Government of India, Ministry of Rural Development, *NO. 1-12011/33/87-IRD, Credit, dated 25-3-91,* New Delhi; Chief Officer, RBI, *Ref. No. SS. 277/SS. 41-90/91, dated 9-3-93,* Mumbai.

17. Reserve Bank of India, *4, Feb. 1994/C. 568 (CD)-93-94,* Mumbai.

18. Government of India, Ministry of Rural Development, *Circular No. 1, 12011/56/83-CIP, dated 29-6-1983,* New Delhi.

19. Government of Haryana, Department of Rural Development, *Memo no. APO (IRD)-92/6007-22, dated 12-3-92,* Chandigarh.

20. ADC - cum-CEO, *DRDA/91/Credit/3130-50, dated 21-6-1991,* DRDA, Bhiwani District.

21. Government of India, Department of Rural Employment and Poverty Alleviation, *Letter No. I-12001/17/93- IRD (Credit), dated 12-2-96,* New Delhi.

22. Government of India, Ministry of Rural Areas and Employment, *Circular No. 1 12011/1/95 - IRD, Credit, dated 1-1-1996,* New Delhi.

23. Government of India, Department of Rural Development, *Letter No. 12012/4/87 - IRD-III, dated 9-12-93,* New Delhi.

24. Government of India, Department of Rural Development, *Circular No. 20011/1/83 - IRD -III, dated 9-5-1983,* New Delhi.

25. Government of India, Department of Rural Department, *Manual for IRDP and Allied Programmes, 1991, op. cit.,* p. 56; Government of India, Department of Rural Development, *Circular No. I-12011/33/87 - IRD, Credit, dated 25-3-1991,* New Delhi.

26. Government of India, Department of Rural Development, *Manual for IRDP and Allied Programmes, 1991, op. cit.,* p. 43.

27. Government of India, Ministry of Rural Areas and Employment, *Circular No. I-12011/1/95 - IRD, Credit, dated 26-10-1995,* New Delhi.

28. The Director and Joint Secretary to Government of Haryana, *Memo No. IF and CC - 3-3-89-RC (N)/758, dared 4-4-90,* Institutional Finance and Credit Control Department, Chandigarh.

29. Government of India, Ministry of Rural Areas and Employment, *Circular No. I-12011/1/95 - IRD, Credit, dated 1-1-1996,* New Delhi.

30. Government of India, Department of Rural Development, *Manual for IRDP and Allied Programmes, 1991, op. cit.,* pp. 35-36.

31. Government of India, Ministry of Rural Development, *Circular No. M. 14013/1/83 - IRD -III, dated 20-5-1983,* New Delhi.

32. Government of India, Ministry of Rural Areas and Employment, *Circular No. I-12011/1/95 - IRD, dated 1-1-1996,* New Delhi.

33. Government of India, Ministry of Rural Areas and Employment, *Circular No. I-12011/23/93 - IRD, Credit, dated 5-5-1995,* New Delhi.

6

IRDP: The Implementation

Integrated Rural Development Programme (IRDP) is a poverty alleviation programme in which families living below the poverty line in rural areas are provided financial assistance in the form of loan and subsidy so that they can cross the poverty line by increasing their productivity in agricultural and allied sectors. The viability of such activities depends to a larger extent upon the potentialities of that particular area. In this chapter an attempt has been made to describe the performance of IRDP at the State as well as at the District levels. It discusses in detail the composition of BPL families, number of families assisted under IRDP, their category-wise and sector-wise distribution, financial allocation and per capita investment. It consists of two parts–the first one deals with the performance of IRDP in Haryana and the second with that of District Bhiwani.

The state has adopted various programmes of rural development since the inception of Community Development Programme (1952) on the initiative of Central Government and has made significant development in certain areas of economy particularly in the field of agricultural and industrial development. The programme of IRDP was introduced in the state in 1978-79 in certain selected Blocks which was later on extended to all the Blocks on 2nd October, 1980. To identify the families below the poverty line, the first household survey was conducted by the State Government in 1980-81 and got it completed by 1984. As per the survey, 5,19,444 families were found below the poverty line in the state out of the total 12,35,066 families surveyed which constitutes 42.06 per cent of the total rural families. The number of schedules caste families below the poverty line was 2,04,983 which constituted 39.46 per cent of the total BPL families in the state. Among the total 5,19,444 BPL families identified, 80,200 were small farmers,

99,985 marginal farmers, 1,63,770 agricultural labourers, 1,28,769 non-agricultural labourers, 23,721 rural artisans and 22,999 others. The agricultural labourers and non-agricultural labourers constitute thirty per cent and twenty-five per cent respectively of the total BPL families. The second survey of this kind was conducted by the State Government during 1991-92. To have a better understanding of the incidence of poverty in various Districts of the state, the figures of BPL families have been presented District-wise in Table 6.1.

Table 6.1
District-wise distribution of BPL families

Sl. No.	*Name of District*	*No. of Blocks*	*Total Rural Popul. (1991)*	*Total Rural Families (Surveyed)*	*Total BPL Families*	*Percentage of BPL Families*
1.	Ambala	7	709705	94109	30050	32
2.	Bhiwani	8	926117	113313	48241	42.6
3.	Faridabad	5	752819	94402	28399	30
4.	Gurgaon	9	897370	122456	63579	52
5.	Hisar	14	1446869	234868	81965	35
6.	Jind	7	792702	113910	46261	41
7.	Kaithal	5	697766	97687	40272	41
8.	Karnal	6	637256	93390	48119	52
9.	K/Shetra	4	481516	66066	32196	49
10.	M/Garh	5	580876	84313	25584	30
11.	Panipat	4	605864	61801	20064	32.5
12.	Rewari	5	528288	76707	24304	32
13.	Rohtak	10	1395179	156728	52656	34
14.	Sirsa	7	711237	105580	28215	27
15.	Sonipat	7	567388	121482	23259	19
16.	Y/Nagar	5	541593	73628	35696	48.5
	Total	108	12272545	1710440	628860	36.8

Source: Rural Development Department, Government of Haryana.

The figures given in Table 6.1 demonstrated that the poverty is not evenly distributed in the state, it varies from District to

District. The BPL families constitute 36.8 per cent of the total rural families in the State of which Karnal and Gurgaon Districts have the highest percentage i.e. 52 each and Sonipat District has the lowest i.e. 19 followed by Sirsa having 27 per cent.

Income-wise Distribution of BPL Families

To highlight the intensity of poverty in different parts of the state, it has been demonstrated on the basis of economic strata of various Districts. The number of rural families below the poverty line on the basis of income identified by the 1991-92 household survey have been given in Table 6.2.

Table 6.2
Income-wise distribution of BPL families

Sl.. No.	*Name of Distt.*	*No. of Rural Families Below Poverty Line*				
		Income Up to Rs. 4000	*Income Between 4001-6000*	*Income Between 6001-8500*	*Income Between 8501-11000*	*Total BPL Fami.*
1.	Ambala	4702	9306	9248	6794	30050
2.	Bhiwani	10889	7729	17781	11842	48241
3.	Faridabad	4463	7526	9068	7342	28399
4.	Gurgaon	7431	6615	36138	13395	63579
5.	Hisar	25305	29009	19482	8169	81965
6.	Jind	13968	18673	10059	3561	46261
7.	Kaithal	4845	7675	18346	9406	40272
8.	K/Shetra	4043	7484	15498	5171	32196
9.	Karnal	7468	8545	20260	11846	48119
10.	M/Garh	3741	6436	10909	4498	25584
11.	Panipat	6697	5319	5962	2086	20064
12.	Rewari	582	5239	8567	4616	24304
13.	Rohtak	6208	31773	10249	4426	52656
14.	Sirsa	7864	5601	10792	3958	28215
15.	Sonipat	10006	7319	3977	1957	23259
16.	Y/Nagar	4000	7806	16583	7307	35696
	Total	127512 (20)	172055 (27)	222919 (36)	106374 (17)	628860 (100)

Note: Percentage have been given in parentheses.
Source: Rural Development Department, Government of Haryana.

Table 6.2 shows that the size of BPL families varies in income strata from District to District. In some Districts the lower two strata of income constitute more than two-thirds of the total strength of BPL families i.e. in Hisar, Jind, Sonipat and Rohtak.

This indicates that in these District the economic position of most of the BPL families seems to be very weak whereas in some other District like Bhiwani, Gurgaon, Kaithal, Kurukshetra, Karnal. Mahindergarh and Yamunanagar the economic position of these BPL families appears comparatively sound and almost about two thirds of the BPL families fall in two upper income groups. This indicates that these districts are industrially or agriculturally advanced or have larger land holdings. As far as the general picture of poverty is concerned almost two-thirds of the total BPL families fall in the middle two strata of income.

Category-wise Classification of BPL Families in Haryana

The category-wise classification of the BPL families on the basis of 1991-92 household survey is given in Table 6.3.

Table 5.3 shows that the agricultural labourers constitute a major part i.e. forty-two per cent of the total BPL families in the state followed by non-agricultural labourers twenty per cent and marginal farmers sixteen per cent. The small farmers, others and rural artisans constitute eleven per cent, eight per cent and three per cent respectively of the total BPL families. A close look at the figures reveals that the agricultural labourers constitute the major part of the BPL families in all the Districts except Kaithal and Mahendergarh.

Caste-wise Distribution of the BPL Families

The case-wise distribution of the families below the poverty-line according to 1991-92 household survey may seen in Table 6.4.

Table 6.4 indicates that out of the total BPL families in the state forty-one per cent are scheduled caste, twenty-two per cent are backward caste and thirty-seven per cent are others. Sirsa, Hisar and Ambala Districts have the highest percentage of scheduled castes i.e. more than half of their total BPL families whereas Gurgoan, Mahendergarh and Rewari have the lowest percentage of scheduled castes in their respective BPL families.

Table 6.3
Category-wise Distribution of BPL Families

Sl. No.	Name of Distt.	Small Farmers	Marginal Farmers	Agri. Labourers	Non-Agri Labourers	Rural Artisans	Others	Total BPL Fam.
1.	Ambala	2461	3128	19554	4297	238	372	30050
2.	Bhiwani	5202	16806	16845	8457	323	608	48241
3.	Faridabad	2768	5752	6979	8426	1213	3261	28399
4.	Gurgaon	9043	9995	23719	11568	2026	7228	63579
5.	Hisar	7150	8446	43417	17055	1289	4608	81965
6.	Jind	5286	6213	31670	2840	230	22	46261
7.	Kaithal	5455	4532	6236	19469	2363	2217	40272
8.	Karnal	3641	4410	22567	12997	3522	982	48119
9.	K/Shetra	2272	2245	22700	2720	296	1963	32196
10.	M/Garh	2915	9371	3207	7463	1205	1423	25584
11.	Panipat	2594	2196	14031	241	943	59	20064
12.	Rewari	1485	5430	5824	5556	1115	4894	24304
13.	Rohtak	7457	12354	12249	12679	1738	6129	52656
14.	Sirsa	1700	1887	19999	2817	510	1302	28215
15.	Sonepat	2745	3285	4668	5390	709	646	223259
16.	Y/Nagar	5213	4695	9822	6840	1907	7166	35696
	Total	67387 (11)	100745 (16)	263487 (42)	128815 (20)	19730 (3)	48696 (8)	628860 (100)

Note: Percentage have been given in parentheses.
Source: Rural Development Department, Government of Haryana.

Table 6.4
Caste-wise Distribution of BPL Families

Sl. No.	*District*	*SC/ST*	*BC*	*Others*	*Total*
1.	Ambala	15716	7598	6786	30050
2.	Bhiwani	17103	10133	21005	48241
3.	Faridabad	8226	5039	15134	28399
4.	Gurgaon	10541	11823	41215	63579
5.	Hisar	44159	15800	22006	81965
6.	Jind	21992	10386	13886	46261
7.	Kaithal	18140	10558	11574	40272
8.	Karnal	18598	13815	15706	48119
9.	K/Shetra	13479	11820	6897	32196
10.	M/Garh	7359	2966	15259	25584
11.	Panipat	7854	5676	6534	20064
12.	Rewari	8136	3109	13059	24304
13.	Rohtak	20230	9118	23308	52656
14.	Sirsa	17389	2985	7841	28215
15.	Sonipat	9599	4660	9000	23259
16.	Y/Nagar	16866	9431	9399	35696
	Total	2,55,387 (41)	1,34,917 (22)	2,38,556 (37)	6,28,860 (100)

Note: Percentage have been given in parentheses.
Source: Rural Development Department, Government of Haryana.

Initially, a uniform target of assisting 3000 families per Block at the rate of 600 families per year was set up for the 6th Five Year Plan (1980-85). The criteria for allocation of funds was also uniform per Block in the 6th Five Year Plan. However in the 7th Five Year Plan the criterion for allocation and fixation of targets for selecting the families was changed from uniformity basis to the incidence of poverty basis, in view of the inter-state variations and disparities. The state-wise figures of the incidence of poverty have been given by 32nd, 38th and 42nd rounds of survey of the National Sample Survey Organization (NSSO).

However, the figures of NSSO in its 32nd and 38th rounds of survey, have wide difference with that of the stated figures.

According to NSSO survey the incidence of poverty in the state was 23.2 per cent, 15.2 per cent and 11.7 per cent as per its 32nd, 38th and 42nd rounds of survey carried out in the years 1977-78, 1983-84 and 1987-88 respectively.[1] Since the criteria for allocation of funds under IRD for poverty alleviation have been changed from uniformity to incidence of poverty from 1988-89. Thus the NSSO figures have adversely affected the allocation of resources for the state of Haryana. The figures of poverty brought out by state household surveys, carried out at various intervals, have not been taken into account by the Central Government for the allocation of resources to the State Government under Poverty Alleviation Programmes.

Physical Targets and Achievements

The physical targets and achievements regarding the number of families assisted so far under IRDP has been presented in Table 6.5. The percentage of achievements have been calculated from the figures of Physical targets which have been presented in Table 6.5.

Table 6.5
Physical Targets and Achievements

Year	*Targets*	*Achievements*	*Percentage*
1980-85	268200	194599	72.56
1985-90	239240	266158	111.25
1990-91	17236	34179	198.30
1991-92	16326	24756	151.64
1992-93	13606	23349	171.61
1993-94	17989	34026	189.15
1994-95	14715	28285	192.22
1995-96	0	17473	—
Total	587312	622825	106.05

Source: Rural Development Department, Government of Haryana.

Table 6.5 illustrates that the physical achievement has been higher than the physical target fixed during various periods except the 6th Five Year Plan (1980-85). The percentage of target achievement has almost doubled in various years during 1990-96.

The overall percentage of target achievement is also more than the target fixed. The Government of India has stopped to fix the physical target since 1995-96, now only the financial target is fixed by the government.

Coverage of Scheduled Caste Families

The Scheduled Caste had remained amongst the most vulnerable section of rural society since ages. They constitute the bulk of rural BPL population in the country. Though special coverage has been provided to this section of the rural society under IRDP. Hence it becomes very meaningful to highlight the coverage of scheduled caste in the state at various intervals. The families of Scheduled Caste and non-Scheduled Caste assisted under IRDP since 1980-96 can be seen in Table 6.6.

Table 6.6
Coverage of Scheduled Caste & Non Scheduled Caste

Year	*SC*	*NSC*	*Total*	*% of SC*
1980-85	91771	102828	194599	47.2
1985-90	90156	176002	266158	33.9
1990-91	14551	19628	34179	42.6
1991-92	12019	12737	24756	48.5
1992-93	11645	11704	23349	50.0
1993-94	16490	17536	34026	48.5
1994-95	13751	14534	28285	48.5
1995-96	8283	9190	17473	47.4
Total	2,58,666	3,64,159	6,22,825	41.5

Source: Rural Development Department, Government of Haryana.

Table 6.6 reveals that the coverage of SC families under IRDP has been to the tune of 41.5 per cent since 1980 to 1996 which is in accordance with the target fixed by the Government of India. The performance of SC coverage ranges between fifty per cent in 1992-93 to thirty-four per cent in the Seventh Plan.

However, in the initial years there was no target of the coverage of SC families. But in the 7th Plan, it was envisaged that thirty per cent of the benefits under the programmes should go to the

Beneficiaries belonging to the Scheduled Caste category. This limit was raised to fifty per cent in 1990-91. The State Government has also fixed the target of fifty per cent for SC coverage under the programme simultaneously and the achievement has almost been the same except the 7th Plan period when the coverage has been reduced to the level of thirty-four per cent.

Coverage of Women and Physically Handicapped under IRDP

Women and physically handicapped were also among the under privileged and neglected sections of rural society. Though the programme of IRDP is basically for these weaker sections of rural society, they could not get desired benefits under the programme. Hence, the Government of India has to fixed target for their coverage. Here an attempt has been made to present their coverage in the state of Haryana. The figures regarding the coverage of women Beneficiaries under IRDP during the 6th Plan were not available as there was no fixed target for women during this period, similar is the position about physically handicapped during the 6th and 7th Plans. The Table 6.7 shows the coverage of women Beneficiaries under IRDP during 1985 to 1996 and that of physically handicapped during 1990-96.

Table 6.7
Coverage of Women and Physically Handicapped Beneficiaries

Year	*Total Families assisted*	*Women Beneficiaries*	*% age*	*P.H. benef.*	*% age*
1985-90	266158	85802	32.2	N.A.	—
1990-91	34179	14545	42.5	651	1.9
1991-93	24756	10447	42.2	357	1.4
1992-93	23349	9812	42.0	452	1.9
1993-94	34026	13968	41.0	706	2.1
1994-95	28285	11190	39.6	624	2.2
1995-96	17473	6461	37.0	349	2.0
Total	4,28,226	1,52,225	35.5	3,139	1.9

Source: Rural Development Department, Government of Haryana.

Table 5.7 reveals that the women coverage under IRDP has been 35.5 per cent during the period 1985 to 1996. During 1985-86 for the first time, a target of thirty per cent was fixed for the coverage of women Beneficiaries under the programme. This target has been raised to forty peer cent during 1992-93. However, during the whole period of the 7th Plan (1985-90) the coverage of women Beneficiaries has been 32.2 per cent of the total families assisted which is higher than the target fixed for the said period. Although there is a continuous decline in the percentage of women assied since 1990-96 yet it is almost equal to the percent age reserved for the women Beneficiaries during this period. The target for the physically handicapped families under IRDP was fixed to 3 per cent for the first time in 1990-91 but it has remained between 1.4 per cent in 1991-92 to 2.2 per cent in 1994-95 which is lower than the percentage reserved for them.

As endeavour has been made to express clearly the percentage of scheduled castes, women and physically handicapped Beneficiaries covered under IRDP in Haryana since 1980 to 1996 with the help of graph 6.1 given below.

SC, Women and Physically Handicapped Beneficiaries coverage under IRDP since 1980 to 1996.

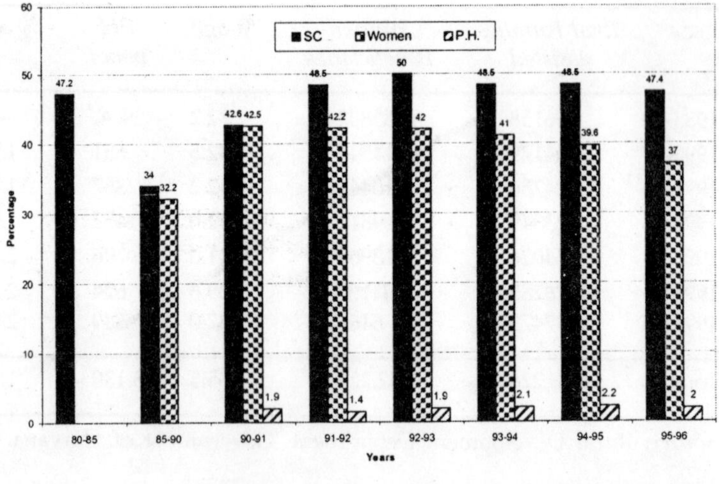

Graph 6.1 : Category-wise Coverage of Beneficiaries under IRDP in Haryana since 1980 to 1996

Sector-wise Coverage of Families under IRDP

The Beneficiaries under IRDP are provided assistance for various activities depending upon the choice of the Beneficiaries and availability of potentialities in that particular area. These activities are broadly divided in to three sectors-Primary, ISB and Tertiary. It has been tried here to present the broad idea of activities provided to Beneficiaries under various sectors in the state. The sector-wise coverage of families assisted under IRDP in Haryana since 1980 to 1996 has been presented in Table 6.8.

Table 6.8
Sector-wise Coverage of Families under IRDP

Year	*Primary*	*%*	*ISB*	*%*	*Tertiary*	*%*	*Total*
1980-85	137502	70.7	26079	13.4	31018	15.9	194599
1985-90	150476	56.5	56677	21.3	59005	22.2	266158
1990-91	18742	54.8	7893	23.1	7544	22.1	34179
1991-92	11823	47.8	7424	30.0	5509	22.2	24756
1992-93	10029	43.0	8675	37.0	4645	20.0	23349
1993-94	14313	42.1	12403	36.5	7310	21.5	34026
1994-95	11290	40.0	10822	38.3	6173	21.7	28285
1995-96	6250	36.0	7860	45.0	3363	19.0	17473
Total	360425	57.9	137833	22.1	124567	20.0	622825

Source: Rural Development Department, Government of Haryana.

Table 6.8 elucidates that the percentage of Beneficiaries in Primary sector is higher than seventy (70) per cent during the 6th plan which was reduced to 56.5 per cent in 7th plan. There is a spontaneous decrease in the percentage of Beneficiaries in Primary sector during the 1990-91 to 1995-96 from 55 per cent to 36 per cent. The figures reveal that the percentage of families assisted in Primary sector in Haryana has decreased continuously. However, the reasons might be the lack of interest among beneficiaries for this sector, saturation of activities under this sector or increase in interest for ISB or tertiary sectors.

On the contrary, the percentage of Beneficiaries assisted in ISB sector has increased from 13.4 per cent in the 6th plan to 21.3 per cent in the 7th plan. It has increased from 23.1 per cent in 1990-91 to 45 per cent in 1995-96 whereas the percentage of Beneficiaries assisted in tertiary sector has remained almost the same.

The overall assessment of the sectors-wise coverage of Beneficiaries shows that the Primary sector is still dominating over ISB and tertiary sectors in matter of assistance to the Beneficiaries under IRDP which alone constitutes more than fifty-eight per cent. However, the average percentage of ISB sector is merely twenty-two per cent and that of tertiary sector is twenty per cent.

This sector-wise coverage of families under IRDP can also be seen in Graph 6.2.

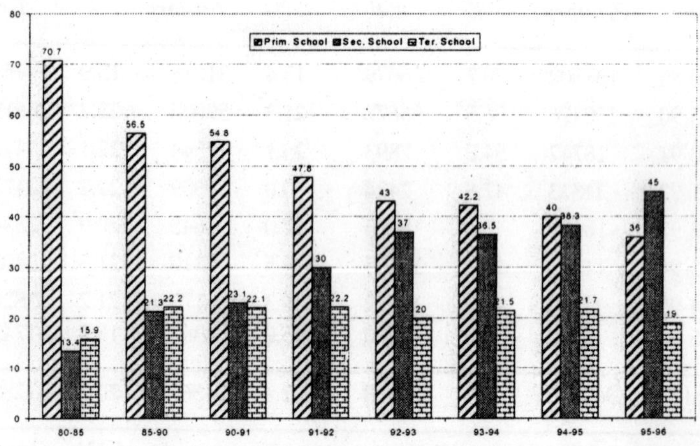

Graph 6.2 : Sector-wise Coverage of Families under IRDP since 1980-1996

Financial Assistance

The funds allocated and utilized for the implementation of IRDP in Haryana since 1980-96 have been presented in Table 6.9.

As elucidated in Table 6.9, an amount of Rs. 12145.26 lakh has been allocated for this programme in Haryana during the period 1980-96. Against this allocation, the total expenditure has been Rs. 14552.85 lakhs. The percentage utilization of funds has been 120. The percentage of utilization of funds against allocation has remained higher from 1980-85 to 1995-96. It has been varying from 102 per cent in 7th plan to 184 per cent in 1994-95. However, it may be pointed out here that the expenditure shown in Table 6.9 also includes the expenditure of infrastructural support.

Table 6.9
Financial Assistance

(Rs. in Lakh)

Plan/Year	*Allocation*	*Expenditure*	*Percentage*
1980-85	3141.00	3343.17	106
1985-90	4856.98	4958.09	102
1990-91	943.76	1002.65	106
1991-92	510.19	756.84	148
1992-93	480.00	796.25	166
1993-94	742.00	1318.31	178
1994-95	736.00	1351.32	184
1995-96	735.33	1026.22	140
Total	12145.26	14552.85	120

Source: Rural Development Department, Government of Haryana.

Credit Mobilization (Loan + Subsidy)

The total credit mobilized in the state under IRDP since 1980 to 1996 can be seen in Table 6.10.

Table 6.10
Credit Mobilization (Loan + Subsidy)

(Rs. in lakh)

Year/Plan	*Subsidy*	*Loan*	*Total Investment*
1980-85	2141.31	4789.57	6930.88
1985-90	4052.03	8443.19	12495.22
1990-91	795.82	1267.83	2063.65
1991-92	620.50	978.80	1599.30
1992-93	665.07	1067.36	1732.43
1993-94	1157.29	1819.70	2976.99
1994-95	1125.44	2066.81	31.92.25
1995-96	799.21	1931.46	2730.67
Sub Total (1990-96)	5163.33	9131.96	14295.29
Grand Total	11356.67	22364.72	33721.39

Source: Rural Development Department, Government of Haryana.

Table 6.10 reveals that the total investment of Rs. 33721.39 lakh has been invested on IRDP in Haryana since 1980 to 1996. It consists of Rs. 11356.67 lakh as subsidy and Rs. 22364.72 lakh as credit/loan. The investment sharply raised and became almost doubled in Seventh Plan as compared to 6th Plan. It has further increased about two and half folds in 1990-96 as compared to 6th Plan. Similar is the position with loan and subsidy. The ratio of loan and subsidy is 2:1 in the whole period. This shows that there is a constant rise in subsidy as compared to loan. The reason is clear as the Government of India has raised the limits of subsidy from time to time for various categories.

Per Capita Investment

The per capita investment made under IRDP in Haryana during 1980 to 1996 has been presented in Table 6.11.

Table 6.11
Per Capita Investment

Year/Plan	*Total Fam. assisted*	*Total Investment (Rs. In Lakh)*	*Per Capita investment in Rs.*
1980-85	194599	6930.88	3562
1985-90	266158	12495.22	4695
1990-91	34179	2063.65	6078
1991-92	24756	1599.30	6460
1992-93	23349	1732.43	7425
1993-94	34026	2976.99	8749
1994-05	28285	3192.25	11286
1995-96	17473	2730.67	15627
Sub Total (1990-96)	162068	14295.29	8223
Grand Total	622825	33721.39	5414

Source: Department of Rural Development, Government of Haryana.

The above figures demonstrates that there is a constant rise in per capita investment. It was Rs. 3562 in 6th Plan, Rs. 4695 in 7th Plan and Rs. 8223 for the period 1990-96. The per capita investment has increased more than four folds in 1995-96 as compared to 6th Plan. This indicates that the government is cautious about the rising prices, hence modified the unit cost of the assets accordingly.

The rise in per capita investment can also be seen in Graph 6.3.

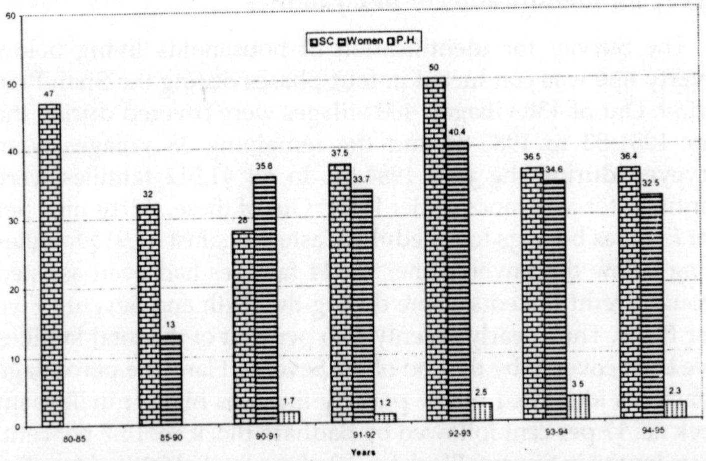

Graph 6.3: Per Capita investment under IRDP since 1980-96

The Position of IRDP in District Bhiwani

IRDP was initially started in five selected Blocks of Bhiwani District viz. Dadri-I, Badhara, Loharu, Tosham and Bawani Khera in 1978-79. With effect from October 2, 1980, it was extended to the remaining two Blocks also i.e. Bhiwani and Dadri-II and since then it continues to be implemented in all the Blocks of the District. Siwani Block was carved out in August, 1983 and it was taken under the programme since the very year. At present there are eight Blocks in Bhiwani District and all are covered under the IRDP programme. During 1980-81 and 1981-82 Rs. 6.00 lakh per Block were provided while the funding was raised to Rs. 8.00 lakh per Block for the next 3 years of the Sixth Plan.

In the beginning, the programme was implemented through the then existing Small Farmers Development Agency (SFDA). Later on when SFDA was merged and restructured in the form of IRDP, this organization was renamed as District Rural Development Agency (DRDA). At the District level this programme with other rural poverty alleviation programmes is administered by the DRDA from the District headquarters with the help of various Block level officials of various departments.

Survey for Identification of BPL Families

The Survey for identification of households living below poverty line was conducted in four phases during the Sixth Plan period. Out of 438 villages, 400 villages were covered during the year 1981-82 to 1983-84 and the remaining 38 villages were surveyed during the year 1984-85. In all 41,912 families were identified for assistance under IRDP. Out of these, thirty-nine per cent families belongs to Schedules Castes. Against 41,912 families living below the poverty line, 30,344 families had been assisted through credit linked scheme during the Sixth and Seventh Five Year Plans. Thus nearly seventy-two per cent of the total families have been covered by the end of the Seventh Plan. The percentage of families identified below poverty line was highest in Tosham Block i.e. 17 per cent followed by Badhara Block i.e. 14.7 per cent. It was lowest in Siwami Block i.e. 2.2 of the total identified families in the District. Similarly the strength of Scheduled Castes in the identified BPL families varied from 2.5 per cent in Siwami Block to eighteen per cent in Tosham Block.[2]

Due to Change in income criteria, a fresh survey of the whole District for identification of households below poverty line was conducted during 1991-92. In all, 48,241 families were identified for assistance under IRDP to be covered under the 8th plan period. Out of total families identified, 17,103 belong to Scheduled Castes and 10,133 to Backward Castes.[3] The percentage of BPL families was 34.25 of the total households. These figures don't include the present Siwani Block, which was shifted to Hisar District during this period. This increase was forced by the intervention of the State Level Steering and Coordination Committee to get the survey conducted a fresh in view of numerous complaints from the people and due to rise in poverty line from Rs. 3500 to Rs. 6400 per annum and cut off line for identification having been raised to Rs. 4800 per annum. As IRDP is a target group programme and small farmers, marginal farmers, agricultural and non-agricultural labourers, rural artisans etc. constitute the most vulnerable section of rural society. However, majority of them are from SC/ST and Backward Castes. The composition of both castewise and category-wise of the District can be seen in tables to follow.

Table 6.12 shows caste-wise and block-wise number of households below poverty line in District Bhiwani as per 1991-92 survey.

Table 6.12
Caste-wise and Block-wise Distribution of BPL Families

Sl. No.	*Name of Block*	*SC*	*BC*	*Others*	*Total*	*% age*
1.	Bhiwami	2925	1481	2935	7341	15.2
2.	Tosham	3536	2606	3784	9926	20.6
3.	B/Khera	3462	1195	1960	6617	13.7
4.	Dadri-I	1786	876	2819	5481	11.3
5.	Dadri-II	1604	1272	3086	5962	12.4
6.	Badhara	1795	1318	3096	6209	12.8
7.	Loharu	1995	1385	3325	6705	13.9
	Total	17103 (35.4)	10133 (21.0)	21005 (43.6)	48241 (100)	100

Note: Percentage have been given in parentheses.
Source: Annual Action Plan for IRDP, 1995-96, Bhiwani District.

Table 6.12 shows that Tosham Block has the highest strength of BPL families i.e. 9,926 followed by Bhiwami Block with 7,341 constituting 20.6 per cent and 15.2 per cent of the total in the District. Dadri-I and Dadri-II are at the bottom with a strength of 5,481 and 5,962 BPL families constituting 11.3 per cent and 12.4 per cent respectively. On the other hand, the caste-wise distribution of the BPL families in the District shows that there are 35.4 per cent scheduled castes, twenty-one per cent backward castes and 43.6 per cent others.

Category-wise Distribution of BPL Families

The category-wise break up of households below poverty line in Bhiwani District may be seen in Table 6.13.

Table 6.13
Category-wise Distribution of BPL Families

Sl. No.	*Name of Block*	*SF*	*MF*	*AL*	*NAL*	*RA*	*Others*	*Total*
1.	Bhiwani	713	1783	3125	1604	27	89	7341
2.	Tosham	1126	3404	3747	1500	68	81	9926
3.	B/Khera	604	1272	2717	1728	44	252	6617
4.	Dadri-I	599	1987	2117	673	80	25	5481
5.	Dadri-II	604	2268	1826	1112	50	102	5962
6.	Badhara	807	2808	1453	1098	26	17	6209
7.	Loharu	749	3283	1860	742	28	43	6705
	Total	5202 (10.8)	16805 (35)	16845 (35.7)	8457 (17.5)	323 (0.7)	608 (1.26)	48241 (100)

Note: Percentage have been given in parentheses.
Source: Annual Action Plan for IRDP, 1995-96, DRDA, Bhiwani.

Table 6.13 shows that the strength of marginal farmers and agricultural labourers together is maximum i.e. 70 per cent of the total BPL families in the District whereas that of rural artisans and others is minimum with a strength of 1.9 per cent of the total BPL families. There are 10.8 per cent small farmers and 17.5 per cent non-agricultural labourers of the total BPL families in the District. On the basis of another survey for identification of BPL families (1992-93) Rs. 11000/- per annum was fixed as the income level for poverty alleviation programmes. This was up dated again in 1995-96. The latest figures of BPL families in the District are 61,101 constituting 43.4 per cent of the total households in rural areas. A close look of data would show that instead of any significant reduction in the poverty, it has increased over the years. It is observed that the base line survey in the villages was not conducted properly. The information collected in the survey does not include information regarding the number of earning members in the family, their income, land owned by them in different parts of the village and its utilization, assistance required under the programme etc. Due to lack of data, proper assessment cannot be made therefore, many underserving families were included in the list of BPL families. Apart from it, surveys have been conducted in a casual manner and that too by Block officials and untrained persons.

Physical Targets and Achievements

The physical targets and achievements of Beneficiaries under IRDP during the 6th Plan, 7th Plan and between 1990 to 1995 year-wise of the District has been presented in Table 6.14.

Table 6.14 reveals that during 1980-95 period physical target of 35,016 was fixed and the real achievement was 39,324 which constitutes 112 per cent of the target in the District. There seems to be variation between the physical target and its achievement in the District at different intervals. During the 6th Plan, the target and achievement were almost equal but it increased to 111 per cent in 7th plan. The physical achievement was maximum against target i.e. 201 per cent in 1990-91, followed by 174 per cent in 1993-94 and minimum sixty-seven per cent in 1991-92. The average physical achievement during 1990-95 was much more i.e. 133 per cent against the target fixed. Since 1995-96 the Government of India has stopped the fixing of physical target, now only financial target is provided to DRDAs.

Table 6.14
Physical Targets and Achievements

S.No.	*Year/Plan*	*Targets*	*Achievements*	*% age*
1.	1980-85	11458	11673	102
2.	1985-90	16825	18671	111
3.	1990-91	1277	2567	201
4.	1991-92	2473	1663	67
5.	1992-93	883	1314	149
6.	1993-94	1155	2013	174
7.	1994-95	945	1423	151
	Sub Total (1990-95)	6733	8980	133
	Grand Total	35016	39324	112

Source: DRDA, Bhiwani District.

Block-wise Coverage of Beneficiaries

As the Blocks have been selected on the basis of total number of Beneficiaries under IRDP during 1980-95. Hence the data regarding it has been presented here. The block-wise coverage under IRDP in Bhiwani District since 1980 to 1995 is given in Table 6.15.

Table 6.15
Block-wise Coverage of Beneficiaries

S.No.	Block	1980-85	1985-90	1990-95	Total	% age
1.	Tosham	1658	3431	1292	6381	16.2
2.	Badhara	1766	2535	1288	5589	14.2
3.	B/Khera	1623	2519	1363	5505	14.0
4.	Bhiwani	1767	2096	1190	5003	12.7
5.	Dadri-I	1352	2250	1019	4621	11.8
6.	Loharu	1614	1925	1005	4544	11.5
7.	Dadri-II	1634	1758	844	4236	10.8
8.	Siwani	309	2157	979	3445	8.8
	Total	11673 (29.7)	18671 (47.5)	8980 (22.8)	39324 (100)	100

Note: Percentage have been given in parentheses.
Source: DRDA, Bhiwani District.

The data in Table 6.15 reveals that 11,673 families were assisted during 6th plan period in Bhiwani District which constitutes 29.7 per cent of the total families assisted since 1980-95 period in the District. During the 7th plan (1985-90) special emphasis was led on poverty alleviation programmes and the number of Beneficiary families assisted under IRDP in the District was increased significantly i.e. 18,671 which constitutes 47.5 per cent of the total families covered under IRDP during the total period. The coverage of families under IRDP in next five years (1990-95) was again poor and it was less than half of the total strength of families assisted during 7th plan. Tosham Block is at the top in the District having 16.2 per cent of the total assisted families followed by Badhara Block with 14.2 per cent. Siwami Block was found at the bottom with only 8.8 per cent of the total Beneficiaries followed by Dadri-II having only 10.8 per cent.

Coverage of Scheduled Castes

The Scheduled Castes which form the most weaker section of our society, has been subjected to social discrimination and economic exploitation since ages. This resulted in their deep rooted poverty, illiteracy and general backwardness. After independence special attention has been paid for the upliftment of these depressed castes. The Government of India directed the state governments to cover at least forty per cent of the scheduled castes families under IRDP during 6th and 7th plans which was later on increased to the level of fifty per cent of the total assisted families. The Scheduled Castes population constitutes nineteen per cent of the total population of the District Bhiwani. At the time of survey during 1981-82 to 1983-84, 16,742 scheduled castes families were found below poverty line in the District. Out of which 11,500 had already been assisted under IRDP. As per new survey of 1990-91 total scheduled castes families identified below poverty line were 17,103 against the total identified families of 48,231 which constitutes 28 per cent. The number of scheduled castes families assisted under IRDP in Bhiwani District during 1980-95 have been given in Table 6.16.

Table 6.16
Coverage of Scheduled Castes Beneficiaries

S.No.	*Year*	*SC*	*% age*	*Others*	*% age*	*Total*
1.	1980-85	5487	47	6186	53	11673
2.	1985-90	6013	32	12658	68	18671
3.	1990-91	723	28	1844	72	2567
4.	1991-92	625	37.5	1038	62.5	1663
5.	1992-93	657	50	657	50	1314
6.	1993-94	735	36.5	1278	63.5	2013
7.	1994-95	518	36.4	905	63.6	1423
Sub Total		3258	36.3	5722	63.7	8980
Grand Total		14758	37.5	24566	62.5	39324

Source: Annual Action Plan 1995-96, IRDP Bhiwani District.

Table 6.16 reveals that of the total 39,324 assisted families since 1980-95 in the District, 37.5 per cent were the families of scheduled castes. However, this strength is comparatively low to that of the percentage reserved for scheduled caste. But the coverage of SC families under IRDP was comparatively good in 6th plan period which was 47 per cent. There was a sudden fall in coverage of scheduled castes families in 7th plan period i.e. 32 per cent. During 1990-91, it was at the lowest with only 28 per cent of scheduled castes families. The coverage of scheduled castes was fifty per cent only once in 1992-93. By and large it has remained between 36.4 per cent to 37.5 per cent in most of the years during 1980-95 period.

Coverage of Women and Physically Handicapped Families

In rural areas women are the victims of socio-economic exploitation, social customs, misinterpretation of religious norms. Poverty and illiteracy have neglected rural women to inferior status. Though they put in more hours of work in economically productive activities, they have no control over income or properties. Rural women whether they belong to farm sector or are landless agricultural labourers, put in 50-60 per cent more hours of work than their manfolk. In spite of this they have no ownership or legal control over productive resources.

Keeping these facts in view, a number of schemes to provide women with skills and means for development activities have been introduced in the 7th plan period under IRDP. It was targeted to cover 30 per cent of the total Beneficiaries as women headed households for the 7th plan period. However this strength was increased to 40 per cent since 1990-91. The coverage of physically handicapped persons was negligible during 6th and 7th plans. Hence to give special coverage to them under IRDP, it was decided that at least three per cent of the total Beneficiaries in each Block should be from the handicapped. Table 6.17 shows the coverage of women and physically handicapped under IRDP in Bhiwani District since 1980-95.

Table 6.17 reveals that 14.2 per cent of the women beneficiaries have been covered since 1980-85 under IRDP in Bhiwani District. The coverage of women Beneficiaries was lowest i.e. 12.9 per cent in 1985-90 and highest i.e. 40.4 per cent in 1992-93. It was nil during 6th plan period. However the coverage of women

Beneficiaries was comparatively better after the fixation of their target. The coverage of Physically Handicapped was about half per cent during the above mentioned period in the district. Before 1990, the coverage of physically handicapped was nil under IRDP. It was lowest (1.2 per cent) in 1991-92 and highest (3.5 per cent) in 1993-94. The category-wise coverage of Beneficiaries has also been in Graph 6.4.

Table 6.17
Coverage of Women and Physically Handicapped

Sl. No.	*Year*	*Total Assisted Families*	*Women*	*% age*	*P.H.*	*% age*
1.	1980-85	11673	–	–	–	
2.	1985-90	18671	2402	12.9	–	–
3.	1990-91	2567	919	35.8	45	1.7
4.	1991-92	1663	560	33.7	20	1.2
5.	1992-93	1314	531	40.4	33	2.5
6.	1993-94	2013	697	34.6	71	3.5
7.	1994-95	1423	477	33.5	33	2.3
	Total	39324	5586	14.2	202	0.5

Source: Annual Action Plan of IRDP, DRDA, Bhiwani District.

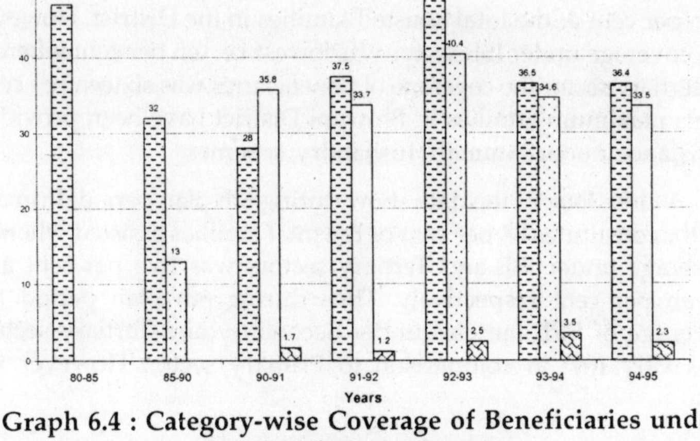

Graph 6.4 : Category-wise Coverage of Beneficiaries under IRDP in Bhiwani District.

Sector-wise Coverage

The sector-wise coverage of Beneficiaries under IRDP during 1980 to 1995 in Bhiwani District can be seen in Table 6.18.

Table 6.18
Sector-wise Coverage

	Primary Sector				*ISB*		*Tertiary*		
Year/Plan	*Agri.*	*%*	*Ani.*	*%*	*Sector*	*%*	*Sector*	*%*	*Total*
1980-85	3461	30	6772	58	635	5	805	7	11673
1985-90	3307	18	10403	56	1234	6	3727	20	18671
1990-91	892	35	884	34	148	6	643	25	2567
1991-92	293	18	605	36	251	15	514	31	1663
1992-93	232	18	484	37	321	24	277	21	1314
1993-94	326	16	688	34	661	33	338	17	2013
1994-95	–	–	677	48	516	36	230	16	1423
Sub Total (1990-95)	1743	19	3338	37	1897	21	2002	23	8980
Grand Total	8511	22	20513	52	3766	10	6534	16	39324

Source: Annual Action Plan of IRDP, DRDA, Bhiwani District.

The data in Table 6.18 show that out of the total 39,324 families assisted so far under IRDP in Bhiwani District, 74 per cent were covered under Primary sector which constitutes almost three-fourths of the total Beneficiaries. Animal Husbandry constitutes a major part in Primary sector and coverage under this part is fifty-two per cent of the total assisted families in the District. However the coverage under ISB sector was lowest i.e. ten per cent whereas in Tertiary sector the coverage of Beneficiaries was sixteen per cent. Thus maximum families in Bhiwani District have been provided assistance under Animal Husbandry schemes.

A close look of the data show during 6th plan period, Primary sector constitutes 88 per cent of the total families assisted whereas coverage under ISB and Tertiary sectors was five per cent and seven per cent respectively. Thus during 6th plan period the coverage of BPL families under Secondary and Tertiary sectors was very low in comparison to Primary sector. However the activities under Animal Husbandry schemes were given maximum preference i.e. 58 per cent of the total Beneficiaries assisted. During the 7th plan also the Primary sector constituted about three-fourths of the total Beneficiaries assisted. But there was a sudden fall in coverage under agriculture schemes which were reduced from 30 per cent in 6th plan to 18 per cent in 7th plan. However there was a significant rise under Tertiary sector. The coverage almost increased three times during this period. The ISB sector almost remained the same during this period. During 1990-95, there was significant fall in the coverage of families under Primary sector, of course, it remained more than 50 per cent of the total families assisted during this period. Interestingly a three fold rise in the coverage was found in ISB sector during this period. These figures have also been presented in Graph 6.5.

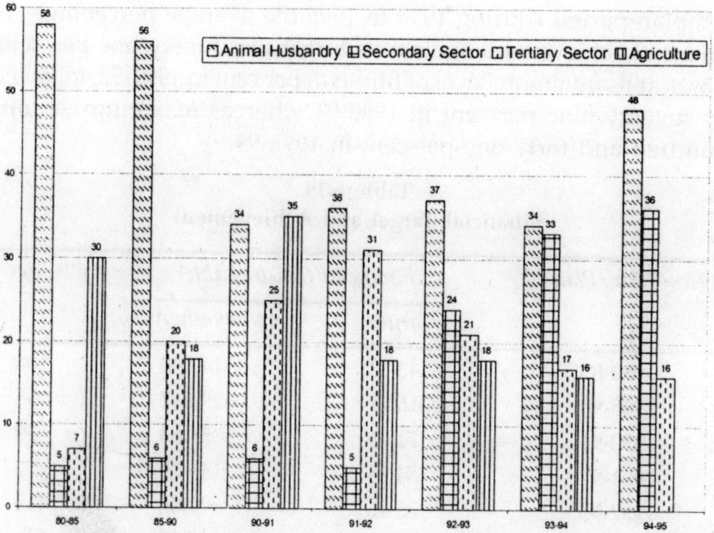

Graph 6.5: Sector-wise Coverage of Beneficiaries under IRDP in Bhiwani District.

On the basis of the above data overall picture emerges is that the Primary sector has shown a constant and significant decline in coverage whereas ISB sector has shown a constant and significant rise in the coverage of assisted families under IRDP. In spite of variations of we take consolidated figures of this period

(1990-95) then Tertiary sector seems to have constant upward movement in coverage. This might be due to diversification of activities from Primary sector to ISB and Tertiary sectors on direction of Government of India from time to time.

Financial Target and Achievement

The financial target and achievement of IRDP in Bhiwani District during period 1980-95 have been presented in Table 6.19.

Our data in Table 6.19 show that the total financial achievements against its target in Bhiwani District during 1980-95 is ninety-five (95) per cent which is comparatively low against the target provided. There is variation between financial target and its achievement if we look on the Table minutely. In the 6th plan financial achievement was better than its target i.e. one hundred and four per cent whereas it was ninety-five per cent in 7th plan period. During 1990 to 1995 the average percentages of financial achievement against its target was ninety-one per cent. It was at its minimum level of fifty-two per cent in 1991-92, followed by seventy-nine per cent in 1990-91 whereas maximum i.e. one hundred and forty-one per cent in 1993-94.

Table 6.19
Financial Target and Achievement

S.No.	*Year/Plan*	*Financial (Rs. in Lakh)*		*% age*
		Target	*Achievement*	
1.	1980-85	143.32	147.60	104
2.	1985-90	310.77	294.17	95
3.	1990-91	71.68	56.83	79
4.	1991-92	84.75	43.29	52
5.	1992-93	35.56	40.86	115
6.	1993-94	48.10	68.23	141
7.	1994-95	47.27	53.12	112
	Sub Total (1990-95)	287.36	262.33	91
	Grand Total	741.45	704.10	95

Source: DRDA, Bhiwani District.

Sector-wise Financial Coverage

To have a better understanding about the unit cost of various activities under different sectors an attempt has been made to present the sector-wise financial coverage in the District. The sector-wise financial coverage of IRDP in Bhiwani District during 1980 to 1995 has been in Table 6.20.

Table 6.20
Sector-wise Financial Coverage

(*Rs. in Lakh*)

S.No.	*Year/Plan*	*Primary Sector*		*ISB Sector*	*Tertiary Sector*	*Total*
		Agri.	*An. Hus.*			
1.	1980-85	38.806	86.819	5.580	16.401	147.60
		(26)	(59)	(4)	(11)	(100)
2.	1985-90	37.27	162.63	18.63	75.67	294.14
		(13)	(55)	(6)	(26)	(100)
3.	1990-91	12.81	28.07	2.76	13.19	56.83
4.	1991-92	4.61	21.19	5.75	11.74	43.29
5.	1992-93	4.46	17.94	9.51	8.95	40.86
6.	1993-94	6.04	25.92	24.75	11.52	68.23
7.	1994-95	—	22.55	20.89	9.68	53.12
	Sub Total	27.92	115.67	63.66	55.08	262.33
	(1990-95)	(11)	(44)	(24)	(21)	(100)
	Grand Total	103.99	365.12	87.84	147.15	704.07
		(15)	(52)	(12)	(21)	(100)

Note: Percentages have been given in parentheses.
Source: Annual Action Plans of IRDP, DRDA, Bhiwani District.

Table 6.20 shows that out of the total subsidy released during 1980-95, 67 per cent was given to Primary sector in which animal husbandry constitutes a major part, whereas it was twelve per cent in ISB sector and twenty-one per cent in Tertiary sector. There was sudden fall in subsidy released for agricultural activities in 7th plan as compared to 6th plan period and also later on. Thus in Primary sector, there was constant decline in financial assistance whereas the ISB and Tertiary sectors had shown a constant increase in financial assistance from 1980 to 1995 period.

Credit Mobilization

The credit mobilized which consists of loan and subsidy, has been presented separately to have a clear view of unit cost and loan-subsidy ratio. The credit mobilized for various schemes under IRDP in District Bhiwani during 1980-85 may be seen in Table 6.21.

Table 6.21
Credit Mobilization

(Rs. in Lakh)

S.No.	*Plan/Year*	*Subsidy*	*Loan*	*Total*	*Ratio of Loan And Subsidy*
1.	1980-85	147.60	299.49	447.09	2:1
2.	1985-90	294.14	680.13	974.27	2.3:1
3.	1990-91	56.83	91.48	148.31	1.6:1
4.	1991-92	43.29	69.43	112.72	1.6:1
5.	1992-03	40.86	63.82	104.68	1.6:1
6.	1993-94	68.23	113.67	181.90	1.7:1
7.	1994-95	53.12	105.60	158.72	2:1
	Sub Total (1990-95)	262.33	444.00	706.33	1.7:1
	Grand Total	704.07	1423.62	2127.69	2:1

Source : DRDA, Bhiwani District.

The data in Table 6.21 show that during 1980 to 1995 the loan of Rs. 1423.62 lakh was distributed whereas the subsidy given was of Rs. 704.07 lakh. Thus the total credit mobilized during this period was Rs. 2127.69 lakh. The loan and subsidy' ratio during the whole period was 2:1. However it was 1.7:1 for the period of 1990-95. This shows a significant increase in subsidy given to the Beneficiaries under IRDP in the District Bhiwani.

Per Capita Investment

The per capita investment has direct link with the creating of assets. For purchasing a potential and standard assets, it is essential that unit cost should be revised with the rising prices in the market. The per capita investment under IRDP in District Bhiwani during 1980 to 1995 is given below in Table 6.22.

Table 6.22
Per Capita Investment

Plan/Year	*Total Families assisted*	*Total Credit Mobilized (Rs. in Lakh)*	*Per Capita Investment*
1980-85	11673	447.09	3830
1985-90	18671	974.27	5218
1990-91	2567	148.31	5778
1991-92	1663	112.72	6778
1992-93	1314	104.68	7967
1993-94	2013	181.90	9036
1994-95	1423	158.72	11154
Sub Total (1990-95)	8980	706.33	7866
Grand Total	39324	2127.69	5410

Source : DRDA, Bhiwani District.

Our data in Table 6.22 show that there was a significant increase in per capita investment in 7th plan period i.e. Rs. 5218 as compared to 6th plan i.e. Rs. 3830. During 1990-95 the average per capita investment i.e. Rs. 7866 was almost doubled during 6th plan period. There was a constant increase in per capita investment in this period. So that the Beneficiaries can create/purchase a potential asset. The per capita investment in 1995 has become Rs. 11154, almost doubled to that of 1991 i.e. Rs. 5778.

Per Capita Investment

The per capita investment (Loan + Subsidy) under IRDP in District Bhiwani during 1980-85 may be seen in Table 6.23.

Table 6.23 indicates that there was a constant and considerable increase in per capita subsidy since 1980-1995 and it has increased almost three folds during this period i.e. 3733 in 1995 to Rs. 1264 in 1980. As far, the per capita loan is concerned, there was also a constant and considerable increase and it has reached to Rs. 7421 in 1995 as compared to Rs. 2566 in 1980 i.e. almost three times. A close appraisal of Table shows that the per capita subsidy was increased significantly (almost doubled) during 1990-95 as compared to 1985-90. The per capita investment (loan + Subsidy) under IRDP in Bhiwani District during 1980-95 can also be seen in graph 6.6.

Table 6.23
Per Capita Investment

Year/Plan	*Loan*	*Subsidy*	*Total Investment*
1980-85	2566	1264	3830
1985-90	3643	1575	5218
1990-91	3564	2214	5778
1991-92	4175	2603	6778
1992-93	4857	3110	7967
1993-94	5647	3389	9036
1994-95	7421	3733	11154
Sub Total (1990-95)	4944	2922	7866
Grand Total	3620	1790	5410

Source: DRDA, Bhiwani District.

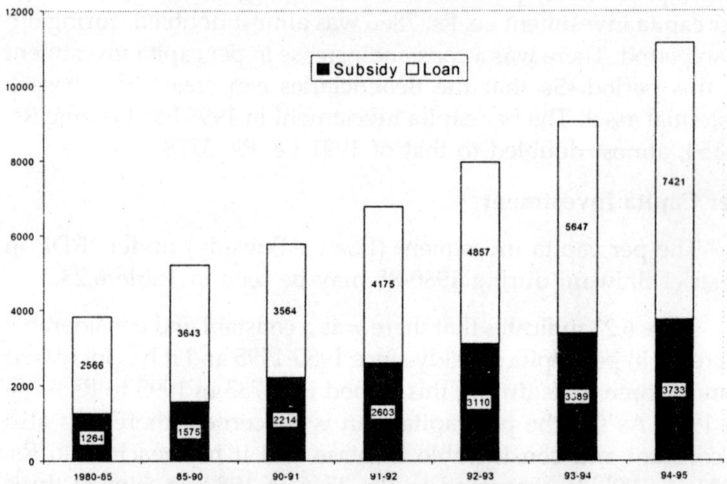

Graph 6.6 : Per Capita Investment (Loan + Subsidy) under IRDP in Bhiwani District during 1980-1995

In brief we can say that the state has adopted various programmes of rural development since its inception on the initiative of Central Government. The IRDP was introduced in the state in 1978-79 in certain selected Blocks which was later on extended to all the remaining Blocks from October 2, 1980. For implementation, the first household survey was conducted by the state government during 1980-84 in which 519444 families (42 per cent) were found below poverty line in rural areas. Among these families about (39 per cent) were families of Scheduled castes. The second survey of this kind was completed during 1991-92 and the number of BPL families identified were 628860 in the state constituting about thirty-seven (37) per cent of the total rural households. Out of these about two-thirds were from the middle strata of income. Majority of them (42 per cent) were from agricultural labourers followed by non-agricultural labourers (20 per cent). Forty-one (41) per cent were Scheduled Castes and twenty-two (22 per cent) Backward castes. The incidence of poverty varied from District to District. The number of families assisted under IRDP in Haryana since 1980-1996 were 622825 of which about forty-two (42) per cent were Scheduled Castes, twenty-five (25) per cent women and half per cent physically handicapped persons. Majority of Beneficiaries (58 per cent) were assisted under Primary sector, followed by ISB sector (22 per cent) and Tertiary sector (20 per cent) during this period. The number of Beneficiaries assisted under Primary sector has continuously decreased to significant extent whereas ISB sector has shown a sharp rise. A total sum of Rs. 145.52 crore has been spent as administrative expenditure and subsidy during this period. The total credit mobilized was Rs. 113.56 crore as subsidy and Rs. 223.65 crore as loan and the per capita investment was Rs. 5414 for the whole period.

IRDP was initially started in five selected blocks of Bhiwani District in 1978-79 and was extended to all the seven blocks since October 2, 1980. For its implementation, the first household survey for identification of BPL families was conducted during 1980-84 and 41912 families were identified below the poverty line of which 30,344 families had been assisted during 6th and 7th plans. The second survey of this kind was completed in 1991-92, in which 48,241 families were identified below the poverty line of these 17103 were from Scheduled Castes (35.4 per cent) and 10133 from Backward Classes (21 per cent). The percentage of BPL families was 32.25 per cent of the total households. The strength of BPL families varied from Block to Block. It was highest in Tosham Block (20.6 per cent) and lowest in Dadri-I (11.3 per cent). Majority of these BPL families belong to marginal farmers and agricultural labourers. The total number of families assisted under IRDP in this District since 1980-95 were 39324 of these maximum were in Tosham Block (16.2 per cent) and minimum in Siwani Block (8.8 per cent). Among the total assisted families 37.5 per cent were Scheduled Castes, 12.8 per cent women and 0.5 per cent were from Physically Handicapped persons. The coverage of latter two groups has significantly increased since 1990-91. About three-fourths of total Beneficiaries were assisted under Primary sector followed by Tertiary sector (16 per cent) and ISB sectors (10 per cent). The coverage under Primary sector has been reduced to a significant level whereas it has been increased about seven times in ISB sector during this period. A sum of Rs. 704.1 lakh has been spent on this programme in the District so far, of which about two-thirds (67 per cent) have been spent on Primary sector followed by Tertiary sector (21 per cent) and ISB sectors (12 per cent). The total credit mobilized during 1980-95 was Rs. 2127.69 lakh of which Rs. 704.07 lakh were spent on subsidy and Rs. 1423.62 lakh on loan. The average per capita investment during the whole period was Rs. 5410 though it has increased more than three folds during 1994-95 as compared to 6th plan period (1980-85).

7

IRDP: Officials-Beneficiaries Perceptions

In this chapter, a discussion on the actual implementation of Integrated Rural Development Programme (IRDP) and the perception of the Beneficiaries as well as that of the Officials concerned in Bhiwani District has been presented. Besides the background information of the respondent Beneficiaries and Officials, their perceptions about the administrative structure, process of implementation of the IRDP, its impact on poverty alleviation and their perceptions about each other have been described in this chapter. The views of public opinion leaders and concerned Branch Managers of Rural Banks have also been taken about the programme to ensure the objectivity of the study. Here our prime objective was not to test the correlation between various variables, yet efforts have been made to correlate them whenever and wherever it became possible.

The chapter consists of three parts. The first part deals with the socio-economic background of Beneficiary respondents. However, not much variations were found on the background data of the Officials. Hence their background information has not been given in tables. Their background information has been explained in percentage. The second part deals with their perception about the administrative structure, process of implementation and impact of IRDP. The third part discusses the Officials-Beneficiaries perceptions about each other.

Background Information of the Respondents

The success of any programme of development like IRDP is determined to a greater extent by the perceptions of Officials concerned and that of Beneficiaries towards each other as well as that of the programme as a whole. The environment in which the individual lives, has a definite role in shaping and reshaping of his perceptions. Hence the perceptions of Officials and Beneficiaries can be examined in a better manner by making a close investigation of the environment in which they are born and grew up. Hence it was thought essential and appropriate here to give the background information of the respondent Officials and Beneficiaries.

As per programme guidelines, proper identification of eligible target group families in rural areas is essential. The guidelines envisage to ascertain the income and social status of the families through a detailed household survey and classify these families on the basis of their annual income. The families falling in the lowest income group are to be provided assistance on priority basis. In order to ascertain the factual position, we collected the background information from the chosen 240 respondent-Beneficiaries and twenty Officials of IRDP. The information, thus collected have been presented in tables given in the chapter.

Sex-wise Distribution of Respondents

The government has directed to give forty per cent coverage for women under IRDP since 1991. Hence it becomes fruitful to describe their strength covered under IRDP. The sex-wise distribution of the selected Beneficiaries has been given in Table 7.1.

Table 7.1
Sex-wise Distribution of Respondent Beneficiaries

Sr. No.	*Block*	*Male*	*Female*	*Total*
1.	Bhiwani	49	31	80
		(61.3)	(38.7)	(100)
2.	Badhara	48	32	80
		(60.0)	(40.0)	(100)
3.	Loharu	50	30	80
		(62.5)	(37.5)	(100)
	Total	147	93	240
		(61.3)	(38.7)	(100)

Note : Percentages have been given in parentheses.

Table 7.1 shows that out of 240 selected Beneficiaries, 61.3 per cent males and 38.7 per cent of them were females. The proportion of women Beneficiaries under the IRDP programme was in tune with the prescribed guidelines. The sex-wise distribution of the respondents was almost the same in all the selected Blocks.

However, among the Officials eighty per cent were males and twenty per cent were females. Three-fourths of them had rural background and one-fourth of them were from urban areas.

Caste-wise Distribution of the Respondents

The main objective of IRDP is to assists the BPL families living in rural areas and majority of them should be from SC and ST. The Government has directed to ascertain their maximum coverage. At present it is fifty per cent for scheduled castes and at least three per cent for physically handicapped persons of the total assisted Beneficiaries in a particular area. Hence we decided to know their coverage out of the total respondent Beneficiaries. The caste-wise distribution of the respondent Beneficiaries has been presented in Table 7.2.

Table 7.2
Caste-wise Distribution of Respondents

S. No.	*Block*	*SC*	*NSC*	*PH*	*Total*
1.	Bhiwani	38	40	2	80
		(47.5)	(50.0)	(2.5)	(100)
2.	Badhara	36	41	3	80
		(45.0)	(51.3)	(3.7)	(100)
3.	Loharu	37	39	4	80
		(46.2)	(48.8)	(5.0)	(100)
	Total	111	120	9	240
		(46.3)	(50)	(3.7)	(100)

Note : Percentages have been given in parentheses.

Over data in Table 7.2 show that out of the 240 selected Beneficiaries, 46.3 per cent belonged to SC, 3.7 per cent from physically handicapped persons, whereas half (50 per cent) of them were from Non Schedules Castes. The coverage of SC under the programme was slightly lower and that of Physically

Handicapped persons was more than their prescribed strength. Thus, their respective coverage under the programme in our sample respondents is by and large similar to the guidelines.

Out of the official respondents more than fifty five (55) per cent were from the SC and forty-five (45) per cent of them belonged to Non-Scheduled Castes.

Family Size

The initial IRDP guidelines envisaged a family consisting of five members as a unit for purposes of identification and assistance. As per seventh plan period a family of five members having annual income of Rs. 11,000 or less per annum was supposed to be below the poverty line. Low level of income and large sized families have been seen as the major causes of poverty in rural areas. Hence as attempt has been made here to collect information about the family size of the respondents. The information, thus collected from the chosen respondents has been included in Table 7.3.

Table 7.3
Family Size of the Respondents

S. No.	*Block*	*up to 5 members*	*6-8 members*	*9-10 members*	*above 10 members*	*Total*
1.	Bhiwani	15	46	12	7	80
		(18.8)	(57.5)	(15.0)	(8.7)	(100)
2.	Badhara	13	35	31	1	80
		(16.3)	(43.8)	(38.7)	(1.2)	(100)
3.	Loharu	12	39	27	2	80
		(15.0)	(48.8)	(33.7)	(2.5)	(100)
	Total	40	120	70	10	240
		(16.7)	(50.0)	(29.2)	(4.1)	(100)

Note : Percentages have been given in parentheses.

Our data in Table 7.3 clearly indicate that half (50 per cent) of our respondents have the family size between 6-8 members. However, a very small number (16.7 per cent) of them have a family of 5 members and a sizeable number (29.2 per cent) of them have 9-10 members in their family. Only a small number (4.1 per cent) of them have bigger families having more than 10 members. Hence, more than four fifths of the respondent Beneficiaries had enlarge families to the criteria and it has been observed as one of the main reasons of their poverty. So it is suggested that adequate steps needs to be taken to strengthen the family welfare programme for the rural poor and to awaken them about their causes of poverty.

However, the size of the families of Officials by and large were small. Majority (60 per cent) of them belong to the families of 6-8 members, whereas a good number (40 per cent) of them have small families of five members.

Occupational Status of Respondents

Under IRDP the emphasis is on the weaker sections of society consisting of small farmers, marginal farmers, agricultural and non-agricultural labourers and rural artisans living below the poverty line. Here an attempt has been made to know the occupational status of the respondent-Beneficiaries. The occupational distribution of the chosen respondents has been given in Table 7.4.

Table 7.4
Occupational Status of the Respondents

S.N.	*Block*	*SF*	*MF*	*AL*	*RA*	*OT*	*Total*
1.	Bhiwani	14	29	34	3	0	80
		(17.5)	(36.3)	(42.5)	(3.7)	(0.0)	(100)
2.	Badhara	7	30	39	4	0	80
		(8.7)	(37.5)	(48.8)	(5.0)	(0.0)	(100)
3.	Loharu	12	32	23	2	0	80
		(15.0)	(40.0)	(42.5)	(2.5)	(0.0)	(100)
	Total	33	91	107	9	0	240
		(13.8)	(38.0)	(44.6)	(3.6)	(0.0)	(100)

Note : Percentages have been given in parentheses.

Table 7.4 illustrates that all the respondent Beneficiaries belonged to target groups of the programme. Agricultural labourers constituted nearly half (44.6 per cent) of the respondent Beneficiaries, followed by marginal farmers thirty-eight (38) per cent and small farmers (13.8 per cent). The strength of rural artisans was found insignificant only 3.6 per cent. However, there was variations in occupational status of our respondents if we look at the figures of the Blocks. The strength of the small farmers was 8.7 per cent in Badhara block is almost half of their strength in Bhiwani and Loharu Blocks individually. The cumulative strength of marginal farmers and agricultural labourers is more than four fifths (82.6 per cent) of the total respondents under this programme.

Among the officials about one third were from officers category, forty-five per cent from class III and one-fourth were from class IV. Sixty per cent of the Officials dependent upon their salary exclusively whereas a small number (15 per cent) had agricultural income as supportive means and the same number had other position. Only 10 per cent of them had business income as a subsidiary means of assistance.

Income of Respondents Before Assistance

As per the guidelines, Beneficiaries have been selected for assistance under IRDP from the BPL families. Under the programme poorest of the poor are given the preference. To ascertain the economic condition of our respondent Beneficiaries before assistance under the programme, we asked them about their income. The information on income thus, collected has been presented in Table 7.5.

Table 7.5
Income of Respondents Before Assistance

S. No.	*Block*	*Up to Rs. 1725*	*Rs. 1726-3500*	*Rs. 3501-4800*	*Rs. 4801-6400*	*Total*
1.	Bhiwani	10 (12.5)	52 (65.0)	14 (17.5)	04 (5.0)	80 (100)
2.	Badhara	08 (10.0)	37 (46.3)	33 (41.2)	02 (2.5)	80 (100)
3.	Loharu	07 (8.8)	40 (50.0)	29 (36.2)	04 (5.0)	80 (100)
	Total	25 (10.4)	129 (53.6)	76 (32.6)	10 (4.4)	240 (100)

Note : Percentages have been given in parentheses.

The data in Table 7.5 show that out of 240 selected Beneficiaries, 10.4 per cent belonged to the lowest income group.

However, more than half (53.6 per cent) of them belonged to the income group of Rs. 1726-3500. A significance number (32.6 per cent) of them were having an annual income between Rs. 3501-4800 and a very small number (4 per cent) of them belonged to the income group of Rs. 4801-6400. Thus, the instruction of the guidelines to assist the poorest of the poor first seems to have been adopted only in 10.4 per cent cases. More than four-fifths of the Beneficiaries were from the middle two income groups. However, income-wise distribution of the respondents varies from Block to Block. Our data in Table 6.5 reveals that more than four-fifths (82.5 per cent) of the respondents of Bhiwani Block were from the income group between Rs. 1726-3500 to Rs. 3501-4800. By and large the similar was the economic position of the respondents of Loharu Block.

Educational Status of Respondents

Education plays an important role in determining ones socio-economic status and his outlook towards life. An educated person would certainly be better informative. Hence, we wanted to know the educational status of our respondents. The information collected from the respondents about their educational qualification has been presented in codified from in Table 7.6.

Table 7.6
Educational Status of the Respondents

S. No.	*Blocks*	*Illiterate*	*Literate*	*Metric*	*Inter*	*Total*
1.	Bhiwani	39	27	11	3	80
		(48.7)	(33.8)	(13.8)	(3.7)	(100)
2.	Badhara	53	22	4	1	80
		(66.2)	(27.5)	(5.0)	(1.3)	(100)
3.	Loharu	51	24	3	2	80
		(63.8)	(30.0)	(3.7)	(2.5)	(100)
	Total	143	73	18	6	240
		(59.6)	(30.4)	(7.5)	(2.5)	(100)

Note : Percentages have been given in parentheses.

Our data in Table 7.6 indicates that a large number (59.6 per cent) of our respondents were found illiterate. Hardly about one-thirds (30.4 per cent) of them were just literate knowing only ABC of education. A very small number (7.5 per cent) of them were educated up to Matriculation. Interestingly only a few (2.5 per cent) of them were educated up to Intermediate. Thus, the educational status of most of the Beneficiaries in the sample is very poor which has been observed as a major cause for their poverty. Therefore, it is suggested that special attention needs to pay towards improving the educational standard of the BPL families in rural areas. Whereas among the Officials, forty per cent were educated up to Matriculation, fifteen per cent Intermediate and forty-five per cent Graduate and above. Majority of the Officials belong to the lowest strata of education.

Awareness of Respondents

Awareness of the target group families about the IRDP programme is very important. Unless the Beneficiaries understood the real spirit of the programme, one cannot expect their full involvement and participation in the programme. In the absence of knowledge, generally the beneficiaries feel more concerned with subsidy without bothering about the viability of the scheme opted. Therefore, it is essential that proper awareness about the programme is created amongst the Beneficiaries by the Extension staff and also its long term benefits be made known to them.

Under IRDP scheme the job of awareness of the Beneficiaries has been entrusted to the concerned APO and the Gram Sachiv. These Officials are supposed to explain the programme and its benefits in detail to the prospective Beneficiaries so that they could actively participate in the programme. It has been observed time and again that the Gram Sachiv hardly bothers to educate the people about the benefits of the programme. The APO has no time for this purpose as he has to see two or three Blocks besides a lot of work at the Head Quarters. Lack of interest toward programme is also one of the major reasons for majority of DRDA functionaries who are supposed to educate the Beneficiaries. The village panchayats are also supposed to enlighten the masses about the likely benefits from the IRDP programme. The data on the role of Gram Sachiv, IRDP staff (Assistant Project Officer) and Panchayats in information dissemination to the Beneficiaries have been presented in Table 7.7.

The data in Table 7.7 show that about three-fourths (72.5 per cent) of the respondents came to know about the programme through Assistant Project officer and fifteen (15.0 per cent) of them came to know about the programme through Gram Panchayat. A small number of them have reported that Gram Sachiv and fellow villagers informed them about the programme. On the basis of the above analysis we are inclined to conclude that the Extension activities were not found satisfactory and needed to intensify and improve upon them. Hence seems there a great need to post more specific Extension staff for educating the people about the programme and its future benefits. The present Gram Sachiv and the Assistant Project Officer need some activism so that the rural people can take the maximum benefits of the programme under the IRDP.

Table 7.7

Role of Various Functionaries in Information Dissemination

S. No.	*Block*	*Gram Sachiv*	*APO*	*Gram Panchayat*	*Fellow Villagers*	*Total*
1.	Bhiwani	05	58	11	06	80
		(6.3)	(72.5)	(13.7)	(7.5)	(100)
2.	Bhadara	06	60	10	04	80
		(7.5)	(75.0)	(12.5)	(5.0)	(100)
3.	Loharu	06	56	15	03	80
		(7.5)	(70.0)	(18.8)	(3.7)	(100)
	Total	17	174	36	13	240
		(7.1)	(72.5)	(15.0)	(5.4)	(100)

Note : Percentages have been given in parentheses.

Selection Procedure of Beneficiaries

As the process of development has not much benefited a large section of rural population. As a result the Government had to initiate special target group programmes for these sections and thus IRDP is the most important step undertaken in this direction. The general feeling among the people was that most of the benefits from the rural development programmes have gone to the richer section of rural society. It was also admitted by the late Prime Minister Rajiv Gandhi. To ensure that the benefits of IRDP should reach to the target groups, their proper identification is highly essential. For proper identification of Beneficiaries, it is important that the BPL list be prepared honestly and sincerely. The BPL families are selected for IRDP activities through village survey which is recommended by the Gram Sabha. For selection of Beneficiaries under IRDP a camp is organized in each village by the DRDA with the help of local staff of various concerned departments and Gram Sabha where the prospective Beneficiaries are asked to fill up the application forms. We thought it worthwhile to collect the information on selection procedure adopted for the Beneficiaries. The information, thus, collected has been given in Table 7.8.

Table 7.8
Selection Procedure of Beneficiaries

S. No.	*Block*	*BPL List*	*Credit Camp*	*Both (a+b)*	*Another*	*Total*
1.	Bhiwani	—	—	80	0	80
				(100)	(0.0)	(100)
2.	Bhadara	—	—	80	0	80
				(100)	(0.0)	(100)
3.	Loharu	—	—	80	0	80
				(100)	(0.0)	(100)
	Total	—	—	240	0	240
		—	—	(100)	(0.0)	(100)

Note : Percentages have been given in parentheses.

Table 7.8 reveals that all the respondents were selected from BPL list and the loan application forms were filled up in credit camps organized at village level. The BPL lists were finalized after the recommendation of Gram Sabha. This indicates that Gram Sabhas were taking active part in the process of identification of Beneficiaries under IRDP. No single Beneficiary has been selected by any other mean except the above mentioned.

Processing of Loan Applications

After identification of the Beneficiaries, educating them about the programme and identifying productive activities for them, it is very important for smooth implementation of the programme that the loan applications should be processed quickly. Timely availability of financial assistance is an important factor helping the Beneficiary to acquire the right type of asset at the lowest price, particularly in case of seasonal activities. The delay in sanctioning of loan and grounding of the scheme has always burdened the Beneficiaries with undue sufferings. Therefore, to avoid any type of delay and to process the loan application quickly, survey camps is organized in the concerned village/s by the District Rural Development Agency which is attended by all the concerned Officials including Bank representatives so that the loan applications can be disbursed or handed over to the Bank Officials on the spot. However, in practice these applications are collected by the concerned Assistant Project Officer who dispatched them to the concerned Bank after completing all the formalities and this takes one to three months time.

The data regarding processing of loan applications for assistance both at DRDA and Banks levels and the difficulties faced by the Beneficiaries during the processing of their loan applications were collected from the sample respondents. These data in codified form have been presented in Tables 7.9, 7.10 and 7.11 respectively.

Time taken by DRDA in Processing of Loan Applications

The guidelines of IRDP directed to organize credit camps for speedy disposal of the loan applications of Beneficiaries to the Banks, so that the timely help can be provided to them. The data collected from the Beneficiaries regarding the time taken by the DRDA for processing their loan application forms have been included in Table 7.9.

Table 7.9

Time taken by DRDA in Processing of Loan Applications

S. No.	*Block*	*0-1 month*	*1-2 month*	*2-3 month*	*Total*
1.	Bhiwani	0	21	59	80
		(0.0)	(26.3)	(73.7)	(100)
2.	Bhadara	0	25	55	80
		(0.0)	(31.3)	(68.7)	(100)
3.	Loharu	0	23	57	80
		(0.0)	(28.8)	(71.2)	(100)
	Total	0	69	171	240
		(0.0)	(28.8)	(71.2)	(100)

Note : Percentages have been given in parentheses.

Our data in Table 7.9 indicate that the DRDA could not clear even a single loan application within the prescribed period. The time taken in more than one-fourth (28.8 per cent) cases was up to 1-2 months. However, in nearly three-fourths (71.2 per cent) cases the application forms were processed between 2-3 months. This shows the disposal of the cases were very slow and time consuming. After the clear-cut directions of Government of India to process promptly the loan applications of Beneficiaries, the DRDA is not able to fulfil the requirements of the guidelines and has not completed even a single case of the respondents within one month. It took 2-3 months time in processing of loan application of most of the Beneficiaries at the DRDA level itself.

Time Taken by Banks in Processing of Loan Applications

The Reserve Bank of India has directed all the concerned Banks to clear the loan applications of IRDP Beneficiaries within a fortnight after receiving them fro DRDA. To ascertain the factual position we asked out respondents about the time taken by the Banks for completing the formalities for final release of loan. Their replies in codified form have been presented in Table 7.10.

Table 7.10
Time Taken by Banks in Disbursement of Loan

S. No.	*Block*	*0-1 month*	*1-2 month*	*2-3 month*	*above 3 month*	*Total*
1.	Bhiwani	0 (0.0)	16 (20.0)	45 (56.3)	19 (23.7)	80 (100)
2.	Badhara	0 (0.0)	19 (23.7)	52 (65.0)	09 (01.3)	80 (100)
3.	Loharu	0 (0.0)	15 (18.7)	47 (58.8)	18 (22.5)	80 (100)
	Total	0 (0.0)	50 (20.8)	144 (60.0)	46 (19.2)	240 (100)

Note : Percentages have been given in parentheses.

Our data in Table 7.10 clearly suggest that the Banks could not clear even a single application for loan within the stipulated time period. The time taken by the Banks in sanctioning and disbursing the loans was found to be between 1-2 months in the cases of twenty-one per cent and between 2-3 months in case of sixty (60) per cent loaness. However, in a significant number (19.2 per cent) of cases the time taken by the Banks was found more than three months. Thus, the Banks have failed to comply with the guidelines of Reserve Bank of India. Regarding the delay in sanctioning the loan, on enquiry, most of Bank Officials told that the recovery position of IRDP loans is very poor. As a result the Banks have to appraise every application with care and caution. This naturally will take more time. However, Government has started Back-End-Subsidy system to check the problem of poor recovery of loans. Here we are inclined to conclude from the above analysis that the processing and disbursement of loans appear to be a time consuming process both at the Bank as well as District Rural Development Agency levels. It is, therefore, suggested that the loan applications should be processed promptly and needs to adhere the guidelines issued regarding this.

Problems in Getting Loans

The guidelines of IRDP clearly suggest that the Beneficiaries should not face any difficulty in getting loans. For this purpose credit camps are organized at the village/s level for filling up their loan applications and completing all the formalities on the spot so that the loan applications of the Beneficiaries can be processed promptly. In spite of these clearly guidelines the Beneficiaries have to face many difficulties in getting the loan under the scheme in time. To ascertain the fact regarding the difficulties, we asked our respondents whether they faced or not any difficulty in getting the loan. Their responses have been presented in codified form in Table 7.11.

It is clear from data in Table 7.11 that a very large number (70.0 per cent) of our respondents faced difficulties in obtaining their loans under IRDP. However, nearly one-third (30.0 per cent) of the did not face any difficulty in getting their loans. The reasons cited regarding difficulties were the large quantum of formalities attached with land and also the unhelpful attitudes of the concerned Officials. Some of the respondents told in private that many of the concerned Officials demanded bride. As a result in many cases the assets of the Beneficiaries were under estimated by the Officials. Thus the difficulties, many times are created by the bribery taker officials. Most of the Beneficiaries who had not faced any difficulty in getting the loan, pointed out that they had already paid or committed to pay the amount demanded by the Officials as a bribe at the time of the sanction of loan. Hence there was no problem of under-estimation of their assets for this group of Beneficiaries. This kind of adjustment between the concerned officials and Beneficiaries has been observed as one of the major reasons for misappropriation of assistance provided. Therefore, it is suggested that vigilance network needs to be further tightened and complaints regarding this should be heard by Additional Deputy Commissioner himself and strict action should be taken against the corrupt officials.

Table 7.11
Difficulties faced in Getting Loans by Beneficiaries

S. No.	*Block*	*Yes*	*No*	*Total*
1.	Bhiwani	59	21	80
		(73.7)	(26.3)	(100)
2.	Badhara	53	27	80
		(66.2)	(33.8)	(100)
3.	Loharu	56	24	80
		(70.0)	(20.0)	(100)
	Total	168	72	240
		(70.0)	(30.0)	(100)

Note : Percentages have been given in parentheses.

Identification of Productive Activities/Schemes

During the time of basic survey, the preference of Beneficiary towards the proposed economic activity is invariably obtained. This is done in order to know the intention and choice of the Beneficiary. However, the activities are finalized after ascertaining the resource potential and infra-structural facilities. The list of activities in a particular area is prepared by the Nodal Bank and approved by the Governing Body of DRDA. By and large the Beneficiaries receive the activities according to their choice. The choices/options are determined mainly by the perception of the Beneficiaries regarding the likely distribution of activities. Therefore, the Beneficiary's options depend upon what the programme provides. Another factor which seems to determine the preference of the Beneficiary is the amount of subsidy involved. Generally, the Beneficiaries opt for the activities in which subsidy component is relatively high. The information, thus, collected from the respondents regarding their choice of activities/schemes have been given in Table 7.12.

Table 7.12
Respondents Choice about the Scheme

S. No.	*Block*	*First Choice*	*Second Choice*	*No Choice*	*Total*
1.	Bhiwani	42 (52.5)	29 (36.2)	09 (11.9)	80 (100)
2.	Badhara	40 (50.0)	32 (40.0)	08 (10.0)	80 (100)
3.	Loharu	41 (51.2)	33 (41.3)	06 (7.5)	80 (100)
	Total	123 (51.2)	94 (39.2)	23 (9.6)	240 (100)

Note : Percentages have been given in parentheses.

Our data in Table 7.12 show that more than half (51.2 per cent) of our respondents succeeded in receiving the scheme of their first choice whereas more than one-third (39.2) per cent) of them could succeed in getting the schemes of their second choice. However, a very insignificant number (9.6 per cent) of them did not have any choice in getting the schemes/assets. Thus, it can be concluded by and large that most of our respondents could get the schemes/assets of their choice whether it may be of their second choice. Simultaneously, we can not undermine that significant part of respondents who reported poor choices about the assets. Hence more attention is required to enhance the opportunities for better choice.

Kind and Cost of Schemes

IRDP guidelines provides for financial assistance to the Beneficiaries in form of loan and subsidy to enable them to acquire the economic assets which generate additional income for the Beneficiaries over a period of time. The size and number of the schemes should be determined in relation to the income gap required to be covered to bring the family above the poverty line. The assets/projects are broadly classified into three categories viz; Primary, Secondary (ISB) and Tertiary. The Primary sector comprises mostly land based activities like animal husbandry, agriculture, forestry, irrigation etc. The Secondary sector consists of village industries, handicrafts and handlooms etc. and Tertiary sector comprises of supportive services required by Primary and Secondary sectors such as : mule/camel carts, donkey units, motor cycle with milk cane, rickshaw etc.

Kind of Schemes

The viability of a particular scheme depends upon various factors which include: location, availability of infrastructure support, interest shown by the Beneficiaries etc. The kind of schemes opted by the Beneficiaries have a direct correlation with these factors. Hence, these factors should be kept in mind while providing assistance to the Beneficiaries for schemes. Our respondents were asked questions about the kind of schemes they had received. The information thus, collected from them has been given in Table 7.13.

Table 7.13 elucidates that out of the total 240 respondents, forty per cent were assisted under Primary sector, 38.7 per cent under Secondary sector and 21.3 per cent under Tertiary sector. Milch cattle constitutes about 38.5 per cent of the total assets created under Primary sector followed by plough camel/bullocks i.e. 33.3 per cent. Thus these two schemes constituted about three-fourths of the total assets created in Primary sector. In the Secondary sector, 47.3 per cent of the Beneficiaries were assisted with the village industries, handicraft and handloom activities, followed by twenty-four per cent for kiryana shop and eighteen per cent for tailoring. The strength of Beneficiaries who have been assisted under various other activities in this sector was insignificant. The majority (47.1 per cent) of Beneficiaries in Tertiary sector were assisted for camel carts and mule carts. Thus most of the Beneficiaries got the schemes according to the local profile of the area.

Table 7.13
Sector-wise/Scheme-wise Classification of the Respondents

S. No.	Scheme	Bhiwani	Badhara	Loharu	Total
I.	Primary Sector				
1.	Milch Cattle	14	13	10	37 (38.5)
2.	P/Camel	08	11	13	32 (33.3)
3.	Sheep	06	05	06	17 (17.7)
4.	Others	04	01	05	10 (10.5)
	Sub Total	32 (40.0)	30 (37.5)	34 (42.5)	96 (40.0)
II.	ISB Sector				
1.	Vill. Ind.	13	16	15	44 (47.3)
2.	Kirana Shop	08	08	06	22 (23.7)
3.	Tailoring Shop	06	05	06	17 (18.3)
4.	Others	03	02	05	10 (10.7)
	Sub Total	30 (37.5)	31 (38.7)	32 (40.0)	93 (38.7)
III.	Tertiary Sector				
1.	Mule/Camel carts	12	07	05	24 (47.1)
2.	Donkey	02	03	04	09 (17.6)
3.	Others	04	09	05	18 (35.3)
	Sub Total	18 (22.5)	19 (23.8)	14 (17.5)	51 (21.2)
	Grand Total	80 (100)	80 (100)	80 (100)	240 (100)

Note : Percentages have been given in parentheses.

Unit Cost of Scheme

The unit cost has a direct correlation with the creation of assets. If it is not adequate, the chances of misutilization of assistance provided will be higher. Thus it is essential that the unit cost be revised at different intervals. The Government with consultation of Nodal Bank and NABARD revised the unit cost at different intervals. The data collected from respondent Beneficiaries regarding the per unit cost of the scheme/s have been presented in Table 7.14.

Our data in Table 7.14 reveal that the average cost of all schemes in Bhiwani Block worked out was Rs. 11,720, in Badhara Block Rs. 11,225, and in Loharu Block it was calculated Rs. 11,362.

Thus, Bhiwani Block has the highest average value of all the schemes under the IRDP programme followed by Loharu Block. However, the per unit cost in Badhara Block was found to be the lowest average values of all the schemes. As far as the sector-wise average value is concerned, ISB sector has ranked the highest average value of Rs. 12,937 followed by Primary sector which was of Rs. 11,458. However, it was found lowest in Tertiary sector consisting Rs. 8,666. The highest average value in Primary and Tertiary sectors was found in Bhiwani Block whereas in Badhara Block the highest average value was calculated in ISB sector.

Table 7.14
Unit Cost of the Scheme(s)

Blocks		*Bhiwani*		*Badhara*		*Loharu*	
S. No.	*Scheme*	*No. of Units*	*Average value*	*No. of Units*	*Average value*	*No. of Units*	*Average value*
I.	Primary Sector						
1.	Milch Cattle	18	14500/-	16	14900/-	20	14800/-
2.	Plough camel	10	5300/-	11	5400/-	13	5700/-
3.	Sheep/goats	06	12900/-	05	12700/-	06	12500/-
4.	Others	04	11700/-	01	11900/-	06	12100/-
	Total	38	11532/-	33	11309/-	45	11504/-
II.	Secondary Sector						
1.	Village Ind.	13	15300/-	16	15800/-	15	15600/-
2.	H. craft/H. loom	8	12700/-	08	12600/-	06	12900/-
3.	Shop (kirana)	06	8000/-	05	8300/-	06	8500/-
4.	Others	03	9600/-	02	9900/-	05	9700/-
	Total	30	12577/-	31	13384/-	32	12841/-
III.	Tertiary Sector						
1.	Camel/Mule	12	14300/-	07	14600/-	05	14670/-
2.	Donkey	02	3700/-	03	3900/-	04	3500/-
3.	Others	04	3500/-	09	3300/-	05	3600/-
	Total	18	10722/-	19	7558/-	14	7525/-
Grand Total		86	11272/-	83	11225/-	91	11362/-

Note : Percentage have been given in parentheses.

Adequacy of Assistance

The assistance provided has a direct bearing on the purchasing and operating parts of the assets. If it is sufficient, the chances of proper utilization of the assistance provided will be higher. We have asked our respondents whether the assistance i.e. loan and subsidy provided under IRDP is sufficient for the purpose, their replies in the codified form have been given in Table 7.15.

Our data in Table 7.15 clearly show that more than two-thirds (69.2 per cent) of the respondent Beneficiaries considered the assistance provided as sufficient for purchasing or creating the assets. However, about one-third (30.8 per cent) considered it insufficient to purchase or create a standard asset. As a result, in such cases they were forced to create/purchase substandard assets or had to adopt other short-cuts. The majority of respondents who had not actually created/purchased the assets were from the later category. Besides other reasons, they considered inadequacy of assistance as one of the major causes for misutilization of assistance.

Table 7.15
Adequacy of Assistance

S. No.	*Block*	*Yes*	*No*	*Total*
1.	Bhiwani	56	24	80
		(70.0)	(30.0)	(100)
2.	Badhara	57	23	80
		(71.3)	(28.7)	(100)
3.	Loharu	53	27	80
		(66.2)	(33.8)	(100)
	Total	166	74	240
		(69.2)	(30.8)	(100)

Note : Percentages have been given in parentheses.

Procurement of Assets

As per the guidelines of IRDP, the assets procured should be of standard quality, at economic prices and to the satisfaction of the Beneficiaries. DRDAs have been made responsible for making the assets available to the Beneficiaries. Generally two systems viz., purchase committee system and cash disbursement system are followed in procurement of assets under IRDP. Before 1991-92, in all the Blocks the assets were purchased by a Purchase Committee consisting of Assistant Project Officer, Veterinary Surgeon, Bank official, Gram Sachiv and representative of village Panchayat. However, this scheme could not be found satisfactory for the Beneficiaries. Under the scheme major benefit went to the traders or middleman. As a result the Government decided to introduce Cash Disbursement Scheme in half of the Blocks from 1991-92. In these Blocks, the Beneficiary could purchase the assets himself and was at liberty to purchase it from anywhere he/she liked. Though this system has been adopted to check the loopholes of the Purchase Committee system, it came under severe attack owing to certain odd difficulties. In most of the cases, it was found that the asset was actually not purchased. The data regarding the purchase of assets collected from our respondent Beneficiaries have been codified and given in Table 7.16.

Table 7.16

Whether the Asset Actually Created/Purchased

S. No.	*Block*	*Asset Created Purchased*	*Asset not Created*	*Total*
1.	Bhiwani	47	33	80
		(58.8)	(41.2)	(100)
2.	Badhara	65	15	80
		(81.2)	(19.8)	(100)
3.	Loharu	64	16	80
		(80.0)	(20.0)	(100)
	Total	176	64	240
		(73.3)	(26.7)	(100)

Note : Percentages have been given in parentheses.

Our data in Table 7.16 show that out of the total 240 respondent Beneficiaries about three-fourth (73.3 per cent) had actually created/ purchased the assets. Interesting more than one-fourth (26.7 per cent) did not create/purchase the assets. The reason may vary from Block to Block and Beneficiary to Beneficiary. The tendency not to create the assets and to grab the money with the consent of the officials was much higher (41.2 per cent) in Bhiwani Block as compared to Badhara and Loharu Blocks.

Further, we asked our respondents the reasons for not creating/purchasing the assets. Their replies in codified form have been presented in Table 7.17.

Data in Table 7.17 clearly indicate that out of the total 64 respondents who had not created/purchased the assets, one-fourth (25.0 per cent) were not interested in purchasing the assets. A significant number (42.2 per cent) of them found the financial assistance inadequate for purchasing the assets. Interestingly about one-third (32.8 per cent) of them bribed the concerned Officials and misutilized the money provided in form of assistance for purchasing the assets. Bhiwani Block topped in the case of misutilization of funds provided under IRDP for creating assets. In Badhara Block more than half of them reported the inadequacy of assistance as the main reason for not purchasing the assets followed by one-fourth as lack of interest. It was also observed that some of the Beneficiaries have nothing to do with assets. Their sole motto was to gobble up the subsidy provided under the programme. However, in Loharu Block majority of the Beneficiaries considered the inadequacy of the assistance as the main reason for not purchasing/creating the assets.

Table 7.17
Reasons for not Purchasing/Creating the Assets

S. No.	*Block*	*Lack of Interest*	*Assistance was inadequate*	*Consultanance with officials*	*Total*
1.	Bhiwani	07 (21.2)	12 (36.4)	14 (46.4)	33 (100)
2.	Badhara	04 (26.7)	08 (53.4)	03 (20.0)	15 (100)
3.	Loharu	05 (31.3)	07 (43.7)	04 (25.0)	16 (100)
	Total	16 (25.0)	27 (42.2)	21 (32.8)	64 (100)

Note : Percentages have been given in parentheses.

Quality of Schemes/Assets

As per the guidelines of Government of India, the Beneficiary has to be provided a good quality of scheme/asset either through the Purchasing Committee or it is purchased by the Beneficiary himself. The survival of the schemes/assets will depend on its quality. The respondents were asked the quality of scheme/assets provided to them/purchased by them. Their replies in the tabulated form have been given in Table 7.18.

The data in Table 7.18 reveal that out of the total 176 respondents who had actually created/purchased the assets, 56.8 per cent of them replied that the assets given to them or purchased by them were of good quality. However nearly one-third (31.3 per cent) of them reported that the assets were of average quality and 11.9 per cent of them found the assets of poor quality. In Bhiwani Block about two-thirds (63.1 per cent) of the respondents considered the assets as of good quality. Similar was the situation in Loharu and Badhara Blocks were more than half of the beneficiaries considered the assets of good quality. On the contrary, a significant number of the beneficiaries were not satisfied with the quality of their assets and reported underestimation of unit cost and escalation of prices as the major reasons for this.

Table 7.18
Quality of Schemes/Assets

S. No.	*Block*	*Good*	*Average*	*Poor*	*Total*
1.	Bhiwani	30	12	05	47
		(63.1)	(25.5)	(10.4)	(100)
2.	Badhara	37	21	07	65
		(56.0)	(32.3)	(10.7)	(100)
3.	Loharu	33	22	09	64
		(51.6)	(34.4)	(14.8)	(100)
	Total	100	55	21	176
		(56.8)	(31.3)	(11.9)	(100)

Note : Percentages have been given in parentheses.

Present Status of the Scheme

Status of the assets is a significant indicator showing the viability of the units provided under different schemes. The success or failure of schemes depends on the effective life span of the asset provided under the scheme and its capacity to provide a regular income to the Beneficiaries. To assess the actual position of the assets purchased or provided for income generating activities, our respondent Beneficiaries were asked about the present status of the scheme. Their replies in codified form have been presented in Table 7.19.

It can be seen from the data in Table 7.19 that total 260 assets were provided to the sample respondents. Out of these, about one-third (30.4 per cent) were found intact, 34.6 per cent of them were sold and an equal number (35.0 per cent) of them were either perished fully or partly. The percentage of assets intact was found maximum (33.7 per cent) in Badhara Block and was found minimum (27.9 per cent) in Bhiwani Block. The respondents reported that in case of milch cattle the Beneficiary was compelled to sell the animal whenever it went dry and stopped generating enough income. In the remaining thirty-five per cent cases the reasons stated were unexpected contingencies, diseases, lack of enough income generations, costly maintenance and in some cases defective assets. Thus, as a result of inadequate infrastructural support many of the Beneficiaries could not maintain their assets provided to them for income generation under the IRDP. However, in some cases the role of the Beneficiaries in putting the assets into operation has been observed dubious.

Table 7.19
Present Status of the Scheme

S. No.	*Block*	*Total No. of Assets Supplied*	*Intact*	*Sold*	*Fully/ Partly perished*
1.	Bhiwani	86	24	28	34
		(100)	(27.9)	(32.6)	(39.5)
2.	Badhara	83	28	32	23
		(100)	(33.7)	(38.6)	(27.7)
3.	Loharu	91	27	30	34
		(100)	(29.6)	(33.0)	(37.4)
	Total	260	79	90	91
		(100)	(30.4)	(34.6)	(35.0)

Note : Percentages have been given in parentheses.

Supplementary Assistance

The main goal of IRDP was to enable the selected families living below the poverty line in rural areas to cross it. This involves not only a small help, but sufficient assistance capable of bringing the poor above the poverty line. The resource potential of the target group is so poor that a single economic activity may be sufficient to generate enough income to bring that family above the poverty line. Therefore, supplementary assistance in terms of two or more activities was considered essential under the guidelines of IRDP. In this connection our respondents were asked about the extent of supplementary assistance provided to them. Their replies in the codified form have been presented in Table 7.20.

The data in Table 7.20 show that more than half (56.7 per cent) of the respondents were given assistance only for a single activity. However, more than one-third (37.9 per cent) of them were given the assistance for two activities. Only a very few (5.4 per cent) of them were provided the assistance for multiple activities under IRDP. As the majority of respondent Beneficiaries were provided assistance for single activity, it is essential to increase the assistance to a large number of Beneficiaries for multiple activities so that they can get supplementary assistance from various sources and raise their family income.

Table 7.20
Supplementary Assistance

S. No.	*Block*	*Single Activity*	*Double Activities*	*Multiple Activities*	*Total*
1.	Bhiwani	45	32	03	80
		(56.3)	(40.0)	(3.7)	(100)
2.	Badhara	43	31	06	80
		(53.8)	(38.7)	(7.5)	(100)
3.	Loharu	48	28	04	80
		(60.0)	(35.0)	(5.0)	(100)
	Total	136	91	13	240
		(56.7)	(37.9)	(5.4)	(100)

Note : Percentages have been given in parentheses.

Economic Position of the Beneficiary After Assistance

As we have already stated that the main objective of IRDP is to help the below poverty line families of rural areas to generate enough income from the assets provided. For generating sufficient income, it is essential to extract the asset to the optimum level and all this is determined to a larger extent by the availability of infrastructural support and the intention of Beneficiary towards the operation of the asset. To what extent the Beneficiary was capable of putting the asset into income generating position, can be assessed by getting information about his economic position after putting the asset into operation. The information, thus obtained from the respondents has been given in Table 7.21.

Table 7.21
Improvement in Economic Position of Beneficiaries

S. No.	*Block*	*Significant*	*Marginal*	*A little*	*No diff.*	*Indebted*	*Total*
1.	Bhiwani	23	28	14	09	06	80
		(28.8)	(35.0)	(17.5)	(11.2)	(7.5)	(100)
2.	Badhara	17	32	20	08	03	80
		(21.2)	(40.0)	(25.0)	(10.0)	(3.8)	(100)
3.	Loharu	13	29	27	09	02	80
		(16.2)	(36.3)	(33.8)	(11.2)	(2.5)	(100)
	Total	53	89	610	26	11	240
		(22.1)	(37.1)	(25.4)	(10.8)	(4.6)	(100)

Note : Percentage have been given in parentheses.

Our data in Table 7.21 clearly reveal that 22.1 per cent of our respondents have made a significant improvement in their economic condition after the operation of the assets provided to them under IRDP. More than one-third (37.1 per cent) of them improved marginally whereas one-fourth (25.4 per cent) of them could achieve a little improvement in their economic position. However, a small number (10.8 per cent) of our respondents did not find any change in their economic condition after receiving assistance under IRDP. Interestingly, 4.6 per cent of them complained of indebtedness as they had consumed the money given to them under the scheme. It was observed that some of them had taken the loan of IRDP just to repay the money borrowed from local financers. Thus a significant part of the respondents admitted that their was no fruitful change in their economic position. Hence the monitoring process needs to be further strengthen besides the available infrastructural facilities.

Repayment of Loans

As stated earlier the main objectives of IRDP is to help BPL families to cross the poverty line by generating extra income from the assets provided. However, the Beneficiary has to repay the loan provided to him under IRDP. Favourable maintenance of an asset and economic viability of the assistance or success or failure of any scheme can be observed from the amount of overdues standing against the Beneficiaries. Regular and timely recovery of Bank loans is an important parameter to judge the success of a loan-based development programme, as recovery is closely dependent on adequate income generation. To ascertain about the extent of the repayment of loan, we asked our respondents, whether they were paying the loan according the guidelines of the IRDP. Their responses in the codified form have been presented in Table 7.22.

Table 7.22
Repayment of Loans

Sl.. No	*Block*	*Cleared the loan*	*Paying regularly*	*Wanted to clear, but not in position at present*	*Only few instalments have paid*	*Defaul-ter*	*Total*
1.	Bhiwani	20	36	08	10	06	80
		(25.0)	(45.0)	(10.0)	(12.5)	(7.5)	(100)
2.	Badhara	14	41	09	09	07	80
		(17.6)	(51.3)	(11.2)	(11.2)	(8.7)	(100)
3.	Loharu	16	35	07	15	07	80
		(20.0)	(43.8)	(8.7)	(18.8)	(8.7)	(100)
	Total	50	112	24	34	20	240
		(21.0)	(47.0)	(10.0)	(14.0)	(8.0)	(100)

Note : Percentages have been given in parentheses.

The data in Table 7.22 reveal that a sizeable number (21.0 per cent) of the Beneficiaries have cleared their loans in time. Forty-seven per cent of them are repaying their loan's instalments regularly. However, ten per cent of them wanted to clear it but were not in position at the moment to pay the instalments of the loan. Interestingly (14.0 per cent) of them could pay only few instalments of their loans. Only a very small number (8.0 per cent) of them could not pay even the single installment of their loans.

Thus, on the basis of the above analysis, we can conclude that a good number of Beneficiaries have utilized the loan for generating the regular income. Thus, the IRDP scheme for rural poor has come as a boon for them.

Officials-Beneficiaries Perceptions

Broadly speaking the term perception means the quality of understanding of an individual about an object. It is a significant variable particularly for development activities and ascertains one's preferences or choices. The success of a development programme depends to a great extent upon the various factors among which perception of the people who are involved in its implementation and the people for whom it is going to be implemented is a major one. The actions/involvement of the people concerned in a particular programme depend upon how they considered the utility and the effectiveness of the concerned programmes for the achievement of its goal. To ascertain the views of our respondents regarding the utility and effectiveness of IRDP for elimination of poverty, we asked them various questions about the administrative structure of IRDP, role of financial institutions, adequacy of assistance provided under IRDP, number of Beneficiaries who actually created assets, process of implementation, infrastructural facilities available, monitoring process, sector-wise performance of the programme, its purchasing system, number of families crossing the poverty line, views regarding its future and the general assessment of the programme have been described in this part. As the perception of respondent Beneficiaries as well as the Officials have been described simultaneously, in the following tables, so it is not possible to give Block-wise information about the Beneficiaries. Hence, the information collected from the respondent Beneficiaries and Officials concerned have been consolidated at district level and presented into codified form in the following tables.

Perception About Administrative Structure of IRDP

The type of administrative structure has a direct relation with the performance of the programme. The administrative structure does not function in isolation. The perception of persons working in it and that of people for whom it is created has an immediate effect on its performance. Their satisfaction will certainly increase its efficiency. The data collected from the respondents regarding their satisfaction of the administrative structure of IRDP, have been presented in Table 7.23.

Table 7.23
Perception About Administrative Structure

S. No.	*Perception*	*Officials*	*Beneficiaries*	*Total*
1.	Satisfactory	09 (45.0)	98 (40.8)	107 (41.2)
2.	Unsatisfactory	11 (55.0)	131 (54.6)	142 (54.6)
3.	DK/Uncertain	—	11 (4.6)	11 (4.2)
	Total	20 (100)	240 (100)	260 (100)

Note : Percentages have been given in parentheses.

Table 7.23 indicates that forty-five per cent of the officials and 40.8 per cent of the Beneficiaries were found satisfied with the administrative structure of IRDP. However, more than half (55.0 per cent) of the Officials and almost the same number of the Beneficiaries were not satisfied with the present administrative setup of IRDP. They wanted the establishment of Block level machinery of IRDP. Interestingly, both the Officials and Beneficiaries blamed each other for not responding according to the needs and requirements of the IRDP. However, most of the Officials found the low salary, poor working conditions, stress and overload of work as the major reasons of their dissatisfaction with the present administrative system of IRDP. Similarly, a majority of Beneficiaries found the non-cooperative attitude, lack of interest and non-availability of the Officials as the main reasons of their dissatisfaction with the present administrative structure of IRDP. Hence the larger part of the respondents was not satisfied with it and desired changes both at structural and functional levels. It has been observed that the approach of Officials on key posts in the administration as Director, Project Experts and Chief Executive Officers is very much ad hoc towards the programme which has a direct effect on the performance of the programme. Therefore, it is suggested to create Block level machinery of IRDP, strengthening the existing setup and raise the morale of the officials. The officials on key posts should be appointed for a definite period with fixed accountability. Change in their attitudes towards the programme and Beneficiaries is the need of the hour.

Perception about Financial Institutions

The financial institutions have an important role to play in the implementation of IRDP. They have direct dealings with the Beneficiaries as well as with those of the IRDP Officials. The sanctioning of loan to Beneficiaries and deciding the actual unit cost is the responsibility of the Officials of the concerned Bank. To ascertain the views of both the Officials and Beneficiaries regarding their difficulties in dealing with the financial institutions, they were asked whether they were satisfied in their dealing with financial institutions. Their replies in the codified form have been presented in Table 7.24.

Table 7.24
Perception about Financial Institution

S. No.	*Perception*	*Officials*	*Beneficiaries*	*Total*
1.	Satisfied	12 (60.0)	102 (42.5)	114 (43.8)
2.	Unsatisfied	06 (30.0)	113 (47.1)	119 (45.8)
3.	DK/U	02 (10.0)	25 (10.4)	27 (10.4)
	Total	20 (100)	240 (100)	260 (100)

Note : Percentages have been given in parentheses.

Our data in Table 7.24 suggest that sixty (60.0) per cent of the Officials were satisfied with performance of the financial institutions whereas 42.5 per cent of the Beneficiaries also perceived the functioning of these institutions as satisfactory. However, a large number (47.1 per cent) of the Beneficiaries were not satisfied with the dealings of financial institutions. Similarly about one-third (30.0 per cent) of the Officials of IRDP were not satisfied with the functioning of these institutions. Both the Officials and the Beneficiaries in our informal discussions told the involvement of Bank Officials in bribes while sanctioning the loan to the Beneficiaries. Some of the Beneficiaries reported about under estimation of their assets if they failed to pay the bribe to the concerned Bank Officials. About ten per cent of both the Officials and Beneficiaries were not sure about the functioning of the financial institutions. However, it can be suggested that the supervision of financial institutions needs to be further tightened and strict actions against corrupt officials should be taken.

Perception about the Assistance Provided

The assistance provided under IRDP has a direct concern with the creation of the assets. If it is inadequate, the chances of misutilization will be higher. Though the Government of India, Reserve Bank of India and NABARD are very cautious about the unit cost of the assets and to give more liberty to the programme implementing agencies, they have been given the right to escalate the unit cost up to twenty per cent. The proper utilization of assistance provided to the Beneficiaries depends to a large extent on its adequacy. Here an attempt has been made to know the views of respondent Beneficiaries as well as those of the Officials concerned about the assistance provided under IRDP. Their responses in codified form have been presented in Table 7.25.

It can be seen from the data in Table 7.25 that 80 per cent of the Officials considered the assistance as adequate. A large majority (69.2 per cent) of the Beneficiaries found the provided assistance as adequate. However, about one-fifth (20.0 per cent) of the Officials and nearly one-third (30.8 per cent) of the Beneficiaries found the provided assistance as inadequate. The reasons for inadequacy of assistance perceived by them were underestimation of unit cost, escalation in prices, low level of unit cost fixed by the Government etc. Besides, most of the Beneficiaries reported that they had to spend about one-fourth of total loan sanctioned on fulfilling various formalities or on paying visits to the DRDA or concerned Bank.

Table 7.25
Perception about the Assistance Provided

S. No.	Perception	Officials	Beneficiaries	Total
1.	Adequate	16 (80.0)	166 (69.2)	182 (70.0)
2.	Inadequate	04 (20.0)	74 (30.8)	78 (30.0)
	Total	20 (100)	240 (100)	260 (100)

Note : Percentages have been given in parentheses.

Perception about Creation of Assets by the Beneficiaries

The output of the programme had direct relation with the number of Beneficiaries who have created the assets. If the number of Beneficiaries who have created the assets is higher, the programme will be considered more successful. Hence we have tried to know the views of the respondent Beneficiaries as well as those of the Officials about the number of Beneficiaries who had created the assets. The information, thus, collected have been codified and given in Table 7.26.

Our data in Table 7.26 show that more than one-third (35.2 per cent) of the Officials found the creation of assets by most of the Beneficiaries. One-fourth (20.0 per cent) of them were of the view that all the Beneficiaries created the assets. However, the majority (40.0 per cent) of the Officials perceived that some of them have created the assets. About one-fifth (19.2) per cent) of the Beneficiaries were of the opinion that all of the Beneficiaries did create the assets. More than one-fourth (26.3 per cent) of them perceived the creation of assets by most of the Beneficiaries. However, large number (55.5 per cent) of Beneficiaries viewed that creation of assets by some of them. Thus our data do not suggest a positive picture of the assets really created by the Beneficiaries under IRDP. This indicates towards the existence of forgery in the programme. Hence the seriousness of matter requires special attention from the concerned authorities. Establishment of some what bigger processing units by the DRDA with the help of loan and subsidy provided to the Beneficiaries and then giving permanent employment to these Beneficiaries there, can be a better alternative.

Table 7.26
Perception about Beneficiaries Created Assets

S.No.	Beneficiaries Created assets	Officials	Beneficiaries	Total
1.	All of them	05 (25.0)	46 (19.2)	51 (19.6)
2.	Most of them	07 (35.0)	63 (26.3)	70 (26.9)
3.	Some of them	08 (40.0)	131 (55.5)	139 (53.5)
4.	None of them	0 (0.0)	0 (0.0)	0 (0.0)
	Total	20 (100)	240 (100)	260 (100)

Note : Percentages have been given in parentheses.

Perception Regarding Process of Implementation

The process of implementation has a direct bearing on the results of the programme. If it is sound, results of the programme will be better. Hence, it was thought proper to know the views of respondent Officials and Beneficiaries about the process of implementation of IRDP. The information, thus, collected from the respondents have been given in codified form in Table 7.27.

Our data in Table 7.27 show that ten per cent of the Officials were highly satisfied about the process of implementation of IRDP whereas majority (55.0 per cent) of them expressed only their satisfaction. However, a quite good number (35.0 per cent) of them were not satisfied with the present process of implementation of IRDP. Thus the majority of the Officials have a positive perception regarding the process of implementation of IRDP. On the other hand, among the Beneficiaries a marginal number (16.3 per cent) were found highly satisfied with the process of implementation of IRDP and a large number (40.0 per cent) were just satisfied with it. Interestingly, quite a good number (33.3 per cent) of them were not satisfied at all with the process of the implementation of IRDP and 10.4 per cent of them were found highly dissatisfied with its process of implementation. The reasons of the dissatisfaction of

Beneficiaries may include delay in processing of loan applications, low choice given in selection of schemes/assets, inadequacy of unit cost, poor infrastructural facilities, improper monitoring and rigid recovery system, delay in settling of claims etc. This information was gathered from the Beneficiaries through the informal discussions with them.

Table 7.27

Perception Regarding the Process of Implementation

S. No.	*Perception*	*Officials*	*Beneficiaries*	*Total*
1.	Highly Satisfied	02 (10.0)	39 (16.3)	41 (15.8)
2.	Satisfied	11 (55.0)	96 (40.0)	107 (41.2)
3.	Not Satisfied	07 (35.0)	80 (33.3)	87 (33.5)
4.	Highly Unsatisfied	00 (0.0)	25 (10.4)	25 (9.5)
	Total	20 (100)	240 (100)	260 (100)

Note : Percentages have been given in parentheses.

Perception about Availability of Infrastructural Facilities

The successful operation of a scheme is determined to a large extent by the availability of infrastructural support in that particular area. The availability of requisite input-output linkages like marketing, raw material, maintenance facilities etc. is essential for the potential output of the scheme/project created. The IRDP guidelines of Government of India envisages to spend ten per cent of the total project cost on creating infrastructural support facilities. Of course in District Bhiwani various such infrastructural facilities were created. However, at present most of these facilities require repairs as well as modifications. The respondents were asked about the availability of infrastructural facilities in their respective area. Their replies in codified form have been presented in Table 7.28.

Table 7.28
Perception about Availability of Infra-Structural Facilities

S. No.	*Activity*	*Officials*	*Beneficiaries*
1.	Input	13	132
		(65.0)	(55.0)
2.	Output	11	129
		(55.0)	(53.0)
3.	Repair	12	142
		(60.0)	(59.0)
	Total	20 (100)	240 (100)

Note : (i) Percentages have been given in parentheses.
(ii) Percentages do not add up to 100 because of over lapping responses.

The data presented in Table 7.28 show that a large number (65.0 per cent) of the Officials perceived enough availability of input facilities. The majority (55.0 per cent) of the Beneficiaries also found the enough input facilities for the IRDP. Similarly, a majority (55.0 per cent) of the Officials also were of the view that the output facilities available were sufficient whereas 53.0 per cent of the Beneficiaries were of the same view. As far as the repair/ maintenance facilities were concerned, 60.0 per cent of the Officials and about the same number (59.0 per cent) of the Beneficiaries were satisfied with the availability of the repair facilities. Thus, the majority of the respondents both Officials and Beneficiaries were satisfied with infrastructural facilities available at present under the IRDP scheme.

Monitoring

It is an integrated process consisting of following-up, monitoring, and evaluative activities. For ensuring that IRDP Beneficiary crossed the poverty line, it is not sufficient to provide him assets through subsidy and loan. The progress of the management of his assets for generation of incremental income has to be continuously followed, monitored and evaluated. These factors play a key role in determining the effective operations or maintenance of the assets and their productivity. As the

Beneficiaries are not only weak in economic terms but also in respect of skills and abilities, needed for maintenance and management of assets provided under the programme and therefore, need a continuous support and guidance to ensure maximum output. This system has been provided in IRDP guidelines.

The follow-up of the schemes given to the Beneficiaries has to be made by DRDA (APO concerned), Bank Officials, Gram Sachiv etc. These Officials are responsible for constant evaluation of the proper management of the scheme given to Beneficiaries under the IRDP so that their income continue to be generated. All efforts are made to remove difficulties the Beneficiaries faced during the implementation of the scheme provided to them. An annual physical verification of assets is also to be undertaken on a campaign basis at the end of every year. However, it has been observed that in many cases, it has been confined to the paper work.

By and large-monitoring is done through the mechanism of periodical Reports and Returns. The performance of implementation of IRDP is to be monitored continuously at various levels. At the Block and District levels this is done through reports and physical verification of the assets. At the State and Central levels, the programme is continuously monitored on the basis of telegraphic reports, monthly key indicator reports, annual progress reports etc. Besides, qualitative Monitoring of IRDP at Block and District levels is done through field visits and physical verification of assets by the key official-Chairman of DRDA, Chief Executive Officer of DRDA, Assistant Project Officer (Monitoring), Sub Divisional Magistrate, Block Development Officers etc. The respondents were asked regarding their satisfaction about the follow-up and monitoring process. The responses of those who considered it satisfactory, have been present in Table 7.29.

Table 7.29 shows that two-thirds (65.0 per cent) of the Officials were satisfied with follow-up activities whereas the same opinion is expressed by half (51 per cent) of the Beneficiaries. But in practice, it has been observed that the condition was rather sad. In most of the cases Vikas Patrikas were not found to be given to the Beneficiaries. In few cases where it was given, no information except the initial entries were recorded. The reasons for the non-intact of the assets is largely due to lack of supervision and proper follow-up. As far as the qualitative monitoring is concerned three-fourths of the Officials and less than half of the Beneficiaries were satisfied with it. It has been observed that in most of the cases the qualitative monitoring has been confined to paper work. Therefore, it is the need of the hour that the monitoring process should be updated by ensuring regular field visits through State, DRDA and Block Officials.

Table 7.29
Perception about Monitoring Process

S. No.	*Perception*	*Officials*	*Beneficiaries*	*Total*
1.	Follow-up	13 (65.0)	132 (51.0)	135 (51.9)
2.	Qualitative Monitoring	15 (75.0)	113 (47.0)	128 (49.2)
	Total	20 (100)	240 (100)	260 (100)

Note : (i) Percentages have been given in parentheses.
(ii) Percentages do not add up to 100 because of over lapping responses.

The Government of India, Ministry of Rural Development carries out concurrent evaluation of IRDP through the reputed Institutions and organizations in the state on regular basis. The findings are analyzed and the research results shared with State Governments for suitable follow-up action. In Haryana, there is not special institution on the pattern of NIRD at Central level, to investigate, analyze and evaluate the data exclusively. HIRD, Nilokheri has performed a very limited role in this direction. As per provisions in the programme guidelines, the State Government may get evaluation studies conducted through the reputed institutions and organizations on the areas of the programme thrown up by the concurrent evaluation as meriting detailed studies. No such study was ever conducted in Bhiwani District.

Perception about Sector-wise Performance of the Programme

The results of the various activities provided under IRDP are not the same in all the sectors. It varies from sector to sector. It is generally assumed that the Primary sector has maximum forgery cases as compared to ISB and Tertiary sectors. The views of Officials and Beneficiaries about the success of the programme in various sectors have been taken through asking questions. Their views in codified from regarding the success of programme under various sectors have been presented in Table 7.30.

Table 7.30
Perception about Sector-wise Performance of the Programme

S. No.	*Sectors*	*Officials*	*Beneficiaries*	*Total*
1.	Primary	05 (25.0)	86 (35.8)	91 (35.0)
2.	ISB	09 (45.0)	73 (30.4)	82 (31.5)
3.	Tertiary	06 (30.0)	81 (33.8)	87 (33.5)
	Total	20 (100)	240 (100)	260 (100)

Note : Percentages have been given in parentheses.

It can be revealed from the data in Table 7.30 that nearly half (45.0 per cent) of the Officials considered that IRDP is more successful in ISB sector whereas thirty (30.0) per cent of them found the programme higher in Tertiary sector. Only one-fourth (25.0 per cent) of them found the success of the programme better in Primary sector. On the other hand, more than one-third (35.8 per cent) of the Beneficiaries viewed the success of the programme better in Primary sector. A good number (30.4 per cent) of them also perceived the success of the programme higher in ISB sector. A slightly more than this number (33.8 per cent) of them said the success of the programme much better under Tertiary sector. Thus by and large the success of the programme was judged by both the Officials and Beneficiaries equal in all the sectors. However, in practice, the programme has been observed more successful in ISB and Tertiary sectors. On the contrary, the animal husbandry sector has shown maximum forgery. In this sector, in most of the cases either the animal was not purchased otherwise sold after some time. Therefore, more precautions are required while assisting under this sector.

Perception Regarding the Modes of Purchasing the Assets

Before 1991, it was the responsibility of the Government to provide the Beneficiaries assets of productive and standard quality at economic prices. For the purpose the Government has constituted Purchase Committees in each DRDA. Later on, it as realized that due to interference of middleman, the Beneficiaries were forced to purchase the assets at inflated rates. Hence, the Government of India decided to give the Beneficiaries more liberty regarding the purchase of assets. As a result Cash Disbursement Scheme of loans was introduced in 1991 and was extended to fifty per cent of the Blocks in each District. At present both the systems of purchasing assets are in operation. Regarding the success of the modes of purchasing assets, we asked both the Officials and Beneficiaries to express their views on both the systems of purchasing assets. Their replies in the codified form have been given in Table 7.31.

Table 7.31
Perception about the Modes of Purchasing Assets

S. No.	*Suitability System*	*Officials*	*Beneficiaries*	*Total*
1.	Cash System	05 (25.0)	70 (29.2)	75 (28.8)
2.	Purchase committee	04 (20.0)	60 (25.0)	64 (24.6)
3.	Both	11 (55.0)	110 (44.8)	121 (46.6)
4.	None	—	—	—
	Total	20 (100)	240 (100)	260 (100)

Note : Percentages have been given in parentheses.

Our data clearly indicate in Table 7.31 that majority of both the Officials (50.0 per cent) and Beneficiaries (44.8 per cent) found the operations of both the modes of purchasing assets as successful in their respective areas. However, by and large an equal number of both the Officials (25.0 per cent) and the Beneficiaries (29.2 per cent) favoured the cash system as compared to the system of purchase committee for purchasing the assets. Thus on the basis of the above analysis we can say that both the modes/systems of purchasing the assets seem to be favoured by the Beneficiaries and the concerned Officials. However, in individual cases majority of the respondents were in favour of cash system as compared to purchase committee system. The tendency of misappropriation was observed higher in cash system rather than the purchase committee system.

Perception About Crossing of Poverty Line by the Beneficiaries

If we have to take an objective view about the results of IRDP or its success we have to ascertain how many of the Beneficiaries have succeeded in crossing the poverty line under the programme. There is a direct link between the number of Beneficiaries crossed the poverty line and the success of IRDP. To ascertain the views of both the Beneficiaries and Officials they were asked whether all the Beneficiaries have crossed the poverty line with the assistance under IRDP. Their responses in the codified form have been presented in Table 7.32.

Table 7.32
Perception About Crossing of Poverty Line by the Beneficiaries

S. No.	*No. of Beneficiaries*	*Officials*	*Beneficiaries*	*Total*
1.	All of them	03 (15.0)	26 (10.8)	29 (11.2)
2.	Many of them	04 (20.0)	53 (22.8)	57 (21.9)
3.	Some of them	13 (65.0)	161 (67.1)	174 (66.9)
4.	None of them	—	—	—
	Total	20 (100)	240 (100)	260 (100)

Note : Percentages have been given in parentheses.

Our data in Table 7.32 show a very large number (65.0 per cent) of the Officials perceived that some of the assisted Beneficiaries did cross the poverty line whereas one-fifth (20.0 per cent) of them felt that many of the Beneficiaries have crossed the poverty line under the scheme. However, a small number (15.0 per cent) of them thought all of the Beneficiaries assisted under IRDP had crossed the poverty line. Interestingly, about the same number (67.1 per cent) of the Beneficiaries felt that some of the Beneficiaries have crossed the poverty line. A sizable number (22.8 per cent) of them felt that many of the Beneficiaries had crossed the poverty line. However, a very insignificant number (10.8 per cent) of Beneficiaries thought that all of them crossed the poverty line. Thus, from our data, we can conclude that in the eyes of both the Officials and Beneficiaries under the IRDP many of the chosen Beneficiaries have succeeded in crossing the poverty line. This indicates towards the positive impact of programme over the target groups.

Perception Regarding Continuity of IRDP

IRDP is a poverty alleviation and employment generation programme which is in operation since 1978-79. As the programme is widely published, it has become very significant to assess the impact of the programme so that its future course of action can be decided. The continuity of the programme will be decided to a larger extent by its impact. To assess the future course of the programme, we have asked our respondents whether the programme should continue. The responses of the Officials and Beneficiaries thus collected, have been given in Table 7.33.

Table 7.33
Perception Regarding Continuity of IRDP

S. No.	*Perception*	*Officials*	*Beneficiaries*	*Total*
1.	Be continued	11	169	180
		(55.0)	(70.4)	(69.2)
2.	Be stopped	00	11	11
		(0.0)	(4.6)	(4.2)
3.	Be continued	08	43	51
	with changes	(40.0)	(17.9)	(19.6)
4.	DK/Uncertain	01	17	18
		(5.0)	(7.1)	(7.0)
	Total	20	240	260
		(100)	(100)	(100)

Note : Percentages have been given in parentheses.

Our data in Table 7.33 clearly indicate that a majority of Officials (55.0 per cent) and a large number (70.4 per cent) of the Beneficiaries wanted the continuation of the IRDP in the present form. However, a sizable number (40.0 per cent) of the Officials and a very small number (17.9 per cent) of the Beneficiaries were also in favour of the continuation of IRDP, of course, with certain changes. Only a very insignificant number (4.6 per cent) of the Beneficiaries wanted the complete discontinuation of the IRDP.

Thus on the basis of the above analysis, we are inclined to conclude that the IRDP has certainly benefited the rural poor and therefore, generally both the Officials and Beneficiaries wanted its continuation.

Perception Regarding the Overall Assessment of IRDP

The perception of the Officials concerned and that of the Beneficiaries about the overall assessment of the programme can be an important indicator to give an appropriate idea regarding the success or failure of that particular programme and it will help us a lot to decide the future course of that programme. Hence an attempt has been made to know their views about the overall performance of the programme. The information thus, collected from our respondents regarding it, has been presented in codified form in Table 7.34.

Table 7.34
Perception Regarding the Overall Assessment of IRDP

S. No.	*Perception*	*Officials*	*Beneficiaries*	*Total*
1.	Fully successful	13 (65.0)	138 (57.5)	151 (58.1)
2.	To some extent successful	07 (35.0)	81 (33.8)	88 (33.8)
3.	Failure	00 (0.0)	21 (8.,7)	21 (8.1)
4.	DK/U	00 (0.0)	00 (0.0)	00 (0.0)
	Total	20 (100)	240 (100)	260 (100)

Note : Percentages have been given in parentheses.

Table 7.34 reveals that a large number (65.0 per cent) of Officials and more than half (57.5 per cent) of the Beneficiaries considered the IRDP scheme as fully successful in achieving its goal. However, more than one-third (35.0 per cent) of the Officials and 33.8 per cent of the Beneficiaries thought that the IRDP programme was found to be successful to some extent in achieving its objectives. A very in significant number (8.7 per cent) of the Beneficiaries viewed the IRDP as a total failure in its goal achievement. However, an overwhelming majority of both the Officials and the Beneficiaries found the IRDP either fully or partially successful in the achievement of its goal. Therefore, they have admitted its impact on rural scenario even after the prevailing of some lacuna in the programme.

Officials-Beneficiaries Perception about Each Other

In this part, the perception of the Officials and Beneficiaries towards each-other has been discussed. The perception about each other have direct link with the performance of the programme. If one has good perception about the other, then it will be easy to create an environment of cooperation, mutual understanding which is very much essential for the achievement of the goal of the programme.

Beneficiaries Perception about Officials

An attempt has been made to know the perception of Beneficiaries about the IRDP Officials. Because it will help us to assess the style of functioning of the Officials, their orientation towards their duty and the role played by them for the success of the programme. The Beneficiaries were asked whether the Officials were cooperative and helpful in solving their problems at various stages of the IRDP. Their responses in the codified format have been presented in Table 7.35.

The data in Table 7.35 show that more than half (51.3 per cent) of the Beneficiaries perceived the Officials taking interest in their work. However, an equally significant number 48.7 per cent) of them found the Officials non-interested in their work. Interestingly more than two-thirds (78.8 per cent) of the Beneficiaries perceived the Officials as only concerned about their salaries and a large majority (65.0 per cent) of them believed that the Officials were concerned only about the fulfilment of targets on paper. However, more than one-third (35.0 per cent) of them did not agree with the view that the Officials were only interested in the fulfilment of targets on paper. Interestingly enough, an overwhelming number (82.0 per cent) of the Beneficiaries found the development Officials as arrogant and non-cooperative. This perception of the rural people about the development officials seem to be highly undemocratic and anti-development. This thought of the people regarding the Officials attitude has to be changed by the Officials. The development Officials are required to change their bureaucratic orientation and their style of functioning. It is further suggested that periodic training and workshops to upgrade the skills of the Officials at various levels should be arranged as the existing facilities in the State are not up to the required level.

Table 7.35
Beneficiaries Perception About Officials

S. No.	*Perception*	*Yes*	*No*
1.	Take interest in their work	123 (51.3)	117 (48.7)
2.	Concerned about their salaries	189 (78.8)	51 (21.2)
3.	Interested just to fulfil targets	156 (65.0)	84 (35.0)
4.	Arrogant and non-cooperative	197 (82.0)	43 (18.0)

Note : (i) Percentages have been given in parentheses.
(ii) Percentages do not add up to 100 because of overlapping responses.

Officials Perception about the Beneficiaries

It is not possible for the Government at its own to eradicate poverty. It can only help the Beneficiaries to create some income generating assets and get rid of the evil of poverty by generating extra income. The actual output of this type of development schemes depend to a significant level upon the sincerity of the Beneficiaries. To get a balanced opinion and objective assessment of the perception of Officials as well as the Beneficiaries towards each other, we thought it proper to ascertain the views of Officials about the Beneficiaries of IRDP. The Officials were asked whether the

Beneficiaries take interest in various activities particularly in purchasing the assets and putting them in operation. Their responses regarding the interest taken by the Beneficiaries have been presented in the codified format in Table 7.36.

Table 7.36
Officials Perception about Beneficiaries

S. No.	*Perception*	*Creating assets*	*Putting them In operation*
1.	Take much interest	4 (20.0)	3 (15.0)
2.	Take interest to some extent	10 (50.0)	12 (60.0)
3.	Take little interest	6 (30.0)	5 (25.0)
	Total	20 (100)	20 (100)

Note : Percentages have been given in parentheses.

It can be seen from data in Table 7.36 that twenty per cent of the Officials considered that the Beneficiaries take much interest in creating the assets. Half of them (50.0 per cent) were of the view that the interest taken by the Beneficiaries for purchasing the assets was to some extent. Whereas about one-third (20.0 per cent) of the officials perceived that the Beneficiaries were taking little interest in creating the assets. They just wanted to get the financial assistance by hook or crook. On the other hand, a small number (15.0 per cent) of the Officials were of the opinion that the Beneficiaries were taking much interest in operating the assets. Majority of them (60.0 per cent) observed it to some extent and one-fourth (25.0 per cent) perceived that the interest taken by the Beneficiaries in operating the assets was little. Hence we are inclined to conclude that majority of the Officials were of the view that the interest taken by the Beneficiaries in creating and operating the asset was little to some extent. They further reported that the lack of sincerity among the Beneficiaries in operating the assets has been observed as one of the major reasons of low income generation which later on leads to the misappropriation or decay of assets. Little spirit of work and non cooperative attitudes of the

Beneficiaries have also been reported. Thus the overall perception of the Officials about Beneficiaries is not appreciable and requires some dramatic changes.

However, in reality the position of the Beneficiaries after taking assistance under IRDP has not changed dramatically. It has been observed that most of the Beneficiaries are still not in a position to fulfil their basic requirements. They are living in destitute, unhygienic and rather poor conditions. Their family size are comparatively enlarged to their earnings. Majority of them are illiterate and ignorant. Lack of spirit of work can be observed in these families. Most of them have no future planning and are mingled with their presents needs. Among the families who have crossed the poverty line, majority are those in which some member of that family has got government service. There is a mixed opinion about the programme in the public. However, some of the public opinion leaders considered it as a successful, pragmatic and result oriented programme with specific impacts on rural scenario whereas the others did not perceive it as a successful programme and pointed out various lacuna in this programme.

Briefly we may conclude that of the selected Beneficiaries sixty per cent were males and forty per cent were females, whereas the strength of the females among Officials was twenty per cent. About forty-six per cent of the Beneficiaries were scheduled castes and less than four per cent were from physically handicapped. However among the Officials more than half were from scheduled castes. Half of the Beneficiaries have 6-8 members and one-third have more than 8 members in their families. Thus most of the Beneficiaries have enlarged families against the target of 5 members used in deciding the BPL families list. Hence needs to awaken these families about various causes of their poverty and to strengthen further the Family Welfare Programmes for them. On the contrary, the size of families of Officials by and large were small. The marginal farmers and agricultural labourers constitute about eighty three per cent of the total respondent Beneficiaries. The strength of rural artisans was insignificant. About eighty-six per cent of the respondent Beneficiaries belonged to the middle two strata of income and only ten per cent were from the lower most strata. This shows that the position of the BPL families in the state was not acute and the reasons might be good infrastructural support and sufficient opportunities for labour and wages available. Among the Officials more than two-thirds were from Class III and IV and sixty per cent of them were exclusively dependent on their salary. Three-fifths of our Beneficiaries were illiterate and about one-third were literate with educational qualification up to elementary level. Majority of the Officials were also from the lower standard of education. In about three-fourths (72.5 per cent) of the cases, the source of information dissemination was the concerned Assistant Project Officer (APO). The role of gram panchayats and other village level workers was not satisfactory whose active involvement in rural development programme is highly desired for. Hence the extension services needs to be further strengthened. All the respondent Beneficiaries were selected for assistance from BPL list and their loan application forms were filled up in credit camps. The time taken in processing of their loan applications at DRDA level was 2 to 3 months in more than two-thirds (71.2 per cent) of the cases. Not even a single loan application was reported to be cleared within one month whereas the time taken in disbursement of loan was observed up to three months and above in seventy-nine per cent of the cases. Thus the programme implementing agencies have failed to comply with the directions of government of India, Reserve Bank of India and National Bank for Agriculture and Rural Development. The reasons reported have been technical and documental problems which have to be fulfilled by the concerned Officials. Therefore, it can be concluded from the above observations that processing and disbursement of loan application is a time consuming process. Seventy per cent of the Beneficiaries had to face difficulties in one form or the other in getting their scheme sanctioned. Majority of them have reported to bribe the Bank Officials for it. Otherwise their schemes were either underestimated or not cleared for loans. Half of the respondents reported that they got the schemes of their first choice whereas thirty-nine per cent considered it as their second choice. Thus it can be concluded that the majority of the Beneficiaries were satisfied with their schemes. Majority of them were assisted under Primary sector (40 per cent), followed by ISB (39 per cent) and Tertiary (21 per cent) sectors. Milch cattle and plough camels constitute the major part of the activities under Primary sector. More than two-thirds (69.2 per cent) of the Beneficiaries considered the assistance provided as adequate to establish the assets whereas about one-third (30.8 per cent) considered it as inadequate and further reported that they were either forced to purchase a substandard asset or to go away with the assistance provided to meet their other domestic requirements. About three-fourths (73.3 per cent) of them have actually created the assets and the remaining who did not do so, reported the inadequacy of assistance as the major cause for it, followed by adjustment with concerned officials and lack of interest. The tendency of forgery was maximum in Cash Block (Bhiwani) almost doubled to Purchase Committee Blocks (Badhara and Loharu).

As far as the quality of the assets provided is concerned, fifty-seven per cent of the Beneficiaries considered it good, thirty-one per cent as average and twelve per cent as poor. Beneficiaries 176, who actually created the assets, were provided 260 assets of which thirty per cent were intact, thirty-five per cent were sold and the same number perished fully or partially. The reasons for the last two positions were reported as urgent need to money, unnatural climates, low income generation and costly maintenance. Lack of sincere monitoring has been observed as one of the major causes of perishing of the assets. Majority (57 per cent) of the sample Beneficiaries were single activity holders and only forty-three per cent were benefited for double or multiple activities which is highly required to provide supplementary assistance to the Beneficiaries so that they can generate extra income and cross the poverty line. Only twenty-two per cent of the respondent Beneficiaries reported significant improvement in their economic position whereas thirty-seven per cent considered it marginal, twenty-five per cent a little and eleven per cent found no difference in their economic position. Surprisingly a small number (5 per cent) of them have reported of indebtedness, the reason might be misappropriation of the assistance provided. Thus about forty per cent of them admitted that there was no fruitful change in their economic position. More than two-thirds of them had either cleared the loan or were repaying their instalments regularly. Fourteen per cent had paid only a few installments, eight per cent were defaulters and ten per cent were not in a position to repay at that time. Thus the recovery process of IRDP seems to be satisfactory and IRDP has come as a boon for the poor beneficiaries.

Majority of the respondents have expressed dissatisfaction about the administrative structure of IRDP and desired changes both at structural and functional levels whereas in case of financial institutions, sixty per cent of the officials and about forty-two per cent of the Beneficiaries were of the same opinion. Majority of the respondent Beneficiaries (47 per cent) were dissatisfied with the role of financial institutions and reported about under estimation or rejection of their loan applications in case, they failed to pay a fixed amount to them as bribe. Eighty per cent of the officials considered the amount provided as adequate whereas more than two-thirds (69.2 per cent) of the Beneficiaries were of the same view. Those who considered it as inadequate pointed out that low level of unit cost, escalation in prices and underestimation of the assets were the main reasons for it. Majority of the Officials (40 per cent) and Beneficiaries (55.5 per cent) understood that some of the Beneficiaries actually created the assets whereas only one-fourth of the Officials and less than one-fifth of the Beneficiaries observed that all of them did so. Thus both of the Officials and Beneficiaries admitted the existence of a large section of Beneficiaries who did not actually purchase the assets. About two-thirds (64 per cent) of the Officials and more than half (56.3 per cent) of the Beneficiaries were satisfied with the process of implementation of IRDP. Majority of the Officials and Beneficiaries considered the infrastructural facilities available were sufficient. Two-thirds of the Officials were satisfied with follow-up activities whereas the same opinion was expressed by half of the Beneficiaries. As far as the qualitative monitoring is concerned about three-fourths of the Officials and half of the Beneficiaries were satisfied with it. But the situation in practice was rather sad in both the above mentioned cases. So far as the sector-wise performance of the programme is concerned, majority (45.0 per cent) of the Officials were in favour of ISB sector followed by Tertiary sector (30 per cent) whereas the greater part of the beneficiaries (35.8 per cent) were in favour of Primary sector followed by Tertiary sector (33.8 per cent). Hence, there are mixed results about the performance of IRDP in various sectors. Fifty-five per cent of the Officials and forty-five per cent of the Beneficiaries considered that both the systems of purchasing assets had been successful whereas a greater part of them preferred cash system as compared to purchase committee system. About two-thirds of the Beneficiaries as well as the Officials considered that only some of the families were capable to cross the poverty line whereas about one-fifth of them expressed their views in favour of many of them and a small number of the Officials (15.0 per cent) and Beneficiaries (10.8 per cent) considered that all of them had done so. About seventy per cent of the Beneficiaries have accepted the impact of IRDP and were in favour to continue to it, the same opinion was expressed by more than half (55.0 per cent) of the Officials. However, a sizeable number of the Officials (40.0 per cent) and a small number of Beneficiaries (17.9 per cent) were in favour to continue it with certain changes. Two-thirds of the Officials and more than half of the Beneficiaries considered IRDP as a fully successful programme whereas more than one-third of the Officials and about the same number of the Beneficiaries opined that it is successful to some extent. An insignificant number of Beneficiaries observed the programme as a failure. Hence most of the Officials and Beneficiaries observed that IRDP is fully or partially successful.

Half of the Officials perceived that Beneficiaries were taking interest to some extent in creating the assets whereas one-fifth considered that they were taking very good interest in it and about one-third reported it a little. Sixty per cent of them perceived that the Beneficiaries were taking interest to some extent in putting their assets into operation and one-fourth of them considered it a little. More than half (51 per cent) of the Beneficiaries reported that the Officials took interest in their work and about three-fourths observed that they were more concerned about their salaries whereas about two-thirds considered that they worked just to meet the target. More than eighty per cent pointed out that the Officials were egoist, arrogant and of non-cooperative nature. Thus the overall assessment of Beneficiaries about the Officials is not satisfactory.

After describing the Officials-Beneficiaries perception in this chapter, the conclusion, findings and suggestions about the research work are given in concluding chapter.

8

Conclusion

In the preceding chapters, we have discussed at length some aspects of Administration of Rural Development Programme in Haryana in general and that of the District Bhiwani in particular. Since the summary of each chapter presents a partial picture of the Administration of Integrated Rural Development Programme, in this chapter, we attempt to pick up the threads of the narration so far made and present an integrated picture of the various aspects of the programme under study. Let us recapitulate a little and go back to the broad interest of our study.

Rural Development has today become an objective not only of regional concern but also of national and international importance. It has acquired a central position in the plan endeavour of developing nations. India is a developing country. More than two-thirds of its population has been living in rural areas. The living conditions of these rural masses were very poor before independence. Most of them could not satisfy even their basic needs and there was dominance of illiteracy, poverty, unemployment, diseases and other scourges of mankind. More than eighty (80) per cent of these rural masses depended on agriculture for their livings in 1947. Health, educational and sanitary conditions in the country at that time were far from satisfactory and the situation was rather worse in rural areas. So it was essential for the government to make special arrangements for removal of these evils, without which a smooth and spontaneous progress was not possible. Hence, the Government of India has to adopt various programmes for rural development starting from Community Development Programme (CDP) in 1952 to Integrated Rural Development Programme (IRDP) in 1978-79 and onward. Some of these programmes like CDP, Cooperative Movement, Intensive Agricultural District Programme (IADP), Intensive Agricultural

Area Programme (IAAP), High Yielding Varieties (HYV) etc. have emphasized on the agricultural and infrastructural development in rural areas. Others like Drought Prone Area Programme (DPAP), Desert Development Programme (DDP), Hill Area Development Programme (HADP), Tribal Area Development Programme (TADP) etc. have focussed on the development of a specific area. Still others like Rural Man Power Programme (RMP), Crash Scheme for Rural Employment (CSRE), Food for Work Programme (FWP), National Rural Employment Programme (NREP), Rural Landless Employment Guarantee Programme (RLEGP) etc. have paid attention to rural wage and employment generation. Though specific efforts have been made in different areas of rural development through these programmes and these programmes have shown significant impacts on rural scenario yet these programmes could not satisfy the needs of the weaker sections of rural society. In spite of bringing the weaker sections of rural society above the poverty line, these programmes have largely benefited the richer sections of rural society and led to an enlarged and glaring gap between these sections of rural masses. The benefits of development could not percolate to the weaker sections of the society. Hence in the fourth plan period, target group oriented programmes like Small Farmers Development Agency (SFDA) and Marginal Farmers and Agricultural Labourers (MFAL) were started, because these groups were constituting the bulk of the rural poor. As these programmes could not remain impressive for long in dealing with the acute problem of rural poverty, hence were later on merged into a more comprehensive and integrated programme known as Integrated Rural Development Programme (IRDP). It was launched in 2300 selected Blocks in 1978-79 at national level and extended to all the remaining Blocks since October 2, 1980. It is a target group programme in which persons belonging to the below poverty line (BPL) families have been assisted under various schemes with the help of loan and subsidy so that they can cross the poverty line by generating extra-income and getting employment opportunities. While assisting under IRDP, the concerned authorities have to ensure a minimum percentage coverage of SC/ST, women and physically handicapped persons as directed by Government of India. A sum of Rs. 22,600 crore has been spent on IRDP for providing subsidy to 469.96 lakh Beneficiaries at national level since its inception up to 1995-96. To give special coverage to rural youths, a comprehensive programme known as 'Training of Rural Youths for Self-Employment (TRYSEM) was started at national level in September, 1979 as a sub-scheme of IRDP to provide training and self-employment opportunities to the rural youths from BPL families in the age group of 18-35. Since the commencement of this programme up to 1995-96, 37.09 lakh rural youths have been trained under TRYSEM at national level with the expenditure of Rs. 625 crore. More than half (56 per cent) of these trainees were either self-employed or wage-employed. So far, women were the neglected part of rural population, even after this fact that they were contributing more work hours in rural economy, they had nothing to say in ownership of family property. Hence the Government of India introduced a new programme known as 'Development of Women and Children in Rural Areas' (DWCRA) in 1983 as a sub-scheme of IRDP to give special coverage to rural women belonging to BPL families. Under DWCRA 1,46,562 women groups have been organized at national level with a total strength of 24.69 lakh women Beneficiaries up to March, 1996. A sum of Rs. 191.35 crore has been utilized so far by these groups at national level.

Almost all the rural development programmes have to face challenges at administrative as well as financial levels. The administrative machinery made responsible for implementation of these programmes remained almost the same as was designed by their colonial rulers with a few changes like creation of DRDAs and Block Development Machinery. The Officials concerned with these agencies were not found different from the regular bureaucratic setup. The success of any programme of rural development depends to a great extent on the style of functioning of the functionaries in its implementation, their perception towards the programme and the people for whom it is meant for. Equally the success of the programme will depend upon the active participation of the Beneficiaries. These programmes had remained the hand maid of bureaucracy and desired participation of the people could not be achieved even after the establishment of Panchayati Raj Institutions (PRIs).

However, these programmes gained high publicity during the 6th and 7th Plans. As a result various studies were conducted by the individual scholars as well as by the various institutions at various levels. Having a look at these studies we have to state that no comprehensive work has been done so far on this problem in the state of Haryana. Hence is the importance of the present study. In this study a modest attempt has been made to fill-up the gap. The present study attempts to examine in depth the various aspects of rural development with special reference to IRDP. This includes the study of profile of the area, administrative structure of IRDP, process of implementation, its actual implementation and perception of Officials and Beneficiaries regarding these programmes.

We have selected the IRDP for our study with a view to assess its performance in the state and to find out the validity of the basic assumptions of our study which are as follows. The success of any development programme is determined to a greater extent by the administrative setup responsible for its implementation and its method and procedure of working. The administrative structure of development programmes should be flexible, goal-oriented and development-oriented in nature. The performance of the administrators depends on their mental make-up. The Officials-Beneficiaries perception is equally a determinant of the success of a development programme. Training in management technology specially in areas of project-planning and sharpening of professional skills determine the success of a scheme. The Officials approach towards Beneficiaries through persuasion, co-operation and mutual understanding is needed. A programme of integrated nature like IRDP cannot achieve the expected results without proper coordination and communication among various agencies. For achieving maximum output of development programme, active participation of Beneficiaries becomes essential. Continuous monitoring of the implementation of these programmes is equally important. The more important is the availability of infrastructural facilities for the success of such programme.

The present study on focussed the administration of IRDP in the State of Haryana with special reference to District Bhiwani. The District consists of 8 Blocks and 432 Gram Panchayats. Each Block consists of approximately 50 to 60 Gram Panchayats. The data have been collected for the study up to 1995-96. The period of the study has been 1980-96 whereas for field work Beneficiaries assisted during 1990-95 have been taken. Broadly speaking the study is exploratory in nature and the conclusions are tentative. In terms of scope, the study seeks to provide an initial step towards understanding the various programmes of rural development. The study is primarily based on empirical data collected from the respondent Officials and Beneficiaries through the techniques of interview, personal discussion and observation. For the selection of sample at each level, the following procedure was adopted: First, the District Bhiwani was taken for the purpose of indepth study, though some other factors have paid due consideration in its selection. Second, three Blocks out of eight have been chosen from the District Bhiwani by applying simple random sampling technique on the basis of number of families assisted under IRDP since 1980-95. Thus, the selected Blocks are Bhiwani, Badhara and Loharu. Third, from each of the selected Block, three Gram Panchayats have been selcted by the same method and on the same pattern as was adopted in case of choosing the Blocks. Therefore, the selected Gram panchayats are Devsar, Mitathal and Tigrana in Bhiwani Block, Gopi, Bhandhwa and Pichopa Kalan in Badhara Block and Jhumpa Kalan, Allauddinpur and Gagarwas in Loharu Block. Fourth, respondents were of two types. The Beneficiaries of IRDP and Officials of DRDA, Bhiwani. As the number of Officials in DRDA, Bhiwani was 20, hence all of them were taken for interview. On the contrary, 240 Beneficiaries were taken for sample from the District Bhiwani, taking 80 Beneficiaries from each of the selected Block and the number of Beneficiaries chosen from each Gram Panchayat was proportionate to the size sample. The method applied for selecting the respondent Beneficiaries was simple random sampling for which the lists of the Beneficiaries assisted in each selected Gram Panchayat during 1990-95 were taken from the DRDA Office. Besides all the nine Branch Managers of concerned Banks and nine public opinion leaders/Surpanches of the selected Gram panchayats have also been interviewed to evaluate their perception and participation in this programme. The primary data for the study were collected from the respondents with the help of carefully prepared questionnaires for each group which consists of both structured and unstructured questions. In addition to the interview, the other techniques used in collection of primary data were observation and discussion. These schedules/questionnaires were administrated personally. The responses were collected from the respondents individually and group discussion were also held whenever and wherever deemed necessary. Bank Branches were also visited to verify the facts relating to financial aspects. In addition to the information collected from the respondents, the secondary data were collected from the relevant Official records including various guidelines of the programmes and schemes, the manuals, correspondence between Government of India, State Governments and local level agencies, the progress reports, agenda notes and proceedings of various meetings conducted at Central and State levels. These data have been collected from the office records of the DRDAs, Branches of Concerned Banks, District Statistics Office, District Development and Panchayats Office, Country and Town Planning Office, besides the Directorates of Economics and Statistics and Rural Development. Moreover, a number of publications and evaluation reports of Ministry of Rural Development, Planning Commission, National Institute of Rural Development (NIRD), Rural Development and Panchayat Raj Department and Economics and Statistics Department of Government of Haryana were extensively used in the course of the present study. Besides, Books, Journals, Research Articles and Newspapers were also used for data collection.

Let us add at this stage that we are aware of the limitations of our study. Since the administration of IRDP in an unexplored phenomena, the present study is exploratory in nature. In terms of its scope, it seeks to provide an initial step towards development programmes rather than examining the casual relationship of variables. We hope the study might help to develop hypothesis for further studies. Hopefully greater interest in IRDP can be created and more empirical works will be encouraged.

Having recapitulated some of the theoretical assumptions that went into the spelling out of boarder concerns of this study, we now discuss the findings of the study in a more coherent fashion by pulling together different strands and weaving them in a meaningful pattern in order to draw certain concrete conclusions. The performance of the programme has a direct co-relation with the profile of that area where it is going to be implemented. The profile does not only determine the viability of a particular programme but also the perception of the people to a great extent. Hence a brief review of the profile of the state as well as that of the chosen District has been presented here. The state of Haryana which came into existence on November 1, 1966 as the 17th state of Indian Union, is still predominantly a rural state. It is a small state with an area of 44,212 Sq. Km. constituting 1.35 per cent of the Indian Union. It is situated in the north-west part of the country. Physically, it falls into the broad natural divisions-the sub Himalayan and the Indo-Gangetic Plain which runs in South-Eastern directions almost parallel to each other. The state does not enjoy the passage of any important river through it. Hence, the climactic conditions in the state are not much favourable. It is very hot in summer and markedly cold in winter. There are two well marked seasons in the state. The state has a total population of 1,64,63,648 of which 88,27,474 are males and 76,36,174 are females. The sex ratio is 865 females per 1000 males which is lower to the national average of 927. The state is more densely populated as compared to the national average and three-fourths of its population is dwelling in rural areas. The SCs are about one-fifth of the state's population and there are no scheduled tribes in Haryana. It is a Hindu dominated (89 per cent) state. The literacy rate in the state is somewhat better (55.35 per cent) than the national average (52.21 per cent). However, it is poor on the part of women who constitute only one-third of the total literate population of the state and two-thirds of the literates are residing in urban areas. A satisfactory network of human and animal health services has been established in the state. It has shown significant development in the fields of agriculture, industry and infrastructural facilities in a short period of its existence. Today, it is one of the most developed states of the Indian Union. It has provided all the basic civic amenities to all its towns and villages up to 1981 and enjoys the status of being the first in the country to do the same. Besides, tremendous developments have been made by the state the fields of transport and communication. All the towns are equipped with the facilities of STD/ISD. The state has made remarkable development on economic fronts in the last three decades and is one of the states having highest per capita income which is about one and half times to that of national average. Less than one third of the state's population is engaged in production and two-thirds are non-workers. Among the non-workers three-fourths are inhabiting in rural areas. About sixty per cent of the rural population is engaged in Primary sector and almost the same number derives their earnings from this sector. The average size of land holdings is 2.43 hectares at present which is decreasing day by day. Agriculture is the backbone of the state's economy. Though considerable network of industry has been established. Forty per cent of the state's Gross Domestic Production comes from agriculture and allied sectors. The area under forest in the state is not only poor (2.5 per cent) as compared to the national average but also thinly dispersed. The area under cultivation is about four-fifths of the total cultivable area in the state and half of it is double/multiple cropped. Haryana is the beneficiary of multi-purpose projects on Satluj and Beas. Western Yamuna Canal, Bhakra Canal and Gurgoan Canal are the major irrigation projects. The rural economy of Southern Haryana including Bhiwani District has been transformed after completion of Jui, Siwami and Loharu Lift-Irrigation Schemes and Jawaharlal Nehru (JLN) Irrigation Scheme. The major sources of irrigation in the state are canals (51 per cent) and tube wells (48 per cent). The state government has taken concrete steps to raise the standard of living of the farmers. It has not only written off their cooperative loans but also provided them other supporting facilities. The effects of the Green Revolution can be clearly observed in the state. Today, Haryana is not only self-sufficient in food grains production but also among the top contributors of food grains to the central pool. Besides, the state has a very sound industrial base and it produces the largest number of tractors in the country. One out of every four bicycles is produced here. Panipat, Faridabad, Gurgoan, Hisar, Ambala, Yamuna Nagar etc. have come up as the advanced centres of industries and the future of the state as far as this sector is considered is very bright.

The District Bhiwani came into existence as the 8th district of Haryana on December 22, 1972. It is located on the South-West of the state of Haryana. It shares a long boundary with the state of Rajasthan. Though the district constitutes a part of Indo-Gangetic Alluvial Plain, yet largely it is dry and sandy. Sand Dunes Commonly known as 'Tibbas', can be seen abundantly in the South-Western parts of the district. The climate is very hot and dry in summer and extremely cold in winter. There are frequent dust-storms in May and June. In spite of the fait that Bhiwani is not favourable located, it can be proud of the progress it has made in various fields. It is the second largest district in the state having an area of 5140 Sq. Km. and a population of 11,39,718 constituting

11.6 per cent and 7 per cent of the state respectively. More than four-fifths of the population is living in rural areas. The district is thinly populated as far as compared to the state average. The sex ratio is almost similar to that of the state average. Most of its population consists of Hindus and about twenty per cent of the population is from scheduled castes. The district is not evenly populated. The North-Eastern parts-Bhiwani, Bawani Khera and Charkhi Dadri have more than double density of population is comparison to the South-Western parts-Siwani, Loharu and Tosham. The literacy rate in the district is almost the same as is in the state in general. Similar is the position in case of distribution of workforce and their proportionate strength in various sectors. Among the main workers who form about one-fourth (27.8 per cent) of the total population in the district, more than two-thirds (69 per cent) are engaged in Primary sector, eight per cent in Secondary sector and twenty-three per cent in Tertiary sector. Rural economy of the district is primarily based on agriculture and about eighty per cent of the land holdings are up to 5 hectares. In spite of the unfavourable conditions in existence, the district has achieved eventful growth in all fields of development. All the villages are availing of the facilities of electricity, safe drinking water and metalled roads. Besides, a good network of health, transport and communication services is in existence in the district. The various canal projects completed so far have brought a substantial change in rural economy. The South-Western parts of the district are covered by lift system of irrigation covering about sixty per cent of net area irrigated. Sprinkler system of irrigation has become very popular in Loharu and Badhara Blocks. Industrially the district is not very sound constituting less than two per cent of the total industries in the state which are highly centralized. The profile of all the three selected Blocks is more or less the same. The level of similarity is more in case of Loharu and Badhara Blocks. Thus the profile presents a clear picture of the demographic features of state and that of the District Bhiwani to have a better understanding about the socio, economic and political milieu of the area of study.

Another important set of factors which have an impact on the performance of a development programme is the administrative structure responsible for its implementation. Although the administrative setup may not be the sole determinant of implementation of a development programme, yet it plays a significant role in determining its performance. A glance at the administrative structure clearly reveals that in all the developing nations of Asia and Africa, state is viewed as a unit for social and economic change. The modern state has become a 'welfare-state' engaged in activities of socio-economic development. As the state function through its bureaucracy which is considered as an instrument of modernization and social change, the solution of vital problems of rural development depends to a significant level on the style of working of the bureaucracy. But the bureaucracy in all the developing nations including India has been finding it difficult to generate the required level of confidence in the people and to enlist their active support tend cooperation in the process of social transformation. In India, it has been the victim of its colonial past, though changes were introduced but in a casual manner and those were more marked at the central level than the lower levels of the government. While the central government was looked upon as an agency for development and change, the principle of a 'police-state' continued to govern the functioning of the state machinery at various levels and the layman still perceived the state as government as was the tendency during imperial period. The nation has launched various programmes of rural development starting from Community Development Programme to Integrated Rural Development Programme at different intervals but the administrative setup at various levels by and large remained the same. Though some changes were brought by establishing new institutions for development purposes such as DRDA, Panchayati Raj Institution and Block Development Offices. To ensure the effective implementation of rural development programmes, it was felt that the administrative system should be made more dynamic by strengthening its rational and creative forces. Administrators with development responsibilities must be familiar with different forms or rationality needed for different areas for development administration. Hence the administrative structure engaged in the implementation of various programmes of socio-economic change has been given the name 'development administration'. It was expected that with the passage of time the attitudes of the bureaucracy would change and it would be quite responsive to development. However, the attitudes of bureaucrats in our country have not been changed to the desired extent. In

India, there seems no difference between the regular bureaucracy and personnel engaged in development activities as far as their functioning and service conditions are concerned.

The administrative structure of Integrated Rural Development Programme and allied programmes of poverty alleviation and employment generation at various levels may be briefly mentioned here. The Ministry of Rural Development, Government of India, New Delhi has been made fully accountable for formulating policy, planning, monitoring and evaluating the programmes of poverty alleviation and rural development at national level. It also releases the central share of funds. The Ministry is assisted by Central Level Consultative Committee in performing its responsibilities. The Ministry is headed by the Minister of Rural Development, who is assisted by the Secretary. Besides, there is an additional Secretary, six Joint Secretaries and other administrative as well as technical staff. The other technical institutions operating under the control of the Ministry are National Institute of Rural Development (NIRD), Council for Advancement of People's Action and Rural Training (CAPART) and Directorate of Marketing and Inspection (DMI). In addition to the Minister in charge, the Commissioner, Development and Panchayats is at the top of administrative hierarchy and is the overall incharge of all the rural development programmes including IRDP in the state. Below it, there is the Directorate of Rural Development, headed by Director-cum-Joint Secretary, who with the help of various staff members is actually responsible for planning and implementation of the programme at the state level. Besides, Haryana Institute of Rural Development (HIRD), Nilokheri helps in training of personnel and evaluation of the programme. A State Level Coordination Committee has been instituted to assist the Ministry in discharging its responsibilities. At the District level, all the rural development programmes including IRDP are planned, implemented, coordinated and monitored by the DRDA. In Haryana, these agencies are chaired by the Deputy Commissioners. Besides, the Deputy Commissioner, there is a full time Chief Executive Officer for each DRDA and this post is held by Additional Deputy Commissioner in the State. To help the ADC in formulation of annual action plan, a planning committee has been constituted which consists of an economist, a credit planning officer and a small and cottage industries officer. In the State, there is no separate staff for IRDP at Block level and the DRDA takes help of Block Development Staff and other functionaries of extension services for fulfilling its various requirements.

The performance of a development programme depends to a great extent upon its process of implementation, is another important assumption of our study. Hence, it is worthwhile to have a precise review of the process of implementation of IRDP so that the continuity of analysis can be maintained. This process consists of various steps. The first one deals with the survey for identification of BPL families in rural areas. The survey is conducted by the DRDAs with the help of village level functionaries of various departments, on the directions of state government. However, the active involvement of Gram Panchayats have been ensured through 73rd constitutional amendment at this level to make the survey process more impartial and democratic. The BPL lists so prepared are given adequate publicity and later on sent to the Block Development Officer or DRDA for approval. These lists are compiled at the District level to get a clear picture of the poverty in the district. This type of surveys have been completed twice in the state so far and the third is in operation since 1997. On the basis of the BPL list and the financial allocations, the DRDA prepares perspective as well as annual action plans with the help of its planning team. The perspective plan is prepared keeping in view the local resources, profile, infrastructural facilities and feasible activities in that particular area, besides the financial allocation. It provides detailed information for preparing the annual action plan. The governing body of DRDA approves the annual action plan after taking a critical appraisal of the economic profile, feasibility of activities chosen, forward-backward linkages, assessment of previous year plan etc. Its copies are later on circulated to the Department of Rural Development of the State Government and other concerned agencies for further information and necessary action. Organization of credit camps is the third step in the process of implementation of IRDP. These camps are organized by the DRDA in the proposed village/s to fill up the loan application forms as per the provisions in the annual action plan. The sole criteria for arranging the credit camps is to save the time and resources of both the Beneficiaries and that of concerned staff. These camps are required to be attended by the representative of DRDA particularly by the APO (credit) or the APO of the concerned Block, Patwari, Gram Sachiv, Manager of concerned Bank, representative of District Development Manager (DDM), NABARD, Local Panchayat through Sarpanch and local level functionaries of concerned department and any other person whose presence it felt necessary by the Chairman, DRDA. Processing of loan applications is the fourth step of implementation process. After filling-up the loan application forms of the proposed Beneficiaries in credit camps, these are submitted to the concerned Bank by the Officials of DRDA with subsidy amount and other required documents. The Bank is bound to complete these process within a fortnight of its receipt in its office. However, in practice, it is a time consuming process as the concerned Officials have to appraised of each loan application individually. The State level Committee on Unit Cost has been instituted to ascertain the unit cost for various activities every year. The Regional Office of NABARD is delegated powers to escalate 20 per cent in unit cost decided for various activities. Thus, the revised unit cost is communicated to the State Government, DRDA and Lead Bank. As the unit costs so decided are average one which can further revised by District Level Consultative Committee with the help of Lead Bank. Purchasing of assets is another important step in the process of implementation of IRDP. It is normally the responsibility of DRDA to provide assets to the Beneficiaries of standard quality, at economic prices and to the satisfaction of the Beneficiary. For fulfilling this requirement, Purchase Committee has been constituted in each DRDA which consists of the Beneficiary, a representative each of the DRDA/APO (credit), the financing Institution, the concerned department and a representative of SC/ST. In order to provide more liberty to the Beneficiary while purchasing the assets, the Purchase Committee system was revised in 1991-92 and Cash Disbursement system was introduced up to fifty per cent of the Blocks. In Bhiwani District, Bhiwani, Dadri-I, II, Bawani Khera and Tosham Blocks are under Cash system. In these Blocks, the Bank makes available the whole amount of unit cost to the Beneficiary in advance and Beneficiary is supposed to submit the utilization certificate or cash memo within a month of getting the loan. At present both the systems are in operation. Monitoring is another significant step in the process of implementation of IRDP. It is an integrated process consisting of follow-up, qualitative monitoring and evaluation. It is a process or a strategy to keep a close watch on the implementation of a project so as to ensure the timely completion of its various components within the sanctioned outlay and time frame. It started with the first visit of the Bank and Block Officials of concerned department to the Beneficiary after purchasing the asset. Its main objective is to assist the Beneficiary to put the assets in income generating position and to check their misutilization. For effective and quarterly monitoring of IRDP at DRDA and State level, the Government of India, has suggested two types of schedules. Further the Government of India has also fixed monthly targets for conducting qualitative monitoring by the Inspecting Officers. On the basis of this monitoring, the quarterly consolidated report is prepared by the DRDA for circulation among the BDPOs. The last and most important step in the process of IRDP implementation is the recovery. The Beneficiary has to repay the Bank loan with interest within a period of five years in yearly installments. The routine work of recovery is done by the Officials of concerned Banks. On the recommendations of Expert Committee of RBI on IRDP, the Government has to initiate Back-End Subsidy Process in 1995 to improve the recovery system. In this system the Bank released the full project cost including the subsidy amount as loan to the Beneficiary at the beginning. However, the subsidy is deposited to his account in the Bank with a lock up period of three to five years. It is adjusted to the last few installments of repayment. Besides, taking some concrete steps at administrative level, the Government of India has directed the State Governments to appoint utilization Reporters-cum-Recovery felicitations on commission basis. But in practice nothing such has been done so far in the state.

For a better understanding to asses the reality of programme, a brief review of its performance has been presented here. For implementing IRDP in the state, the first household survey for identification of BPL families was conducted during 1980-84 in which 5, 19, 444 families (42 per cent) were found living below the poverty line in rural areas of which about thirty-nine per cent were from scheduled castes. The second BPL survey was completed in 1991-92 and the number of the families identified below poverty line were 6,28,860 in the state which is about 37 per cent of the total rural households. Among these about two-thirds were from the two middle strata of income. Majority of them (42 per cent) were from agricultural labourers followed by non-agricultural labourers (20 per cent). The schedules castes and Backward Classes were forty-one per cent and twenty-two per cent respectively of the total BPL population in the state. The incidence of poverty varied from district to district. The number of families assisted under IRDP in Haryana since 1980-96 were 6,22,825 which constitutes about eighty per cent of the total BPL families in the state. Among these assisted families about 42 per cent were scheduled castes twenty-five per cent were women and half per cent were physically handicapped. Majority of the Beneficiaries (58 per cent) were assisted under Primary sector, followed by ISB sector (22 per cent) and Tertiary sector (20 per cent) during the above mentioned period. The strength of Beneficiaries assisted under Primary sector has continuously declined to a significant level and a sharp rise has been shown by ISB sector. A total sum of Rs. 145.52 crore has been spent as administrative expenditure and subsidy during this period. The total credit mobilized was Rs. 113.56 crore as subsidy and Rs. 223.65 crore as loan and the per capita investment was Rs. 5414 for the whole period. IRDP was initially started in 5 selected Blocks of District Bhiwani in 1978-79 and was extended to all the seven Blocks since October 2,1980. The first BPL survey was conducted in the district during 1980-84 and 41,912 families were found living below the poverty line of which 30,344 families had been assisted during 6th and 7th plans. According to the second BPL survey (1991-92), 48,241 families were identified living below the poverty line of which 17,103 were from scheduled castes (35.4 peer cent) and 10,133 from backward classes (21 per cent). The total BPL families were 32.25 per cent of total rural households. The strength of BPL families varied from Block to Block. It was highest in Tosham Block (20.6 per cent) and lowest in Dadri-I (11.3 per cent). A significant number of the BPL families hailed from agricultural labourers and marginal farmers i.e. 35 per cent of each group followed by non-agricultural labourers (17.5 per cent). The total number of BPL families covered under IRDP in the District since 1980-95 were 39324 of these maximum pertained to Tosham Block (16.2 per cent) and minimum to Siwani Block (8.8 per cent). Among the total assisted families 37.5 per cent were scheduled castes, 12.8 per cent were women and 0.5 per cent were physically handicapped persons. The coverage of the latter two groups has augmented meaningfully since 1990-91. About three-fourths of the

Beneficiaries were assisted under Primary sector followed by Tertiary (16 per cent) and ISB sectors (10 per cent). The coverage under Primary sector has decreased to a substantial extent whereas increased about seven fold in ISB sector during the whole study period. A sum of Rs. 704.1 lakh has been spent so far on this programme in the District of which more than two-thirds (67 per cent) has been spent on Primary sector followed by Tertiary (21 per cent) and ISB sectors (12 per cent). The total credit mobilized during 1980-95 was Rs. 2127.69 lakh of which Rs. 704.07 lakh were spent on subsidy and Rs. 1423.62 lakh on loan. The average per capita income during the whole period was Rs. 5410. It has amplified more than three folds during 1994-95 as compared to the 6th Plan period (1980-85).

The most important set of assumptions of the present study is that the success of development programmes like IRDP depends to a significant level upon the Officials-Beneficiaries perception about the various aspects of the programme and about their perception towards each other. An endeavour has been made through the responses collected from respondent Officials and Beneficiaries to test the validity of these assumptions. It will be meaningful here to present a precise review of Officials-Beneficiaries perception on various issues about the programme. It consists of three parts. The first part deals with the background information of the respondent Officials and Beneficiaries because the perception of an individual on any problem is designed significantly by it. Hence, it is considered worthwhile to present in brief the socio-economic background of the respondents. It has already been cleared that the Beneficiaries under the programme are persons from BPL families living in rural areas and the programme guidelines indicate clearly that 40 per cent of the Beneficiaries should be from women. However, among our respondents the coverage of women is nearly the same as desired in guidelines. Whereas the strength of women Officials is just twenty per cent. The Government has directed to cover at least 50 per cent of Beneficiaries from SC/ST and at least 3 per cent from physically handicapped persons. Their respective coverage under the programme in our sample respondents is by and large similar to the guidelines. On the other hand, the Scheduled Castes constitute 55 per cent of the respondent Officials. Hence, the category wise coverage of the Beneficiaries in our sample is in accordance with the guidelines issued by the Ministry. A family with five members is considered a parameter for ascertaining its BPL status which is a unit for assistance under IRDP. However, among our respondents it was found that only a small number (16.7 per cent) were from this criteria. Hence more than four-fifths of the respondent Beneficiaries had enlarged families to the set parameter and it has been observed as one of major causes of their poverty. So it is suggested that adequate steps need to be taken to strengthen the family welfare programmes for the rural poor and to awaken them about their causes of poverty. On the other hand, the size of the Officials families by the large was small. The target groups under the programme are the small farmers, marginal farmers, agricultural labourers, non-agricultural labourers, rural artistans etc. These groups constitute the bulk of rural BPL population. Among these marginal farmers and agricultural labourers form a significant part of the population. In our sample the agricultural labourers constitute a major part (44.6 per cent) followed by marginal farmers (38.0 per cent). However, among the Officials more than two-thirds were from class-III and IV categories and majority of them dependent on their salary as a source of income. The income is the sole criteria for identification of BPL families under IRDP. More than half (53.6 per cent) of the respondents were from the lower middle income group i.e. Rs. 1726-3500 and about one-third (32.6 per cent) were from the upper middle income group i.e. Rs. 3501-4800. Thus, it can be concluded that more than eighty per cent of the respondents were from the two middle income groups and the reasons may be that these groups constitute a bulk of rural BPL population. Education has been taken as one of the key indicators while deciding SES background in social sciences and is a determining factor of ones outlook towards life. It is presumed that an educated person would be better informative. About three-fifths (59.6 per cent) of our respondent Beneficiaries were illiterate and nearly one-third (30.4 per cent) of them had elementary knowledge of education. Thus, the educational status of most of the Beneficiaries in the sample is very poor which has been observed as a major reason for their poverty. Therefore, it is suggested that special attention should be paid towards improving the educational standard of the BPL families in rural areas. In spite of it, majority of the Officials were also from lower educational strata. It is essential that the Beneficiaries should have information about the various programmes in operation in that particular area and about the benefits they can derive from these programmes. Unless the Beneficiaries understand the real spirit of the programme, one can not expect their full involvement and participation in the programme. Under IRDP the concerned APO and the Gram Sachiv are entrusted with the job of awareness among Beneficiaries. Besides, a lucrative role of the Gram panchayats has been expected in the process of information dissemination. About three-fourths (72.5 per cent) of our respondents reported that they came to know about the programme through Assistant Project Officer and fifteen per cent got information from the Gram Panchayats whereas an insignificant number (7.1 per cent) of them were informed about the programme by the Gram Sachiv. Therefore, we are inclined to conclude that the extension activities were not found satisfactory. Hence these need to be further strengthened so that the benefits of the programme can be extracted to the optimum level. The Gram panchayats have also to review their position and it is hoped that these institutions will play a liaison role in the rural development programmes. The perspective Beneficiaries have been selected for IRDP assistance from the BPL lists from which credit camps are organized in the village/s by the DRDA with the help of local staff of various concerned departments and Gram Sabha. All the respondents were selected through the above-mentioned procedure and not even a single beneficiary was taken by any other mean. This indicates the active involvement of Gram Panchayats in identification procedure of Beneficiaries. For the smooth implementation of programme and deriving maximum output from the scheme sanctioned, it is essential that the loan applications of the Beneficiaries should be processed quickly. The delay in sanctioning of loan and grounding of the scheme has always burdened the Beneficiaries with undue sufferings. Hence, the government of India has directed to the programme implementing agencies to organize credit camps so that the loan applications could be filled up on the spot without wasting time and resources. These credit camps are attended by all the concerned Officials including Bank representative. The RBI has directed all the concerned Banks to clear the loan applications within a fortnight after receiving them in their office. But in practice, it seems to be a time consuming process. About two-thirds (71.2 per cent) of the respondents have reported that it took 2-3 months time in clearing their loan applications at the DRDA level and less than one-third (28.8 per cent) of them pointed out that the time taken at this level was between 1-2 months. They further informed that the Bank took more than two month period in four-fifths of the cases and in about one-fifth of the cases, loan was disbursed within 1-2 months. Not even a single respondents could get loan within the stipulated period. Therefore, it can be concluded from the above observations that the processing of loan applications is a time consuming process and the reasons might be a lot of formalities and appraisal of every loan application minutely, which the DRDA and Banks have to perform. It is, therefore, suggested that the loan applications should be processed as early as can be possible and needs to adhere the guidelines clearly suggest that the Beneficiaries should not face any difficulty in getting the loans. In spite of these clear guidelines, the Beneficiaries have to face many difficulties in getting the loan under the scheme in time. More than two-thirds (70.0 per cent) of our respondents reported that they have to face difficulties while getting the loan. However, less than one-third (30.0 per cent) of them did not face any difficulty in getting their loans. The reasons cited were large number of formalities, unhelpful attitude of the concerned Officials, besides cases of bribery. In some cases, the assets of the Beneficiaries were reported to be underestimated or the loan was not sanctioned at all. On the other hand, Beneficiaries who did not face any difficulties for getting loans indicated some adjustment with concerned Officials. This kind of adjustment between the concerned Officials and Beneficiaries has been observed to be one of the major causes of misappropriation of assistance provided. Therefore, it is suggested that vigilance system needs to be further tightened and complaint regarding it should be heard by Additional Deputy Commissioner and strict action should be taken against the corrupt Officials. During the time of basic survey, the preference of Beneficiaries towards the proposed economic activity is invariably obtained. This is done in order to know the intention and choice of the beneficiary. However, the activities are finalized after ascertaining the resource potential and infrastructural facilities. Thus, the list of activities in a particular area is prepared by the nodal bank and approved by the Governing Body of DRDA. Efforts are made to provide the beneficiary maximum liberty while selecting a particular scheme. More than half of our respondents (51.2 per cent) got the assets of their first choice and a large number (39.2 per cent) of them preferred it as their second choice. A small number (9.6 per cent) of the respondents reported that they were not given any choice regarding the scheme. Thus, it can be concluded that majority of the respondents could get assets of their choice. Simultaneously, we can not undermine that significant part of respondents who reported poor choices about the assets. Hence more attention is required to enhance the opportunities for better choice. The activities provided under IRDP are broadly divided into three sectors-Primary, ISB and Tertiary. The Beneficiaries can get any activity under these sectors depending upon the profile of that particular area, infrastructural support available and his own interest because these factors determine the survival of a particular asset/scheme created. Forty per cent of our respondents were assisted under Primary sector, followed by 38.0 per cent for ISB sector and 21.3 per cent for tertiary sector. Milch cattle and plough camel constitute about three-fourths (72.8 per cent) of the total assets under Primary sector whereas ISB sector majority lies with village industries, handicarft and handloom activities. The majority of the Beneficiaries in Tertiary sector were assisted for cannel cart and mule cart. Thus most of the Beneficiaries got the schemes according to the local profile of their respective areas. For proper utilization of the assistance provided, it is essential that it should be adequate because there is a correlation between the adequacy of assistance provided and its proper utilization. More than two thirds (69.2 per cent) of our respondents considered the assistance provided as adequate whereas about thirty one per cent of them observed it as inadequate to create a potential asset and they were either forced to purchase a substandard asset or to go away with the assistance provided to meet their other domestic requirements. An interestingly large number (73.3 per cent) of the respondents have actually created the assets and the remaining (26.7 per cent) who did not do so, reported the inadequacy of assistance as the main reason for it, followed by adjustment with concerned Officials and lack of interest of the Beneficiary to create the assets. It was also observed that some of the Beneficiaries has nothing to do with assets. Their sole motto was to gobble up the subsidy provided under the programme. However, in some cases, the role of the Beneficiaries in putting the assets into operation, has been observed dubious. The tendency of misappropriation was highest in Cash Block (Bhiwani) almost doubled to Purchase Committee Blocks (Badhara and Loharu). It is a cause of concern and demands for proper attention from the concerned authorities. Establishment of some what bigger processing units by the DRDA with the help of loan and subsidy provided to the Beneficiaries and then giving permanent employment to these Beneficiaries there, can be a better alternative. The survival of any scheme depends to a great extent upon the quality of scheme provided. The guidelines of IRDP also clearly stated that the Beneficiaries should be provided assets of good qualities. Out the respondents who actually purchased the assets, 56.8 per cent of the them were satisfied with the quality of the assets provided them whereas about one-third (31.3 per cent) of them judged their quality as an average and a small number (11.9 per cent) of them considered the quality of their assets as poor. Thus a significant number of Beneficiaries were not satisfied with the quality of their assets and have reported reasons as under estimation of unit cost and escalation of prices primarily. The present status of the scheme is a significant variable for assessing the success of that particular programme under which it has been provided. Out of the total 260 assets provided to the Beneficiaries, 30.4 per cent were found to be intact, about one-third (34.6 per cent) of them were sold and an equal number of these assets were perished fully or partially. The reasons cited for the non-oretention of these assets were immediate need of money, unnatural calamities, low income generation and costly maintenance of the assets provided. Lack of sincere monitoring has been observed as one of the main reason for perishing of the assets. The main objective of IDRP is to bring the BPL families above poverty line by generating extra income from the assets provided. Not even a single activity is sufficient to break into the vicious circle of poverty, hence these families are provided assistance in form of double or multiple activities. A larger part (56.7 per cent) of our respondents were single activity holders followed by 37.9 per cent who got benefits for double activities and only an insignificant number (5.4 per cent) could have the privileges of being Beneficiaries under multiple activities. Therefore, it can be concluded from the above observations that a significant part of the Beneficiaries were single activity holders which could not prove much effective in breaking their bonds of poverty. So it is suggested that most of the BPL families should be covered under double or multiple activities. The proper utilization of the assistance provided and the success of the programme can be better assessed by knowing the economic position of the Beneficiary after assistance. Only twenty-two per cent of the respondents reported significant improvement in their economic position whereas thirty seven per cent considered it marginal and one-fourth of them observed it a little. However, 10.8 per cent of them found no difference in their economic position. Surprisingly, a small number (4.6 per cent) of them have reported of indebtedness due to misappropriation of assistance provided. Thus, about forty per cent of the respondents admitted that there was no fruitful change in their economic position. Therefore, it needs to strengthen monitoring process besides the infrastructural support available. Repayment of loan is another important indicator for assessing the success of the programme. To what extent the Beneficiaries have properly operated the assets can be assessed by getting information about their repayment of loans. A sizeable (21 per cent) number of our respondents have reported that they had cleared the Bank loans, 47 per cent were repaying regularly. However, 14 per cent of them have paid only a few installments and 10 per cent wanted to clear but not in a position at that time. Interestingly, a small number (8 per cent) of them were defaulters. By and large the recovery process of IRDP seems to be satisfactory.

After assessing the respondent Officials Beneficiaries individual position, their perception about the various aspects of the programme of IRDP here been presented here in second part. Because perception has been observed as a significant parameter for deciding ones preferences so it can be a major determinant for the success of a development programme. The administrative structure responsible for implementing a particular programme determines its performance and the performance of the administrative setup is decided significantly by the perception of people involved in it. Among our respondents, 45 per cent of the Officials and 40.8 per cent of the Beneficiaries expressed their satisfaction about the existing administrative structure. However the large part of the respondents was dissatisfied with it and desired Changes both at structural and functional levels. Both of them blamed each other for not responding according to the needs and requirements of the IRDP. Most of the Officials observed low salary, poor working conditions, stress and overload of work as the main reasons of their dissatisfaction whereas the majority of the Beneficiaries reported that the Officials were not-cooperative, took little interest in their work and were not easily available to them. It has been observed that the approach of Officials on key post in the administration as Director, Project Experts and Chief Executive Officer, is very much casual towards the programme which has a direct effect on the performance of the programme. Lack of Block level machinery of IRDP had been pointed out by both of the Officials and Beneficiaries. Therefore, it is suggested to create Block level machinery of IRDP, strengthening of the existing setup and to raise the morale of the Officials. The Officials on key posts should be appointed for a definite period and their accountability should be fixed. Change in their attitudes towards the programme and Beneficiaries is the need of the hour. The financial institutions have a pivotal role to play in the implementation of IRDP. The respondent Officials and Beneficiaries perception about these institutions show that sixty per cent of the Officials were satisfied with these institutions and 42.5 per cent of the Beneficiaries were also of the same view. Nevertheless, the other significant section of our respondents, who were not satisfied with the financial institutions, have reported privately that the Bank Officials take bribe while sanctioning loans, otherwise their assets were underestimated. Therefore, it is suggested that the supervision over these institutions should be tightened and strict action against corrupt Officials should be taken. Eighty per cent of the Officials considered the amount provided as adequate and more than two-thirds (69.2 per cent) of the Beneficiaries were of the same view. Those who considered the assistance as inadequate pointed out that low level of unit cost, escalation in prices and underestimation of the assets, were the main reasons for it. Majority of the Officials (40.0 per cent) and Beneficiaries (55.5 per cent) were of the view that some of the Beneficiaries actually created the assets. However, one-fourth of the Officials and one-fifth of the Beneficiaries considered that all of them have created the assets. A sizable number (35.0 per cent) of the Officials and a marginal number (26.3 per cent) of the Beneficiaries perceived that most of them have done so. Thus, both the Officials and Beneficiaries admitted the existence of a large section of Beneficiaries who did not actually create the assets. This indicates towards the forgery existing in the programme. Hence this matter needs to pay special emphasis by the concerned authorities. About two-thirds (65 per cent) of the Officials and more than half of (56.3 per cent) of the Beneficiaries have expressed their satisfaction about the process of implementation of IRDP. Interestingly a good number of Officials (35 per cent) and nearly the same number of Beneficiaries (33.3 per cent) were not satisfied with the process of implementation and 10.4 per cent of the Beneficiaries were highly dissatisfied with it. The reasons of dissatisfaction of Beneficiaries include delay in processing of loan applications, low choice in selecting the assets/schemes, inadequacy of unit cost, poor infrastructural facilities, improper monitoring, rigid recovery system, delay in settling of claims etc. Majority of the Officials and Beneficiaries considered that infrastructural facilities available were sufficient. Monitoring is a significant variable for determining the success of a particular programme. Under IRDP special provisions has been made to strengthen the monitoring process. The opinion of the respondent Officials and Beneficiaries regarding it is that majority of the Officials were satisfied with it whereas the number of Beneficiaries who were of the same opinion was relatively low. A significant number of the respondents were not satisfied with the monitoring process. But in practice, the situation was rather sad. The lack of sincere monitoring has been observed as one of the major reasons for misappropriation of the assistance provided. In most of the cases 'vikas patrikas' were not issued to the Beneficiaries and if so done only few entries were marked on. The qualitative monitoring has also confined to paper work in most of the cases. Therefore, it is suggested that the monitoring process should be strengthened by ensuring regular field visits through state, DRDA and Block Officials. Besides, vikas patrikas should be issued in each and every case with latest information recorded on it by the visiting Officials. So far as the sector-wise performance of the programme is concerned, the respondents have expressed mixed opinion. Among the Officials majority (45 per cent) was in favour of ISB sector, followed by Tertiary and Primary sectors whereas the Beneficiaries gave preference to Primary sector (35.8 per cent) succeeded by Tertiary and ISB sectors. Thus, by and large the success of the programme was judged by both the Officials and Beneficiaries equally in all the sectors. However in practice, the programme has been observed more successful in ISB and tertiary sectors. There is maximum forgery in animal husbandry sector. In most of the cases either the animal was not purchased otherwise sold after sometimes. Since 1991, there are two modes of purchasing assets-Purchase Committee and Cash Disbursement systems. Fifty-five (55) per cent of the Officials and 44.8 per cent of the respondent Beneficiaries perceived both the above mentioned systems equally successful whereas in individual cases majority of the respondents favoured Cash system rather than Purchase Committee system. However, in practice the tendency of forgery was observed more in Cash system's Block rather than Purchase Committee system. A remarkable number of the Officials (65.0 per cent) and the same number of the Beneficiaries (67.1 per cent) considered that some of the Beneficiaries were crossing the poverty line. However, a marginal numbers of the Officials (20.0 per cent) and Beneficiaries (22.8 per cent) favoured that most of them crossed the poverty line whereas the strength of the respondents who considered that all of them did so were comparatively lower. Thus, it can be concluded that many of the assisted families were crossing the poverty line. This indicates towards substantial impact of the programme over the target groups. Hence, fifty-five per cent of the Officials and 70.4 per cent of the Beneficiaries were in favour to continue it whereas forty per cent of the Officials and 17.9 per cent of the Beneficiaries wanted to continue it with certain changes. None of the Officials was of the opinion to stop the programme. However, an insignificant number (4.6 per cent) of the Beneficiaries expressed their view in favour to stop the programme. Thus, the overwhelming majority of the respondents were in favour to continue the programme though with certain changes. About two-thirds (65.0 per cent) of the Officials and more than half (57.8 per cent) of the Beneficiaries considered the programme as fully successful followed by about one-third (35.0 per cent) of the Officials and nearly the same number (33.8 per cent) of the Beneficiaries who perceived it successful to some extent. A small number (8.7 per cent) of the Beneficiaries assessed the programme as a failure. Therefore, a surprisingly high percentage of our respondents considered the programme successful and even after some loopholes, they have admitted its impact on rural scenario. The third part concernd with the Officials-Beneficiaries perception about each other, is also an integral part of this study so, it is better to describe it here. More than half (51.3 per cent) of the Beneficiaries considered that the Officials take interest in their work whereas a significant number (48.7 per cent) perceived that they did not take interest in their work. Interestingly, more than three-fourths (78.8 per cent) of them reported that the Officials are more concerned about their salaries and a large number of them (65.0 per cent) observed that the Officials take as much interest in their work as it required to fulfil their targets on paper. More than four-fifths (82.0 per cent) of the Beneficiaries were of the view that the Officials were arrogant and non-cooperative in nature. Thus, the overall assessment of the Beneficiaries about the Officials is not satisfactory and their mental make up is far behind as is required for development oriented programmes. Therefore, we are inclined to conclude here that until the Officials adopt lenient, cooperative and development oriented approach towards Beneficiaries, they can not get fruitful output from these programmes. It is further suggested that periodic training and work shops to upgrade the skills of Officials at various levels should be organized as the existing facilities in the state are highly inadequate. As far as the perception of the Officials about the Beneficiaries is concerned, twenty per cent of the Officials were of the view that the Beneficiaries were taking much interest in creating the assets whereas half of the Officials observed that they took interest in it to some extent. A significant number of (30.0 per cent) the Officials perceived that the interest taken by Beneficiaries in creating the assets was little. However, a small number (15.0 per cent) of the Officials observed that the interest taken by Beneficiaries in operating the assets was much whereas sixty per cent of them perceived it to some extent and about one-fourth of them considered it little. Thus, the overall perception of the Officials about Beneficiaries is not appreciable and requires some dramatic changes. It is hoped that the Beneficiaries would take the assistance sincerely and extract maximum output from it.

However, the actual position of the Beneficiaries regarding IRDP and taking benefits from it, is rather sad. It has been observed that most of the Beneficiaries are still not in a position to meet their basic needs properly. They are living in destitute, unhygienic and rather poor condition. Their family size is too big for their earnings. Majority of them are illiterate and ignorant. Lack of spirit has been observed in these families. Most of them have no future planning and are mingled with present needs. Among the families who have crossed the poverty line, majority are those in which some person of that family has got government service. Some of the public opinion leaders believed that the programmes of rural development including IRDP have not succeeded in alleviation of rural poverty. These programmes have become more politically centred than provided help to the poorest of the poor. The government has been assisting the poor since independence but this help is far from satisfactory. It was also noticed during our study that who have crossed the BPL line were not dependent on IRDP assistance so far. Hence the programmes need to be reviewed. However, the some other public opinion leaders who believed in the usefulness of this programme of poverty alleviation consider that it has benefited a lot of families who have taken the assistance sincerely. They further stated that this programme should continue with certain modifications, if needed. Let's add here that the findings of our study have been endorsed by various studies on the subject and can also be taken for the purposes of generalization.

APPENDIX 1

Explanation of Concepts and Terms

The following concepts and terms are used in the present study:

Agricultural Labourer: A person without any land, but having a homestead and deriving more than 50 per cent of his income from agricultural wages in an agricultural labourer.

Asset: The project or activity provided/purchased by the Beneficiary with the help of financial assistance provided.

Beneficiary: A person who has been assisted under IRDP or other development programme.

Household: The persons connected by blood and marriages and normally living together constitute a household. The income of wife and minor children should be taken into account and added to that of head of the family in determining the status of the head of the family as target group beneficiary.

Marginal Farmer: A person with a land holding of 2.5 acres or below in case of unirrigated land or 1.25 acres or below in case of irrigated (class I) land will be considered as marginal farmer.

Non-Agricultural Labourer: A person whose total income from wage earning does not exceed Rs. 200 per month. Persons who derive their income partly from agricultural and partly from other sources can also be brought under this category, provided at least 50 per cent of their income is from non-agricultural sources.

Poverty: Poverty is a situation in which an individual or a family is unable to fulfil even the basic needs of life. CT Kurien regards poverty, "as the socio-economic phenomenon where the resources available to a society are used to satisfy the wants of the few while the many do not have even their needs met."

Poverty Line: Poverty as it is understood in the planning in India, is defined as that level of income (expenditure) which is sufficient for keeping a family at the subsistence level of existence, measured in terms of basic nutritional requirements. Any one who has an income below this level is said to be poor. According to Sixth Five Year Plan (1980-85), a daily intake of 2400 calories per capita in rural areas and 2100 calories in urban areas, corresponding to a consumption expenditure of Rs. 65 per capita per month in rural areas and Rs. 75 per capita per month in urban areas has been adopted to define poverty line. In the Seventh Plan (1985-90), the definition of poverty line has been revised. According to manual on IRDP and allied Programmes, poverty line has been defined in terms of annual income of a family, a family having an annual income of Rs. 6400 or less is considered to be a family below poverty line (BPL). For the Eight Plan (1992-97), poverty line has been redefined adjusting to the price level of 1991-92. Accordingly, the poverty line to be adopted in rural areas in drawn at income level of Rs. 11,000 per annum for a family.

Primary Sector: Primary sector includes agriculture, animal husbandry, forestry, fisheries and generally encompasses rural activities.

Programme Strategy: The objective of IRDP is achieved by providing productive assets and inputs to the target group. The assets which could be in primary, secondary or tertiary sectors, are provided through financial assistance in the form of subsidy by the Government and term credit advanced by the financial institutions.

Programme: A programme is a plan or a schedule to be followed or a coordinated group of things to be done or performed.

Rural Artisan: A person who is engaged in traditional occupation of Carpentry, Blacksmith, Handloom, Handicraft, Cobbler etc. is called Rural Artisan. The Rural Artisan may be skilled or unskilled but annual income of the family should not exceed Rs. 6400 (or Rs. 11,000 revised) per annum.

Secondary Sector: Secondary sector involves manufacturing of raw material into finished goods. The major component under secondary sector is ISB i.e. Industry, Service and Business sector introduced in IRDP since 1978-79.

Small Farmer: A cultivator with a land holding of 5 acres or below in case of unirrigated land or 2.5 acres or below in case of irrigated (class I) land will be considered as small farmer.

Target Group: The target group of the IRDP consists of small farmers, marginal farmers, agricultural labourers, non-agricultural labourers and rural artisans.

Tertiary Sector: Tertiary sector involves services required by the primary and secondary sectors.

Trickle Down Theory of Development: This is an economic doctrine which believes that benefits of economic growth naturally percolate down to the various strata of the economy. As per this doctrine, it was believed that no special efforts are required to improve the lot of the poor in a country as the benefits of higher growth will automatically reach the poor and improve their lot.

Wage Material Ratio: It is the ratio of total amount spent on wages to the total amount spent on non wage materials for the works.

Working Capital: It is defined as the value of current assets less current liabilities. In the context of IRDP, it is used to denote the capital needed for meeting recurring costs for running a project.

APPENDIX 2

Structure of CLCC

Chairman

1. Secretary, Department of Rural Development.

Members

2. Secretary, Department of Agriculture and Cooperation or his nominee not below the rank of Joint Secretary.
3. Adviser (Rural Development), Planning Commission or his nominee not below the rank of Joint Secretary.
4. Secretary, Expenditure or his nominee not below the rank of Joint Secretary.
5. Secretary, Department of Women and Child Development or his nominee not below the rank of Joint Secretary.
6. Secretary, Department of Small Scale Industries or his nominee not below the rank of Joint Secretary.
7. Secretary, Ministry of Welfare or his nominee not below the rank of Joint Secretary.
8. Director General, CAPART.
9. Additional Secretary, Department of Rural Development.
10. Additional Secretary, Banking Division, Ministry of Finance.
11. Chief Executive Officer, KVIC.
12. Managing Director, NABARD.
13. Executive Director, RBI.
14. Joint Secretary, Finance, Department of Rural Development.

15. State Secretaries of Rural Development of Selected States.

Member Secretary

16. Joint Secretary, IRD, Department of Rural Development.

Other officials/non-officials may be invited to the meetings of this committee if their presence is felt necessary by the chairman.

APPENDIX 3

Composition of SLCC Recommended by Government of India

Chairman

1. Chief Secretary/Agricultural Production Commissioner/ Development Commissioner.

Members

2. Secretary, Department of Rural Development
3. Secretary, Department of Finance.
4. Secretary, Department of Planning.
5. Secretary, Incharge of Women's Programme.
6. Head of Department of Agriculture.
7. Head of Department of Animal Husbandry.
8. Head of Department of Irrigation.
9. Head of Department of Cooperation.
10. Head of Department of Forest.
11. Head of Department of Fisheries.
12. Head of Department of Industries and Mines.
13. Director, Institutional Finance.
14. M.D., S.C./S.T. Development Cooperation.
15. M.D., Women's Development Cooperation.
16. Representative of KVIC.

17. Chief Executive Officer of State KVIB.
18. A representative of the Government of India, not below the rank of Deputy Secretary.

Member Secretary

19. Joint/Deputy Secretary, Department of Rural Development.

The State may include other officials/non-officials whose presence they deem necessary in the meeting.

APPENDIX 4

Composition of State Level Coordination/ Sanctioning Committee in Haryana

The Government of Haryana Reconstituted the SLCC/SLSC in 1994 and the composition is as following:

Chairman

1. Chief Secretary to Government of Haryana.

Members

2. Financial Commissioner and Secretary to Government of Haryana, Planning Department.
3. Financial Commissioner and Secretary to Government of Haryana, Finance Department.
4. Financial Commissioner and Secretary to Government of Haryana, Rural Development Department.
5. Commissioner and Secretary to Government of Haryana, Social Defence and Security Department.
6. Representative nominated by Government of India, Ministry of Rural Development, New Delhi.
7. Chief Executive, Haryana State Khadi and Village Industries Board (KVIB).
8. Managing Director, Haryana Dairy Development Cooperative Federation.
9. Registrar, Cooperative Societies Haryana, Chandigrah.
10. Director, Institutional Training and Vocational Education, Haryana.
11. Director, Industries Department, Haryana.

12. Director, Agriculture Department, Haryana.
13. Director, Institutional Finance and Credit Control Department, Haryana.
14. Director of Panchayats, Haryana.
15. Managing Director, Haryana Women Development Corporation.
16. Managing Director, Haryana Harijan Kalayan Nigam.
17. Principal Chief Conservator of Forests, Haryana.
18. Director, Animal Husbandry Department, Haryana.
19. Director, Horticulture Department, Haryana.
20. Representative of Khadi and Village Industries Commission (KVIC), Haryana.

Member Secretary

21. Special Secretary/Joint Secretary/Deputy-Secretary-cum Director, Rural Development Department, Haryana.

In addition to the above members of the Committee the following would be the standing permanent invites to meeting of the committee.

1. Chief Engineer, Panchayati Raj, Haryana.
2. Convenor, State Level Bankers Committee (SLBC) Haryana-cum-Zonal Manager, Punjab National Bank (PNB), Chandigarh.
3. Deputy General Manager (DGM), NABARD, Regional Office, Chandigarh.
4. Divisional Manager, Syndicate Bank, Chandigarh.
5. State Informatic Officer, National Informatic Center, Chandigarh.

Memo. No. 2975-APO (IRD)-(A-I)-94/9534-9605, dated 28-6-94, Joint Secretary-cum-Director, Rural Development Department, Haryana, Chandigarh.

APPENDIX 5

Composition of Governing Body (Illustrative)

Chairman

1. Deputy Commissioner/Collector.

Members

2. All MPs and MLAs of the District.
3. Head of the Central Cooperative Bank.
4. Chairman, Regional Rural Bank.
5. Chairman of Zila Parishad or his representative.
6. Lead Bank Officer.
7. NABARD representative at District Level.
8. General Manager, DIC.
9. Representative of KVIB.
10. District Officer incharge of Family Welfare Programme.
11. District Employment Officer.
12. Project Officer, ITDP.
13. Regional/District Officer, Scheduled Caste Finance Corporation.
14. APO (Women's Development).
15. One Women Worker/Organizer with actual experience of organizing rural poor.
16. Representative of District Milk Union.

17. Two representatives of the Weaker section. One of whom may be drawn from SC and ST. These representatives may be the beneficiaries of the programme.

18. One representative of rural women.

    Member Secretary

19. Project Officer/Director, DRDA.

    (ADC and Chief Executive Officer).

APPENDIX 6

Composition of Governing Body (District Bhiwani as on Dated 2-6-1994)

Chairman

Deputy Commissioner

Members

1. Sh. Bansi Lal, MLA, Haryana, MLA's Hostel, Chandigarh.
2. Sh. Jagbir Singh, MP, 66, Park Colony, Bhiwani.
3. Sh. Attar Singh, MLA, V & P.O. Madhi Hariya, Tehsil Dadri, District Bhiwani.
4. Sh. Amar Singh, MLA, Advocate Colony, Umra Road, Hansi.
5. Sh. Chattar Singh, MLA, V & P.O. Bond Kalan, District Bhiwani.
6. Smt. Chandrawati, MLA, Charkhi Dadri, District Bhiwani.
7. Sh. Dharam Pal, MLA, Ward No. 8, House No. 34, Dadri, District Bhiwani.
8. Sh. Ram Bhajan, MLA, Cinema Road, Bhiwani.
9. Deputy Secretary, Government of India, Ministry of Rural Development, Krishi Bhawan, New Delhi.
10. Special Secretary-cum-Director, Rural Development Department, Haryana, Chandigarh.
11. Director of Agriculture, Haryana, Chandigarh.
12. Joint Chief Officer, R.B.I. (PBDO PB No. 1003 Minto Road, Delhi).

13. The Lead & District Officer, R.B.I., PBDO PB No. 1003, Minto Road, Delhi.
14. The Director, NABARD, Haryana, Chandigarh.
15. The Director of Animal Husbandry, Haryana, Chandigarh.
16. Sub Divisional Officer (C), Bhiwani, Dadri, Laharu and Tosham.
17. Managing Director, Coop Bank, Bhiwani.
18. Chairman, H.K.G.B., Bhiwani.
19. The Regional Manager, HADCOF, Bhiwani.
20. The Managing Director, HADCOF, Haryana, Chandigarh.
21. The Lead Bank Officer, PNB, Bhiwani.
22. The Supdt. Engineer, HSEB, Bhiwani.
23. S.E. Canal Lining Circle, Bhiwani.
24. S.E., Bhiwani Irrigation Circle, Bhiwani.
25. The Divisional Forest Officer (T) and S.F., Bhiwani.
26. The Divisional Soil Conservation Officer, Bhiwani.
27. The Divisional Forest Officer (AP), Ch. Dadri.
28. The Deputy Director of Agriculture, Bhiwani.
29. The Deputy Director, ICDP, Bhiwani.
30. The District Manager HHK Nigam, Bhiwani.
31. The District Development Officer, NABARD, Bhiwani.
32. The General Manager, DDIC, Bhiwani.
33. The District Manager, PLDB, Bhiwani.
34. The Deputy Registrar, Coop Bank, Bhiwani.
35. The Assistant Soil Conservation Officer, Bhiwani/Dadri.
36. The Assistant Registrar, Coop Society, Bhiwani/Dadri.
37. The District Welfare Officer, Bhiwani.
38. The Executive Engineer, Lift Mech. Division, Bhiwani.

39. The XEN, Loharu Canal Division, Chakbandi Division, Bhiwani.
40. The XEN, Lining Division, MITC, Siwani and Lining Division, MITC, Bhiwani.
41. The Assistance Manager, Agro Industry, Bhiwani.
42. The District Development and Panchayat Officer, Bhiwani.
43. The Chief Medical Officer, Bhiwani.
44. The District Manager, Khadi and Village Industry, Bhiwani.
45. Smt. Bhagwati W/o Sh. Bani Singh V & PO Lohari Jattu, District Bhiwani.
46. Sh. Sita Ram V & PO Milkakpur, District Bhiwani.
47. All BDPO in the district Bhiwani.
48. All APO, Accounts Officer, Project Economist, Head Clerk and HDM, DRDA/CADA, Bhiwani.
49. The Officer on Special Duty, CADA, Bhiwani.
50. The District Planning Officer, Bhiwani
51. The Lady Circle Supervisor, Bhiwani.
52. The Divisional Manger, LIC, Bhiwani.
53. The DSO, Bhiwani.
54. The Settlement Officer, Bhiwani.
55. The District Employment Officer, Bhiwani.
56. Sectt. Municipal Committee in the District Bhiwani.
57. Member Secretary, ADC, Bhiwani.

APPENDIX 7

Questionnaire for the IRDP Beneficiaries

Block ________

Village________

Panchayat________

1. Name of the Beneficiary ____________________
2. Sex — Male/Female
3. Social Classification — SC/NSC/PH
4. Size of the family
   a) Upto 5 members
   b) 6-8 members
   c) 9-10 members
   d) above 10 members
5. Level of Education
   a) Illiterate
   b) Literate
   c) Matric
   d) Inter and above
6. Occupational Status
   a) Small farmer
   b) Marginal farmer
   c) Agricultural Labour
   d) Rural Artisan
   e) Any other
   f) NAL
7. Annual income at the time of inclusion in the IRDP list
   a) Rs. 0-1725 or 0-3200
   b) Rs. 1726-3500 or 3201-6400
   c) Rs. 3501-4800 or 6401-8500
   d) Rs. 4801-above or 8501-above

8. How did you come to know about IRDP Programme?
   a) Gram Sachiv
   b) IRDP Staff (APO)
   c) Gram Panchyat
   d) Fellow Villager/relative
   e) Any other (specify)
9. Does the Gram Sachive/Conerned APO educated Poor people regularly about the various schemes/ Programmes for the poor? Yes/No
10. How do you come to be selected under IRDP?
    a) BPL List
    b) Credit Camp
    c) Both (a) & (b)
    d) Any other
11. What approximate time was spent in processing Loan application in DRDA?
    a) 0-1 Month
    b) 1-2 Months
    c) 2-3 Months
12. What approximate time was spent in getting loan sanctioned and actual disbursement?
    a) One Month
    b) Two Months
    c) Three Months
    d) Above Three Months
13. Did you feel any difficulty in getting the scheme sanctioned? Yes/No
14. If yes, please indicate the type of difficulties faced?
    a) Large No. of formalities Y/N

b) Unhelpful attitude of Bank/IRDP Officials Y/N

c) Have to pay bribe to Bank/IRDP officials Y/N

d) Delay in sanction of loan Y/N

e) Non awareness of different Schemes and their economic importance Y/N

f) Help of intermediate have to be taken Y/N

15. Your choice about the scheme received
    a) High
    b) So so
    c) Low

16. Please indicate the kind of Scheme(s) you received
    a) ___________
    b) ___________
    c) ___________

17. What is the total cost of the Schemes(s)
    a) ___________
    b) ___________

18. How much financial assistance has been provided for the same
    Loan ___________
    Subsidy ___________
    Total ___________

19. Whether the financial assistance provided was adequate:
    a) Yes b) No

20. Whether the assets actually created/purchased :
    a) Yes b) No

21. If the answer is (b) then reasons for not creating the assets:
   a) Lack of interest c) Assistance was inadequate
   c) Adjustment with concerned Officials
22. What is the quality of assets:
   a) Good c) Average c) Poor
23. i) What is the present status of the scheme.
   a) Intact b) Sold c) Fully/partially perished
   d) Other position
   ii) If the answer is other than (a) then reasons:
   1. ___________
   2. ___________
24. What is your position about supplementary assistance.
   a) Single activity b) Double activities c) Multiple activities
25. Whether any improvement in economic position after assistance:
   a) Significant b) Marginal c) A little d) No difference e) Indebtedness
26. What is your position regarding repayment of loans:
   a) Cleared the loan b) Paying regularly c) Wanted to clear but not in position at present d) Only few instalments have been paid e) Defaulter.
27 i) Perception about Administrative Structure:
   a) Satisfactory b) Non-satisfactory c) DK/uncertain d) Desired changes
   ii) If answer is (b) reasons 1. ___________
   2. ___________
28. i) Perception about financial institutions:
   a) Satisfied b) Dis-satisfied c) DK/uncertain
   ii) If answer is (b) then reasons 1. ___________
   2. ___________
29. i) Perception about the assistance provided:
   a) Adequate b) Inadequate

ii) If answer is (b) then reasons 1. ______

2. ______

30. i) Perception about Beneficiaries who actually created the assets:

a) All of them b) Most of them c) Some of them

d) None of them

ii) If answer is (c) and (d), then why

1. ______

2. ______

3. ______

31. i) Perception about the process of Implementation:

a) Highly satisfied b) Satisfied c) Dissatisfied d) Highly Dissatisfied

ii) If answer is (c) and (d) then reasons

1. ______

2. ______

32. Perception about adequacy of infra-structural facilities available

a) Input b) Output c) Repair

33. i) Perception about Monitoring Process:

a) Satisfactory b) Unsatisfactory c) DK/uncertain

ii) If answer is (b) then reasons

1. ______

2. ______

34. Perception about Sector-wise performance of programme:

a) Primary b) ISB c) Tertiary

35. Perception regarding mode of purchasing:

a) Cash b) Purchase system c) Both d) None

36. Perception about Families crossing the poverty line:

a) All of them b) Many of them c) Some of them d) None of them

37. Perception about continuity of IRDP:

    a) Continue b) Be stopped c) Continue with certain changes d) DK/uncertain

38. Perception about Overall assessment of IRDP:

    a) Fully successful b) Successful to some extent c) Failure d) DK/uncertain

39. Any suggestion for its improvement ____________

40. Beneficiaries Perception about Officials:

    a) Take interest in their work Yes/No

    b) Concerned about their salary Yes/No

    c) Work just to fulfil target on paper Yes/No

    d) Egoist, arrogant and non-cooperative Yes/No nature

APPENDIX 8

Questionnaire for IRDP Officials

1. Name of the Official ________
2. Sex Male/Female
3. Age a) Upto 25 b) 26-35 c) 36-45
   d) 46 & above years
4. Caste SC/NSC
5. Size of family
   a) Upto 5 members b) 6-8 c) 9 & above
6. Educational Status
   a) Illiterate b) Literate c) Matric d) Inter
   e) Graduate and above
7. Occupational status
   a) Gazetted b) Class III c) Class IV
8. Income source
   a) Salary Exclusively c) Salary plus agricultural income
   c) Salary plus business d) Salary plus other source
9. i) Perception about Administrative Structure
   a) Satisfactory b) Non-satisfactory c) DK/uncertain
   d) Desired changes
   ii) If answer is (b) reasons 1. ________
   2. ________

10. i) perception about financial institutions:

a) Satisfied b) Dissatisfied c) DK/uncertain

ii) If answer is (b) then reasons 1. ___________

2. ___________

11. i) Perception about the assistance provided

a) Adequate b) Inadequate

ii) If answer is (b) then reasons 1. ___________

2. ___________

12. i) Perception about Beneficiaries who actually created the assets:

a) All of them b) Most of them

c) Some of them d) None of them

ii) If answer is (c) and (d), then why 1. ___________

2. ___________

3. ___________

13. i) Perception about the process of Implementation:

a) Highly satisfied b) Satisfied

c) Dissatisfied d) Highly Dissatisfied

ii) If answer is (c) and (d) then reasons

1. ___________

2. ___________

14. Perception about infrastructural facilities available:

a) Sufficient b) Insufficient c) DK/uncertain

15. i) Perception about Monitoring Process:

a) Satisfactory b) Unsatisfactory c) DK/uncertain

ii) If answer is (b) then reasons 1. ___________

2. ___________

16. Perception about Sectorwise performance of programme:

    a) Primary b) ISB c) Tertiary

17. Perception regarding mode of purchasing:

    a) Cash b) Purchase system c) Both d) None

18. Perception about Families which crossed the poverty line:

    a) All of them b) Most of them

    c) Some of them d) None of them

19. Perception about Continuity of IRDP:

    a) Continue b) Be stopped

    c) Continue with certain changes d) DK/uncertain

20. Perception about overall assessment of IRDP:

    a) Fully successful b) Successful to some extent

    c) Failure d) DK/uncertain

21. Any suggestion for its improvement ___________
22. Official Perception about the Beneficiaries:

    a) Interest taken in purchasing assets

    V. Good/Good/Little (poor)

    b) Interest taken in operating assete

    V. Good/Good/Little (poor)

APPENDIX 9

Questionnaire for Bank Officials/Public Opinion Leader

1. i) Views about IRDP Administrative Setup:

   a) Satisfactory b) Unsatisfactory c) DK/uncertain

   ii) If answer is (b) then reasons 1.___________

   2. ___________

   3. ___________

2. Views about IRDP Officials

   a) Take interest in their work Yes/No

   b) Work just to fulfil target Yes/No

   c) More concerned to status and salary Yes/No

3. Views about Beneficiaries:

   a) Take interest in purchasing assets Yes/No

   b) Take interest in operating assets Yes/No

   c) Have work spirit Yes/No

4. Views about the process of Implementation:

	Satisfactory/Unsatisfactory/Uncertain
– Survey	
Identification of productive activities	— / — / —
Preparation of Annual Action Plan	— / — / —
– Credit Camp and fillings of loan application	— / — / —

- Processing of loan Application & disbursement of loan

  — / — / —

- Beneficiaries' choice about scheme — / — / —
- Adequacy of assistance — / — / —
- Monitoring process — / — / —
- Recovery process — / — / —

5. Views about impact of IRDP: V. Good/Average/Poor

6. General assessment of IRDP:

a) Fully successful b) Successful to some extent c) failure

7. Suggestion if any ____________

Bibliography

Books

Agro-Economics Research Centre, Himachal Pradesh University, *National Rural Employment Programme* (New Delhi: Mittal Publications, 1988).

Arora, R.L., *Integrated Rural Development* (Delhi: S. Chand & Co., 1982).

Barnbas, A.P., *Citizen's Grievances and Administration* (New Delhi: Indian Institute of Public Administration, 1969).

Bata, K. Dey, *Bureaucracy, Development and Public Management in India* (New Delhi: Uppal Publishing House, 1978).

Brayne, F.L., *Better Villages* (Bombay: Oxford University Press, 1946).

Caiden, Gereald E., *Dynamics of Public Administration: Guidelines to Current Transformation in Theory and Practice* (New Delhi: Hort, Rinehart and Winston, 1971).

Chambers, Robert, *Rural Development: Putting the Last First* (London: Longman, 1983).

Chaturvedi, Anil, *District Administration: The Dynamics of Discord* (New Delhi: Sage Publication 1988).

Dahiya, L.N., *Dynamics of Economic Life in Rural India: A Case Study* (New Delhi: Gian Pub. House, 1991).

Das, Kumar B., *Rural Development through Decentralization* (New Delhi: Discovery Publication House, 1991).

Desai, Vasant, *Rural Development, Vol. 1 to 6* (New Delhi: Himalya Publishing House, 1988).

Government of India, Department of Rural Development, *Important Circulars on IRDP, Vol. II* (New Delhi: April, 1983).

Gorwala, A.D., *The Role of Administrator: Past, Present and Future* (Pune: Gokhale Institute of Politics and Economics, 1957).

Hanson, A.H. and Doughlas, J., *India's Democracy* (New Delhi: Vikas Publication House, 1974).

Jain, L.C., Krishanmurty, B.V., et al., *Grass Without Roots: Rural Development under Government Auspices* (New Delhi, Sage Publications, 1985).

Jain, S.C., *Rural Development: Institutions and Strategies* (Jaipur: Rawat Publications, 1985).

Jha, S.K., *Rural Development Administration in India* (New Delhi: Commonwealth Publishers, 1988).

Khan, Waheeduddin (ed.), *Papers and Proceedings of the Workshop Cum Seminar on Rural Institution and Agricultural Development* (Hyderabad, NICD, 1972).

Kothari, C.R. (ed.), *Rural Development, Vol. I, Strategy for Rural Development* (Jaipur: Manak Publication, 1991).

Khanna, B.S., *Rural Development in South Asia-I: India,* (New Delhi: Deep and Deep Publications, 1991).

Lal, Muni, *Haryana: On High Road of Prosperity* (Delhi: Vikas Publishing House, 1974).

Lele, Uma, *The Design of Rural Development: Lessons from Africa* (London: The Johns Hopkins University Press, 1975).

Maheswari, S.R., *Rural Development in India* (New Delhi: Sage Publication, 1985).

Mathur, J.S. (ed.), *Rural Development in India: Some Facets* (Hyderabad: National Institute of Rural Development, 1979).

Mathur, Kuldeep, *Administrative Institutions, Political Capacity and India's Strategy for Rural Development* (Asian Center for Development Administration, 1975).

Mathur, Kuldeep, *Bureaucratic Response to Development* (Delhi: National, 1972).

Mishra, B.B., *District Administration and Rural Development* (Delhi: Oxford University Press, 1983).

Mishra, S.N., *Rural Development and Panchayati Raj* (Delhi: Concept Publishing Company, 1980).

Mishra, S.N., et al., *Participation and Development* (New Delhi: National Book Organization, 1984).

Mishra, S.N. and Sharma, Kaushal, *Problems and Prospects of Rural Development in India* (New Delhi: Uppal Publication House, 1983).

Morris Jones, W.H., *The Government and Politics of India* (Bombay: B.I. Publications, 1974).

National Institute of Rural Development, *Administrative Arrangements for Rural Development—A Perspective* (Hyderabad: NIRD, 1985).

Palombora, Joseph La (ed.), *Bureaucracy and Political Development* (Princeton, N.J.: Princeton University Press, 1963).

Pai Panandikar, V.A. (ed.), *Development Administration in India* (New Delhi: MacMillan, 1974).

Palanithurai, G., *Indian Polity: Myth and Reality* (Delhi: Kanishka, 1993).

Parkash, Buddha, *Glimpses of Haryana,* (Kurukshetra University Press, 1968).

Parshad, Kamta, *Planning for Poverty Alleviation* (New Delhi: Agricole Publishing Academy, 1985).

Prasher, Sharat, *Rural Development Administration* (Jaipur: Arihant Publishing House, 1994).

Randhawa, M.S., *Developing Village in India* (Bombay: Orient Longman, 1951).

Rau, S.K. (ed.), *Rural Development in India: Some Facets* (Hyderabad: NIRD, 1979).

Ray, Ramashray, et al., *Problems in Rural Development* (Delhi: Discovery, 1985).

Reddy, G.N., *The Rural Poor* (Allahabad: Chugh Publication, 1991).

Reddy, Venkta, *Rural Development in India: Poverty and Development* (Delhi: Himalaya Publishing House, 1988).

Shah, S.M., *Rural Development: Planning and Reforms* (New Delhi: Abhinav Publications, 1977).

Sharma, S.K., Malhotra, S.L., *Integrated Rural Development: Approach, Strategy and Perspectives* (New Delhi: Abhinav Publications, 1977).

Singh, Hargian, *Panchayati Raj Administration in Haryana* (Delhi: India Publisher, 1985).

Singh, Hoshiar, *Rural Development in India: Evaluative Study in Politics and Programme* (ed.) (Jaipur: Printwell Publication, 1985).

Singh, Mohinder, *Rural Development Administration and Anti-Poverty Programmes* (New Delhi: Deep and Deep Publication, 1988).

Singh, Kartar, *Rural Development: Principles, Policies and Management* (New Delhi: Sage Publications, 1986).

Singh, S.R., *Bureaucracy and Rural Development* (New Delhi: Mittal Publications, 1988).

Srivastva, A.K., *Integrated Rural Development Programme in India Policy and Administration* (New Delhi: Deep and Deep Publications, 1988).

Sud, O.C., *Administrative Problems of Rural Development in India* (Delhi: Kanishka Publication House, 1992).

Sundaram, I.S., *Anti-Poverty Development in India* (New Delhi: D.K. Publications, 1984).

Upadhaya, Rakesh, *IRD Basic Approach and Policy* (Bombay: Himalaya Publication House, 1989).

Yadav, K.C., *Haryana Ka Itihas* (1803-1966) Part-3 (New Delhi: MacMillan, 1981).

Articles

Alexander, K.C., "Rural Setup and Problems of Planned Change", in *Rural Transformation,* NIRD, Hyderabad, 1984.

Ahmad, R. Furqun, "Development Administration: Need for a New Training Pattern", *Indian Journal of Politics,* Vol. 29, No. 1-2, 1995.

Almond, Gabrial A., "A Development Approach to Political System" in Gable, R.W. and Finkle, J.L. (ed.), *Political Development and Social Change* (New York: John Wiley and Sons, 1966).

Bagchee, Sandeep, "Poverty Alleviation Programmes in 7th Plan: An Appraisal", *Economic and Political Weekly,* Jan 24, 1987.

Bajpai, S.K., "Rural Development: Some Constraints", *Kurukshetra,* Vol. 30, No. 23, 1982.

Bandopadhaya, D., "Direct Intervention Programmes for Poverty Alleviation", *Economic and Political Weekly,* June 25, 1988.

Bala Krishna, S., "Some Demographic Features of Rural India" (ed.) *Rural Development in India* (Hyderabad: National Institute of Rural Development, 1979).

Chaturvedi, T.N., "Rural Development: The Elusive Horizon", *The Administrative Change,* Vol. 6, No. 1-2, July, 1978-June, 1979.

Datta, B.C., "Planning for Rural Areas", *Khadi Gramodyog,* Vol. 21, No. 3, December, 1974.

Dubhashi, P.R., "Approaches to Integrated Rural Development in India: Administrative and Organizational Issues", *The Administrative Change,* Vol. 6, No. 1-2, July 1978-June 1979.

Gosh, Madhusudan, "Agricultural Development and Rural Poverty in India", *Indian Journal of Agricultural Economics,* Vol. 51, No. 3, July-September, 1996.

Ghildial, A.K., "From Steel Frame to Open Structure: Bureaucracy and Social Change in India", *The Administrator,* Vl. 28, No. 1, January-March, 1983.

Gross, Bertran M., "Space, Time and Post-Industrial Society", in James J. Heaphy (ed.), *Spatial Dimension of Development Administration* (Durham, NC, Duke University Press, 1971).

Gupta, Malay, "Planning for Rural Development Programme and its Strategy: A Case Study", *Indian Journal of Agricultural Economics,* Vol. 39, No. 3, July-September, 1984.

Haldipur, R.N., "Bureaucracy's Response to new Challenge", *Indian Journal of Public Administration,* Vol. 12(1), January-March, 1966.

Himachalam, P., "How far has IRDP Alleviated Poverty?", *Kurukshetra,* Vol. 38, No. 2, 1989.

Hirway, Indira, "Critique of Target group Approach: A Study in Gujarat", in *Indian Journal of Agricultural Economics,* Vol. 39, No. 3, July-Sept. 1984.

Hargopal, G. and Murli Manohar, K., "Some Aspects of Morale in the Rank and File of Indian Bureaucracy", *Indian Journal of Public Administration,* Vol. 22, No. 4, October-December, 1976.

Jakhar, Balram, "Plan Policies for Rural Development in India", in Hoshiar Singh (ed.), *Rural Development in India* (Jaipur: Printwell, 1985).

Kahlon, A.S., "Rural Poverty and Land Reforms", *The Administrator,* Vol. 30, No. 1, January-March, 1985.

Khosla, J.N., "Research in Development Administration", in Panandikar, Pai (ed.), *Development Administration in India* (Madras: Macmillan ISSD Press, 1974).

Kothari, Rajni, "Rural Development: Issues and Perspectives", *The Administrative Change,* Vol. 6, No. 1-2, July, 1978-June, 1979.

Kurian, N.J., "Anti-Poverty Programmes: A Reappraisal", *Economic and Political Weekly,* March 25, 1989.

Kutty Krishana, A.C., "A Case Study of Integrated Rural Development Programme in a Kerala Village", *Indian Journal of Agricultural Economics,* Vol. 39, No. 3, July-September, 1984.

Meeta, Krishan, "Poverty Alleviation Programmes", *The Third Concept,* Vol. 10, No. 114, August 1996.

Minhas, B.S., "Rural Poverty, Land Redistribution and Development Strategy: Facts," *Sankhya* (Indian Journal of Statistics), Series C, Vol. 36, No. 2-4, June-December 1974.

Misra, I.S., "Rural Development Change before IRDP: A Fresh Look", *Indian Journal of Agricultural Economics,* Vol. 41, No. 4, October-December, 1986.

Mukherjee, Neela, "Lessons of Poverty Alleviation Programmes", *Yojana,* New Delhi, August 15, 1990.

Montgomery, John D., "A Royal invitation: Variation on three Classical Themes", in Montgomery and William J. Siffin (ed.), *Approach to Development: Politics, Administration and Change* (New York: Mac Graw Hill, 1966).

Nayyar, Rohini, "Does Garibi Hatao Work", *Economic and Political Weekly,* April 29, 1989.

Pai Panandikar, V.A., "Development Administration: An Approach", *Indian Journal of Public Administration,* Vol. 10, No. 1, January-March, 1964.

Pinto, Marina R., "Rural Development and Bureaucracy in India", *The Indian Journal of Political Science,* Vol. 53, No. 3, July-September 1992.

Patil, B.V. and Singh, Gurcharan, "Effective Implementation of IRDP: Some suggestions", *Yojana,* Vol. 35, No. 8, May 15, 1991.

Pondyal, M.P., "Administrative Hurdles to Poverty Eradication: Nepal's Experience with Integrated Rural Development Projects", in T.N. Chaturvedi (ed.), *Rural Development: Some Themes and Dimensions* (New Delhi: IIPA, 1986).

Puranik, S.N., "The Villagers, Perception of the Administrative System: An Empirical Analysis", *The Administrative Change,* Vol. 5, No. 2, July-December, 1977.

Raju, Yerram B., "And Plan Rural Credit better Way", *Yojana,* Vol. 29 (24), January 1-15, 1988.

Rao, B.G., "Community Development in Maharashtra", Panandikar, V.A. Pai (ed.), *Decade of Planning in India* (Bombay: Popular Prakashan, 1969).

Rao, Perumalla D., Natrajan, R, "IRDP Assistance in Andhra Pardesh: An Evaluation", *Kurukshetra,* Vol. 36, No. 6, March, 1988.

Rao, Sudhakar B., "TRYSEM and ISB Component of IRDP", *Kurukshetra,* Vol. 34, No. 8, May, 1986.

Rath, N., "Garibi Hatao: Can IRD Do it?" *Economic and Political Weekly,* Feb. 9, 1985.

Reddy, Uday Bhaskar, "The Role of Voluntary Agencies in Rural Development", *The Indian Journal of Public Administration,* Vol. 33, No. 3, July-September, 1987.

Sanwal, Mukul, "Garibi Hatao: Improving Implementation", *Economic and Political Weekly,* Vol. 20, No. 49, Dec. 7, 1985.

Satya Sunderam, I., "Eighth Plan-Mid-term Appraisal", *Third Concept,* Vol. 9, No. 108, February, 1996.

Sharda, Sarita, "Administrative Structure and Functioning of IRDP-A Case Study", *Administrative Change,* Vol. 17, No. 2, July-December, 1989.

Sharma, P.W., "IRDP and Poverty Alleviation Strategies: An Appraisal", *Kurukshetra,* Vol. 36, No. 6, March, 1987.

Sharma, M.L., et al., "IRDP: Retrospect and Prospect", *Kurukshetra,* Vol. 38, No. 2, 1989.

Shah, S.M., "IRDP - Success or Failure", *Kurukshetra,* Vol. 38, No. 2, 1989.

Singh, Jasbir K., "Socio-Economic Impact of IRDP on Weaker Sections in Punjab", *Guru Nanak Journal of Sociology,* Vol. 9, No. 1, April, 1988.

Singh, Kartar, "IRDP: Some Policies and Management Issues", *Kurukshetra,* Vol. 33, No. 2, Aug. 1985.

Singh, V.S., "An Insight into Poverty Alleviation Programmes", *Yojana,* Vol. 32, No. 6, April 1-15, 1988.

Singh, V.S. and Lal, Banwari, "Poverty Analysis—Where does it lead", *Man and Development,* Vol. 9, No. 3, September, 1987.

Sinha, Sanjay, "Poverty Alleviation: Anything Goes", *EPW,* Vol. 21, No. 19, May 10, 1986.

Taneja, Suresh, "Long Search for Savers", *The Tribune,* February 9, 1989.

Thaha, Mumtaz, "Next Step in Rural Development: Action for Eighties" in (ed.), Lakshaman and Naryana, *Rural Development in India: A Multi-Demensional Analysis.* (Bombay: Himayala Publication, 1984).

Tinaikar, S.S., "Anti-poverty Programme—A Critique", *The Public Administrator* (IIPA, Maharashtra Regional Branch, 1984-85).

Tripathi, R.N., et al., "Evaluation of IRDP in Udhampur and Anantnag Districts of J&K" and "Evaluation of IRDP in Gorakhpur District in UP" both in (ed.), *Research Highlights: Summaries of Studies Conducted in 1987-88* (Hyderabad: NIRD, 1989).

Verson, W. Rutten, "Integrated Rural Development Programme—A Skeptical Perspective", *Agricultural Development Council Review,* Singapore, No. 4, 1975.

World Bank, "Flaws in IRDP", *The Tribune,* September, 3, 1989.

Yadav, et al., "IRDP-Constraints and Remedies", *Indian Journal of Agricultural Economics,* Vol. 41, No. 4, 1986.

Reports and Manuals

DRAD, Bhiwani, *Annual Action Plans of IRDP 1980-81 to 1995-96,* District Bhiwani.

Government of Haryana, Planning Department, *Statistical Abstract of Haryana 1995-96* (Chandigarh: Economics and Statistical Organization, 1997).

Government of India, *India 1990-A Reference Annual* (New Delhi: Revenue and Reference Divisions, Ministry of Information and Broadcasting, 1990).

Government of India, Department of Rural Development, *Manual for IRDP, 1980,* New Delhi.

Government of India, Ministry of Agriculture, *Manual for IRDP and Allied Programmes,* Department of Rural development (New Delhi, April, 1991).

Government of India, Department of Rural Development, *Manual on NREP and RLEGP* (New Delhi: Ministry of Agriculture, 1986).

Government of India, Department of Rural Development, *Manual on JRY 1991* (New Delhi: Ministry of Agriculture, 1991).

Government of India, Department of Rural Development, *NREP: Guidelines* (New Delhi: Ministry of Agriculture, 1985).

Government of India, Department of Rural Development, *Annual Report, 1984-85,* New Delhi.

Government of India, Ministry of Rural Reconstruction, *Annual Report-1980-81,* New Delhi.

Government of India, Department of Rural Development, *Annual Report 1988-89* (New Delhi: Ministry of Agriculture, 1990).

Government of India, Department of Rural Development, *Annual Report 1994-95* (New Delhi: Ministry of Agriculture, 1996).

Government of India, Department of Rural Development and Poverty Alleviation, *Annual Report 1996-97* (New Delhi: Ministry of Rural Areas and Employment, 1998).

Government of India, Department of Rural Development, *Conference of Ministers of Rural Development and Water Supply 29th and 30th October, 1990: Agenda* (New Delhi: Ministry of Agriculture, 1990).

Government of India, Department of Rural Development, *Gramin Vikas News Letter: Rural Development Programme at a Glance,* New Delhi, Jan., 1989.

Government of India, Department of Rural Development, *Basic, Rural Statistics-1990* (New Delhi: Ministry of Agriculture, 1990).

Government of India, Directorate of Economics and Statistics, *Bulletin on Food Statistic 1972,* New Delhi, 1972.

Government of India, Department of Rural Development, *Agenda for the Meeting of States Secretaries of Rural Development on JRY: 21st and 22nd September, 1992,* New Delhi, 1992.

Government of India, Department of Rural Development, *Concurrent Evaluation of IRDP (Jan-Dec. 1987)* (New Delhi: Ministry of Agriculture, August, 1988).

Government of India, Department of Rural Development, Concurrent Evaluation of IRDP (Jan-Dec. 1989) (New Delhi: Ministry of Agriculture, August, 1990).

Government of India, Ministry of Irrigation and Agriculture, *Report of the Review Committee on Pilot Intensive Employment Project* (PIREP), New Delhi, 1977.

Government of India, Planning Commission, *Sixth Five Year Plan,* New Delhi, 1980.

Government of India, Ministry of Agriculture and Irrigation, *Report of Ashok Mehta Committee on Panchayati Raj Institution,* New Delhi, 1978.

Government of India, *Report of the National Commission on Agriculture,* Part-II, Chapter-6, 1976.

Reserve Bank of India, *Report of All India Rural Credit Review Committee,* Bombay, 1969.

Reports of Royal Commission on Agriculture in India (Bombay: Government Central Press, 1928).

Techno-Economic Survey of Haryana (New Delhi: National Council of Applied Economic Research, 1970).

Government of India, Department of Rural Development and Poverty Alleviation, *Concurrent Evaluation of IRDP (September 1992 to August 1993)* (New Delhi: Ministry of Rural Areas and Employment 1996).

Circulars and Official Letters

Government of India, Ministry of Rural Development, *Circular No. M 12012/23/82-IRD III,* dated 13-7-1982, New Delhi.

——, *Circular No. 14012/4/82-IRD-III,* dated 26-8-82.

——, *Circular No. S. 11011/130/81-IRD-I,* dated 24-9-82.

——, *Circular No. 20011/1/83-IRD-III,* dated 9-5-83.

——, *Circular No. M 14013/I/83-IRD-III,* dated 20-5-83.

——, *Circular No. I. 12011/56/83-CIP,* dated 29-6-83.

——, *Circular No. S 11011/18/82-IRD-III,* dated 9--11-83.

——, *Circular No. 14013/1/83-IRD-II,* dated 30-8-84.

Government of India, Ministry of Agriculture, *Circular No. I-12011/33/87-IRD (Credit),* dated 25-3-91 (New Delhi: Department of Rural Development).

——, *Circular No. M. 19010/1/93-REJ-IV,* dated 1-7-93.

——, *Circular No. 12012/4/87-IRD-III,* dated 9-12-93.

Government of India, Ministry of Rural Areas and Employment, *Circular No. I-12011/23/93-IRD Credit,* dated 5-5-95 (New Delhi: Department of Rural Development).

Government of India, Ministry of Rural Areas and Employment, *Circular No. 28012/16/91-IRD-III,* dated 23-1-95.

——, *Circular No. I-12011/1/95-IRD Credit,* dated 26-10-95.

——, *Circular No. I-120016/2/95-IRD-I,* dated 6-11-95.

——, *Circular No. I-12011/1/95 IRD Credit,* dated 1-1-96.

——, *Circular No. I-12011/1/95-IRD Credit,* dated 12-2-96.

——, *Circular No. I-12001/17/03-IRD Credit,* dated 12-2-96.

Government of Haryana, Institutional Finance and Credit Control Department, *Memo No. IFCC-6-2-82-RD,* dated 11-11-1982, Chandigarh.

——, *Memo No. IFCC-3-3-89-RC (N)/758,* dated 4-4-1990.

DRDA, Bhiwani, *DRDA/91.Credit/3130-50,* dated 26-6-91.

Government of Haryana, Department of Rural Development, *Memo No. APO(IRD)-92/6007-23,* dated 12-3-1992, Chandigarh.

Punjab National Bank, Zonal Office, *Ref. No. DGM: DEV: 77/53,* dated 29-7-94, Chandigarh.

Reserve Bank of India, *RPCD No. SP BC/115/09-1-1994-95,* dated 7-2-95, Mumbai.

Reserve Bank of India, *Ref. No. SS 277/SS, 41-90/91,* dated 9-3-93, Mumbai.

Reserve Bank of India, *C. 568 (CD)—93/94,* dated 4-2-1994, Mumbai.

Index